SOLDIER'S TALE
— OF —
COMBATING
HANGOVERS
DEBAUCHERY BEFORE THE INTERNET

S.D. TURNER

outskirts
press

A Soldier's Tale of Combating Hangovers
Debauchery Before the Internet
All Rights Reserved.
Copyright © 2021 S.D. Turner
v2.0

The opinions expressed in this manuscript are solely the opinions of the author and do not represent the opinions or thoughts of the publisher. The author has represented and warranted full ownership and/or legal right to publish all the materials in this book.

This book may not be reproduced, transmitted, or stored in whole or in part by any means, including graphic, electronic, or mechanical without the express written consent of the publisher except in the case of brief quotations embodied in critical articles and reviews.

Outskirts Press, Inc.
http://www.outskirtspress.com

Paperback ISBN: 978-1-9772-3065-2
Hardback ISBN: 978-1-9772-3140-6

Interior Images © 2021 S.D. Turner. All rights reserved - used with permission.
Cover Design © 2021 Design Crowd. All rights reserved - used with permission.

Outskirts Press and the "OP" logo are trademarks belonging to Outskirts Press, Inc.

PRINTED IN THE UNITED STATES OF AMERICA

This book is a work of non-fiction. It is entirely recreated from the author's memory, as well as that of his brothers-in-arms, with whom he has conversed for the creation of this book. As these events happened over twenty-five years ago, the author has made every conceivable effort possible to ensure their accuracy, to the best of his memory.

In some instances, and with explicit written authorization, the author has used the legal names, as well as varying nicknames, for certain individuals. In order to maintain anonymity for others, both living and deceased, some legal names have been replaced with nicknames. In any other instance thereafter, the names of businesses, places, and individuals have been plied with the author's artistic freedom in order to protect their identity, unless the business is otherwise found to be defunct.

As the author has made every attempt to ensure accuracy of information at the time of publication, it stands that any liability to any party, for loss, damage, or disruption caused by errors, the author shall hereby disclaim any such liability, indefinitely.

The year was 1992. I was eighteen years old, fairly good looking, partly intelligent, but moreover, a dumb kid. I was fearless, in the best physical and mental condition of my life, and I could handle myself in a fist-fight. I was trained to load, drive, and gun the M1A1 Abrams Battle Tank—the deadliest tank in the world.

All of my friends back home were either a few months into college or working at their fathers' businesses. I was living on an entirely different continent in an all-together new country; learning a new language, a new culture, and a brand-new world over seven thousand miles away.

Never in a million years would I have ever imagined I would be so lucky. This was our family heritage from long ago, and it was right outside our front gate at Sullivan *Käserne*. It was a dream come true. I was now living in Deutschland… the fatherland.

Kaiserslautern, Mannheim, Frankfurt, Berlin, Paris, Brussels, San Sebastian, Pamplona, München, Lyon, Grafenwöehr, Hohenfels, and Wildflecken would be the names of my new playground. Each with distinct foods, fashion, people, and experiences. These were the places that would change my life forever.

Ein bier, bitte, or *one beer, please,* was the most widely used and first phrase a young soldier learned in Germany. We were stationed in the beer capital of the world and intended to take full advantage of it. Each town had its own version of their beer.

Reinheitsgebot, or German for *purity order,* also known as the Bavarian Purity Laws of 1516, decreed that only barley, hops, and water could be used to make German beer. It was an art form, and still is. Several times was I a patron of the finest beer-art in the finest museums in the known beer world.

So there I was: cigarettes were $4.00 a carton, a half-gallon of top-shelve booze was less than $13.00, and I was living in the beer capital of the world for the first two years of my adulthood. What could possibly go wrong, when everything felt so right?

TABLE OF CONTENTS

PART(Y) TWO—SOLDIER IN EUROPE

INTRODUCTION

My name is S.D. Turner. I served in the United States Army for six years: from 1992 to 1995 in the regular Army (full-time job), and again from 2000 to 2003 in the Nasty Girls (Army National Guard or a part-time job). It was the perfect recipe for a young soldier to have earned a combat patch or two on his right shoulder. Everyone always asks me, *Were you in combat? or Were you in the Gulf War?* I always answer, *"WAR WAS…IT WAS PURE HELL!"* I bow my head a little and be-gin, *"EVERY-SINGLE-DAY I HAD TO COMBAT A HANGOVER IN GERMANY."* It usually elicits a hearty laugh, followed by, *"WHERE IN GERMANY WERE YOU STATIONED?"*

Even as a small child, I was always fascinated with watching WWII and Viet-Nam-era movies. Even at four or five years old, I knew I wanted to join the Army, just like generations of men in my family had previously done. It seemed a family tradition. I wanted to be the desperate hero in a raging battle. I wanted the respect and admiration of my brothers-in-arms; to be known as a man committed to performing his duties when America called. Before the onset of puberty, I already knew what the patch on a man's right sleeve signified. It meant he served his country, his unit, his men—and he served them in combat.

In World War II, my grandfather, Floyd Loraine Robinson, shot down a Japanese Zero over Papua New Guinea, earning him the Silver Star. He spent four years in the Army. My father made it out alive after serving thirteen months in Cha-rang, or Death Valley, Viet-Nam. My brother, Kevin Turner, made a combat jump into Panama during the Noriega ordeal and was also in Saudi Arabia during the Gulf War. My uncle, Chris Robinson, earned the Bronze Star in Iraq. Several of my great-uncles as well as my Great-Great Uncle, Maxie Butler, were in places from Europe to the Pacific during WWII. Even my Great-Uncle, Alton Burks, told me tales about making extra money transporting whiskey during the Korean War. All of them Army veterans. I knew it, I felt it. I was destined to serve my country in the Army. I wanted to serve my country in a combat role; I wanted that patch on my right shoulder. Like Pindar said in the 5th century B.C., *"WAR IS SWEET TO THOSE WHO HAVE NO EXPERIENCE OF IT, BUT THE EXPERIENCED MAN TREMBLES EXCEEDINGLY AT HEART ON ITS APPROACH."*

I had several examples of heroic men in my life that made me want to heed the call. We had a neighbor in Pensacola, Florida, *Old Man Taylor*. His stories, no doubt, would fill an entire book; he was born in 1899! He had lied about his age so that he could serve in the U.S. NAVY during WWI. After his real age was discovered, he was, of course, sent home with a temporary bar to re-enlistment. Some years later, he re-enlisted and retired with more than twenty-plus years of service, but not before serving in WWII, as well. He was the only person I ever knew that served in both of the great World Wars. When I say he was *something*, I mean it. He was a very well-respected and known man in our part of Florida.

He was a monster of a man. Nearing seven feet in height, he towered over most men. To me, at nine years old, he seemed larger than life. After asking him what he was going to do with all of the junk in his yard, he responded, *"JUNK! BOY, THIS ISN'T JUNK. THIS IS*

SELLABLE MERCHANDISE." During the course of his (then) eighty-some-odd years, he'd amassed a collection of boats, lawnmowers, and old vehicles—all sitting proudly on his large piece of property. He had more tools than he would *ever* use or sell. But, if we asked to borrow a tool, rest assured he had it. This is where I learned the valuable lesson of returning something in the same, if not better, condition than when you borrowed it.

Aside from working in the yard or garage for my old man, I had a job at the tender age of nine. I worked at a combination putt-putt golf course/go-kart track for Ed Walton. He could command a book on his own as well. He was a Korean War veteran and, like Mr. Taylor, he too could cuss better than anyone I'd ever met. Thanks in part to these gentlemen, I could out-cuss all the kids in my school. I was a seasoned pro by the age of ten. As both a veteran soldier and now commercial mariner, it's no wonder I do it so frequently.

My dad would never talk about his time in Viet-Nam until I was actually in the Army. I now understand why, as most civilians simply don't understand our world, our brotherhood, or our language. Even though I only had to combat hangovers, I am, more often than not, forced to keep my stories timid for civilians. I need to introduce my brand of insanity very subtly. But, if you get me around another soldier, especially my brothers, I will unload some disgusting shit into the conversation. To others it may seem terrifying or disturbing, but to us, it's as normal as apple pie and baseball.

As I write these words, I debate how much to divulge of my experiences. First: I want these stories documented for my children and heirs to enjoy, as the world will no doubt change. These stories and a few photographs are, thankfully, the only proof of our exploits. There might be a video or two out there (thanks, Spud). Once I am gone, should these stories not be recorded for my children's children, they, like me, will forever disappear into a forgotten past, which happens far too often in life. Second: I have always wanted to write a book. What better subject than my own experiences? Last: I hope you, the reader, will laugh and enjoy the hell out of the wild, crazy, and hysterical stories that are my life as a young soldier in the United States Army.

I should forewarn you, though; there are tales of excessive and repeated drunkenness, sex in strange countries with strange women and animals, international law-breaking, smoking, cussing, and death-defying acts of complete stupidity with little, if any, remorse or regret. I would ask that you bear in mind that I was young. We were all young, and we thought, on more than one occasion, that we were going to war. Besides, I used to load, drive, and shoot an M1A1 Abrams Battle Tank: its 68-tons of pure fucking murder. That said, any expectations of normality should be quickly and immediately dismissed as hearsay and plain old-fashioned bullshit.

Furthermore, I appreciate you taking time from your life to read these stories. I hope you get a little taste of the world in which Joe *Spud* Powell, Tire Iron, Sgt. J, Michael *Tricky Dick* Box, Glenn *Hamburger* Martony, Fritz *Shithouse Lawyer* Kelly, Spive, *Sullivan Slasher* Midge, Ray Weatherford, myself, and the rest of the gang dwelled.

In short, we were uncaged animals that the United States government unloaded in a foreign country *before* the Internet, cell phones, and social medias had the power to destroy so many lives and careers with (sometimes bullshit) evidence of their foolishness. I am pretty sure the statute of limitations will protect us. Cue attorney, now.

Since my time in service, I have been to Italy, France, Spain (including the Canary Islands), Poland, Czechoslovakia, Austria, Liechtenstein, Luxembourg, Belgium, Netherlands, Ireland, Japan, Singapore, Malaysia, South Korea, Trinidad, Bahamas, Guyana, Canada, Mexico, Angola, and the Democratic Republic of Congo, but I have never seen or experienced anything like my Army days in Germany.

Warning: Please read responsibly and remember, we were trained professionals. This novel is screaming fucking hot and will burn the shit out of you. It is dangerous to operate heavy equipment while under the influence of this book. Impalement, inebriated annihilation, damage to health and vital organs, amongst a slew of other radical and *arrestable* offences are all possibilities if you try this shit at home. Into the breach we go. You have been warned!

FOREWORD

Not sure there is too much to say after an introduction like that, but there are a few things I feel should be written in order to lay down some of the groundwork as you venture into the book.

This was the early 1990s. It was a very *different* time. There was a different psyche to humanity back then. Not only in the minds of us young soldiers, but also in Europeans, and especially Germans, as the Berlin wall had come down just a few years before our arrival. It was an exciting time in Europe. *Period.* But Germany, well, it was still magical back then; it was like a fairytale, and we took full advantage of it. Castles, beautiful women, the (then) mystique associated with young American G.I.s (Galvanized Iron, but colloquially dubbed *Government Issued* by U.S. soldiers during WWII)—all were in full-effect. It was a wonderful time to be alive in this beautiful, storybook-like country of beers, blondes, kingdoms, and a not so beautiful and violent history.

We were young men in a combat-arms Military Occupational Specialty (MOS, or our jobs in the Army). We were trained soldiers in the deadliest military on the face of the planet. This was back when women were not allowed to serve in combat roles. As it was the thinking of the time, so we believed it was the way it should have been, as that was the way it had always been. We were, in our minds, indestructible, tougher than the world, and ready for anything it threw our way. That's how we thought, anyway. How we were *made* to feel. And for the most part, after surviving the whole ordeal, it was, for all intents and purposes, very much our truth.

Bear in mind that most Germans liked and appreciated the U.S. Armed Forces presence there. After Communism fell, we brought a much needed financial boost to their economy. The exchange rate was around DM3,30–3,50 (*Deutsch Mark,* German currency before the Euro) to 1 United States Dollar, which stretched a young soldier's budget. We felt it our duty as American ambassadors to single-handedly prop up the beer, bratwurst, and sauerkraut industries, and in some cases, the brothels, too.

We should touch on the subject of rank structure so that you understand exactly with whom you're dealing. This way, the phrase, *Shit Rolling Downhill,* has a better understanding for my *non-military* readers.

There are two types of soldiers in the Army. There are *commissioned officers,* and then there are the soldiers who do the actual work…we call them *enlisted members.* I'll give you three guesses which one I was. *Ding, ding, ding,* we have a winner. Yes, I was an enlisted member. The term *member* has a comical ring to it. It's not like being a member of the local yacht or country club. *A member in good-standing will enjoy all the club's many benefits, fringe or otherwise, entitled to him.* But, after serving, I came to realize that it was an exclusive club, a *member's only* kind of thing: unlike those horrible jackets we all wore in the 1980s. Here it is, from bottom to top:

ENLISTED AND NON-COMMISIONED OFFICERS, or NCOs

Commissioned officers outrank every enlisted and NCO soldier.

E-1/ PVT = PRIVATE. Every soldier in the *whole* of the Army outranks you.

E-2/ PV2 = PRIVATE SECOND CLASS/ MOSQUITO WINGS. Outranks one guy.

E-3/ PFC = PRIVATE FIRST CLASS. Nickname: PRIVATE FUCKING CIVILIAN.

E-4/ SPC = SPECIALIST. Fancies himself a god among the privates.

BEGIN ENLISTED NCO RANKS

E-4P (P = Promotable) CORPORAL OR JUNIOR NCO. New squad leader. *Me!*

E-5/ SGT = SERGEANT. Backbone of the Army. Seasoned squad leader.

E-6/ SSG = STAFF SERGEANT. Runs a platoon. Knows his shit at this point.

E-7/ SFC = SERGEANT FIRST CLASS/ PLATOON DADDY. Nearly untouchable.

E-8/ MSG = MASTER SERGEANT/ 3-UP & 3-DOWN/ END OF AN ENDING.

E-8/ 1SG = FIRST SERGEANT/ We call him Top. LTs *think* they out-rank him.

E-9/ SGM = SERGEANT MAJOR. Forgotten more than you will ever know.

E-9/ CSM = COMMAND SERGEANT MAJOR. Nobody fucks with this guy.

E-9/ SMA = SERGEANT MAJOR OF THE ARMY. Never going to meet this guy.

WARRANT OFFICERS: EXPERT MAINTENANCE PERSONNEL

WO-1/ CW-2/ CW-3 = WARRANT OFFICERS IN TRAINING.

CW-4/ CHIEF WARRANT OFFICER FOUR. This guy definitely knows his shit.

CW-5/ CHIEF. They didn't exist when I served.

COMMISIONED OFFICERS

0-1/ 2LT = SECOND LIEUTENANT/ BUTTER BAR. Knows nothing, thinks he knows it all. A PFC has been promoted more times than this guy.

0-2/ 1LT = FIRST LIEUTENANT. Beginning to understand that most soldiers know more than him.

0-3/ CPT = CAPTAIN. Realizes people have been laughing at him the whole time he was a LT…until now! Usually a Company Commander.

0-4/ MAJ = MAJOR. They are close to power, but still paying their dues. Enters the political realm of the military.

0-5/ LTC = LIEUTENANT COLONEL. Answers phone as if a Bird Colonel, but we all know better. Usually in charge of a battalion.

0-6/ COL = COLONEL/ FULL BIRD COLONEL. They've finally

reached a position of *real* power. Also known as the rank of WAR BIRD.

0-7/ BG = 1 STAR/ BRIGADIER GENERAL. At the bottom of the general pile and courting the Army for a date.

0-8/ MG = 2 STARS/ MAJOR GENERAL. Dating the Army. Still has a boss.

0-9/ LTG = LIEUTENANT GENERAL/ THREE-STARS. Everyone kisses his ass and is now *engaged* to be wed to the Army.

0-10/ GEN = GENERAL/ 4 STARS. Nobody fucks with this guy. Fruit salad adorns his uniform. Honeymoon over. Officially, married to the Army.

GOA = GENERAL OF THE ARMY/ FIVE-STARS/ Rank used only in time of war. God-like mythology follows him. Works directly for the President.

As a military courtesy and custom to signify that a soldier isn't armed, all enlisted personnel must render a salute to both commissioned and warrant officers, when approached. It is extending the right hand in a sharp, snappy manner to the eyebrow to show respect or deference to that officer.

However, there are exceptions. When a soldier, regardless of rank, is met by another that has *earned* the Congressional Medal of Honor, our nation's highest military award, that person will render a salute to that recipient, even if they are of a lower rank. Should you ever meet one of these individuals, know that you are meeting a *real-life* hero and give them the utmost respect. Most soldiers are posthumously awarded the Medal of Honor.

Ac· ro· nym. /ˈakrə,nim/ noun—An abbreviation formed from the initial letters of other words and pronounced as a word. The United States

Army is, after all, a government agency ripe with them, so please, prepare to see shit and tons of acronyms in this book. Normally, unless a book cites an acronym less than three times, it shouldn't be included, but for the sake of my military brothers-and-sisters, I have included most of the common ones associated with the Army.

EXAMPLES:

BOHICA: Bend Over, Here It Comes Again.

OSUT: One Station Unit Training.

LLMF: Lima Lima Mike Foxtrot in the phonetic alphabet, but also known as Lost Like a Mother Fucker.

Military time is based on the 24-hour, or international, system of keeping time. What that means is, there are 24 hours in a day and the military can have no confusion about the time. This book will observe that system.

Translation:

0001 = one minute after midnight.

1201 = one minute after noon.

Normal A.M. times are pretty easy: 0100, 0200, 0300, etc., are 1, 2, and 3 A.M., so-on-and-so-forth until you reach 1 P.M., or the 13th hour of the day. This is translated into 1300 hours. 2 P.M. is 1400 hours, 8:30 P.M. is 2030 hours, etc., etc. When in doubt, anything after 1300, simply subtract 12 hours from it and you have your *normal* times. Who knew I was writing an educational book as well?

PEOPLE I WOULD
LIKE TO THANK

I would like to first thank my father, Paul Turner, a Viet-Nam Veteran... *Welcome home, sir!* Thank you for being tough on me, even when I didn't like it, but needed it the most. Also, my brother Kevin Turner, my uncle Chris Robinson, my grandfather Floyd Robinson, my great-great uncle Maxi Butler, great-uncles Bill Curlee, Gloyd and Robert, cousin Alex, my son Dylan Knowles Dylan Knowles, and an untold number of relatives that have selflessly served in the United States Armed Forces. All of you served the greatest nation on earth, these United States of America. Thank you, one and all.

I'd also like to thank my mother, Brenda Turner, for always encouraging me to be myself. I miss the late-night talks we used to have while the rain poured and the thunder rolled.

I thank my beautiful wife Kristy for her undeterred support in all that I do for our family. Your guidance in love and kindness has been a beacon of light in my life. Remember, I always have a plan, babe.

I would like to thank all of my children: Madeline, Trevor, and Dylan, for their love, acceptance, and understanding. I hope this book serves as some insight as to why I am the way I am.

I would be in big trouble if I didn't pay my respects to the brothers of Echo Company, 2-13 Armor Training Brigade, Fort Knox, Kentucky for Part I of the book's inspiration. And Part II honors go to my lifelong brothers: the Silver Knights of 3rd Battalion, 77th Armor Regiment, First Armored Division, or *Old Ironsides*, Mannheim, Germany. Last, but not least, though not included in the book, are the Men of War of the 1st Battalion, 33rd Armored Regiment, Second Infantry Division (Indian's Head), Fort Lewis, Washington. Gentlemen, you know who you are, and without you these stories wouldn't be possible. My life would not have been as enriched as it was, had it not been for you crazy fuckers. I cannot thank you enough for accepting me as your brother and remaining in my life to this day. I look forward to the next reunion. If you bought this book, the first beer is on me. Iron soldiers!

A couple of individuals that unknowingly made this book possible are fellow veteran and colleague, U.S. Army Infantry Captain, Waylon B, for his continued support of my family through offshore contract work around the world. Armor leads the way, sir. Next is Randy Tompkins, who has now passed through this life, for his assistance and guidance in finding a publisher.

I would also like to give my uncle, Chris Robinson, U.S. Army Intelligence Lieutenant Colonel (Ret), credit for helping me in the editing process and decisions regarding content of the book.

I would be remiss if I didn't give incredible recognition to my editor, Danielle Lake. Thank you for the kind attention and insightful direction you breathed into this book. You are truly a gift to your craft.

I would also like to thank those of you that purchased this book. You could have purchased a million others, but you chose this one. Thank you, and I hope you enjoy a few of the stories of my rich and full youth.

Finally, I would like to thank each and every veteran of this great nation that has served, is currently serving, and will serve in the future to keep these United States of America in safe and capable hands, as our forefathers intended. To each of my *brothers-and-sisters-in-arms* that have taken the oath to defend our constitution, our way of life, and the bright possibility of the American dream, I salute you one and all.

PART I

CIVILIAN
TO
SOLDIER

1

DELAYED ENTRY

I was sixteen when I lied to my parents and told them I was going to a friend's house after school. Instead, I rode my motorcycle to the local Army recruiting office to meet SSG P. Naturally, he told me that I was too young to join. I still wanted to see what jobs they were offering that included the Army College Fund. He informed me about the Delayed Entry Program. Of course, it required my parents' approval. If I would donate $100.00 a month for the first twelve months of my three-year enlistment, the Army would give me over $30K for college. It was a wonderful program.

I should have studied better for the ASVAB (Armed Services Vocational Aptitude Battery, or the exam that determined what job(s) you were qualified to do in the military), but I did well enough, even at six-teen-years old. I did really well on the mechanical section. He offered me all the different MOSs that fell under the College Fund umbrella: Military Police: definitely not; Aircraft mechanic: no. The list endlessly continued. He had these videos that the Army created to show you the *exciting* side of each MOS. Time-after-time the answer from me was, *"No. No. No."* I was thinking I may have to join the infantry, but, I simply didn't want that. I didn't want to make my brother—a Staff Sergeant in the U.S. Army Airborne Rangers—look bad by outper-forming him. Just teasing, Kevin.

That's when he mentioned, *"ARMORED CREWMAN."*

I asked, *"WHAT'S THAT?"*

It certainly didn't sound interesting. It sounded like a cheesy super-hero movie character. *The Armored Crewman is back in this new action thriller where he takes on the Neo-Nazi's of south Chicago. He's out for blood, and this time, he means it.* What could it hurt at this point? He popped a VCR tape into the bottom of the television. Yes, I'm that old. Insert generational gap here: VCR is a Video Cassette Recorder—it's how we watched movies back in those days. Look it up. The struggle was real with rewind fees.

There it was…this big, beautiful tank jumping through the air as it rolled across the desert, leaving dusty mayhem in its wake. It was as if Hell's Hounds had been unleashed onto scorched earth. The M1A1 Abrams Main Battle Tank. The 120mm, M256 smoothbore cannon standing out and tall at attention, waiting to decimate a target. I knew in that moment, I was going to be one of those dusty, crusty, grease-covered, sweaty, bright-eyed, fuzzy-faced, hair-cut-needing, beer-guzzling, under-rated, over-worked, under-paid, over-sexed little shits that can fuck up more battlefield in two minutes than the Infantry can do all day. I was going to be just like the ones I had seen in the movies. I will go ahead and brag and say, wow, did I ever kill it? Especially the beer swilling part.

So, several months later, SSG P and I drove up to the MEPS (Military Entrance Point Station) in Montgomery, Alabama. I can still see the white fence lining a particular piece of property along Highway 231 as you roll into the south of Montgomery. Even years later, that same white fence lines the roadway. I am always reminded of that trip and the many, many life changes that took place soon thereafter.

MEPS involved a lot of waiting in line, and then more waiting in line: eye exam, psychological exam, a turn your head and cough exam, flat-feet exam. It was during this trip that I realized that being a Tanker was far better than the guy that had to pick up men's balls and instruct them to turn their heads and cough. I *DID NOT* want that guy's job. After that, there was more waiting for what seemed like all day, because, quite frankly, it was *all day* and into the evening. There was a waiting line for all manner of medical ins-and-outs. It was exhausting. So far, I thought the Army sucked. I knew this was part of it, though. Hell, I still had more than a year before the real fun even began.

After the dust settled, I was enlisted into the Delayed Entry Program as a 19Kilo (a number/phonetic alphabetical designator is assigned to each specific job in the Army), or Armored Crewman, A.K.A. a Tanker. I was to attend 16½ weeks of OSUT (One Station Unit Training), instead of the normal eight weeks of BT (Basic Training), and umpteen weeks, even months, of AIT (Advanced Individual Training), learning a specific job. I was to report to Fort Knox, Kentucky, a week after my eighteenth birthday.

You would be surprised at how many people ask me if I'd seen or guarded the gold at Fort Knox. *"NO, I NEVER SAW THE GOLD. WAIT, FUCK IT! YOU KNOW WHAT? I WAS IN CHARGE OF THE GOLD. EVERY FUCKING BAR OF IT. I STILL HAVE A COUPLE LAYING AROUND THE GARAGE,"* is what I want to say. Read the book and I'll let you be the judge as to whether you'd want *me* guarding America's gold reserve. We did get to march closer to it than most civilians ever will, but, *no*, not a chance in hell did I see it or even get a whiff of it.

I returned to high school with a whole new outlook, as I was informed that any infractions from here on out, whether in school or civilian life, could potentially screw up my future plans in the Army. I was a whole new kid my last year, much to my parents' and teachers' delight. I don't think they ever had to come pick me up from the dean's office, nor did I ever get suspended one time that year. The operative words here are, *that year*. Hell, I was even selected as one of the Principal's Aides. How the fuck that happened, I'll never know. But I wound up rekindling an old school tradition by organizing the first bonfire pep rally for the football team's homecoming. It was an event that hadn't taken place in an untold number of years. Go Cougars! Go me!

I was proud that I was going to serve our country, serve something larger than myself. Some of my friends had been accepted into college, others were going to work with their fathers or uncles, and others didn't have a clue. I felt I had an edge. I was earning my college money instead of going into debt for it or relying on mommy and daddy to pay for it. We were a working-class family, and this was my shot at success. America was about to enter a war with Saddam Hussein, and I was joining the military. It all seemed so natural to me.

I remember how proud I felt when I raised my right hand and recited,

"I DO SOLEMNLY SWEAR OR AFFIRM THAT I WILL SUPPORT AND DEFEND THE CONSTITUTION OF THE UNITED STATES AGAINST ALL ENEMIES, FOREIGN AND DOMESTIC; THAT I WILL BEAR TRUE FAITH AND ALLEGIANCE TO THE SAME; AND I WILL OBEY THE ORDERS OF THE PRESIDENT OF THE UNITED STATES AND THE ORDERS OF THE OFFICERS APPOINTED OVER ME, ACCORDING TO REGULATIONS AND THE UNIFORMED CODE OF MILITARY JUSTICE. SO HELP ME GOD."

Weird times those were indeed. It was, to say the least, the calm before the storm. As I was known for being a troublemaker, a brawler, a hell-raiser, it is no wonder at all why ARMOR called my name.

2

FORT KNOX—
SCHOOL OF ARMOR

'Twas a cool, rainy night as I flew into Louisville. There waited a man, a civilian that would deliver us into the abyss that surely awaited us. I wore the tennis shoes that would propel me from my first run at Fort Knox, all the way to my last. Little did I know about the journey my life was about to take. The gentleman escorted us onto a bus. I grabbed a seat and looked around at all the other faces and into the eyes of those that were scared. Some tried to hide it, but we were all extremely nervous. What we didn't know was just how fucked our life was about to become.

The bus slugged through the back roads and into the darkness as the rain slacked to a drizzle. Other than passing through Kentucky on the way to my grandparents' home in Detroit, I'd never spent any time there. Even in the dark, it all looked so foreign, but that was mostly fear and uncertainty sinking in. The bus was full of wide-eyed kids. Just a few days prior, all the faces in my life looked so familiar. I was now a stranger in a strange land. After a while, the mood eased, and voices began to get louder and louder. Some guys played off the fear through false arrogance, while others sat in silence. I listened and spoke very little to the guy next to me, less the normal niceties. Simple questions and simple answers filled the void.

The bus approached the gate as the guard smiled and waved us through, despite the cold, drizzling rain. *What's that guy happy about? He's on guard duty.* For he had already been through the hell that we were in route to, which would have made me happy, too, had I known what he did. The lights on post (Army base), were dim, as a collection of both civilian and military vehicles began to dot the landscape. The bus had made countless journeys like this one, with countless numbers of boys on their way to becoming men. Finally, the bus stopped in front of an old, non-descript, white-washed building. A group of men, donned in camouflage, stood attentively in front. Their sleeves were smartly rolled-up with cuffs folded back so that a seamless map of camouflage extended evenly over their upper arms. They had the famous brown and round drill instructor hats pulled low over their brows. We would come to dread these hats, especially the men under them, whom we called Drill Sergeant's (DSs).

One of the DSs stepped onto the bus and calmly spoke. *"ALL RIGHT, GENTLEMEN, GRAB YOUR BAGS AND MOVE OFF THE BUS IN A SINGLE-FILE LINE. STAND ON THOSE YELLOW FOOTPRINTS WITH YOUR BAGS IN FRONT OF YOU."*

We stepped off and found a place at the famous yellow footprints of Fort Knox. As we did, I thought, the [DSs] had gone soft. I thought, my dad, brother, and countless uncles were all full of shit about how mean the drill instructors were in the Army. He seemed pleasant enough. To ensure all [trainees] were present and accounted for, they did a roll call.

"ALL RIGHT, LADIES," began the DS, kindly overlooking the snickers from the boys after being called, *ladies*. With a more commanding voice, he began again. *"ALL RIGHT, LADIES, MAKE YOUR WAY INTO THE BUILDING, ON MY COMMAND, AND ONLY ON*

MY COMMAND. ENTER THE BUILDING AND FOLLOW THE DIRECTIONS OF THE DS IN THERE. DO NOT PICK THE SEAT YOU WANT. SIT NEXT TO ONE ANOTHER IN THE ORDER HE CALLS YOUR NAME. TAKE YOUR BAGS WITH YOU TO YOUR SEAT AND SET THEM ON THE TABLE IN FRONT OF YOU." We did as instructed and without incident. So far, so good.

If you've ever seen the movie *STRIPES,* then you will certainly remember the building/room with all the unit insignias on the wall. That was the building we were in. I was thoroughly impressed at this point, thinking, *This is so cool!* It was a real building, a real place. Coming from a long line of military forefathers and having seen nearly every classic and non-classic military movie, I immediately recognized the unit patches on the wall. First Infantry Division (Big Red One), the 101st Airborne (Screaming Eagles), and Second Armored Division (Hell on Wheels), to name a few. For me, it was a reunion with my childhood heroes plastered right there on those four walls. The First Sergeant (1SG), also known as *Top,* gave us a fine speech about how we were in the hallowed halls of men, of soldiers, on the same grounds as those champions of liberty we'd learned about in school. He said we would be made into men at Fort Knox, that we would be woven from the same military fabric as our forefathers. He also said that some of us would become soldiers and others would not. Like so many men before us, we could feel the warmth of pride in our bellies, in our hearts. Unfortunately, that building, that place of honor has been torn down since our leaving Fort Knox.

One of the DSs took his place in front of the room and thanked Top for his contribution. With a cool, confident voice, he spoke. *"LADIES, THIS IS YOUR ONE AND ONLY CHANCE TO COME CLEAN. ONCE YOU LEAVE THIS ROOM, YOUR ASSES BELONG TO ME AND THE OTHER INSTRUCTORS. THIS PARTY IS ABOUT TO GET STARTED, AND I DON'T CARE WHO YOU WERE WHEN YOU ENTERED THIS ROOM; IF YOU WERE THE FOOTBALL*

CAPTAIN, A FRAT BOY, A MOTOR HEAD, OR A STONER, I DON'T CARE, BECAUSE ONCE YOU LEAVE THIS BUILDING, YOU ARE ALL EQUALLY WORTHLESS TO ME."

A subtle fear started to churn in my belly at this point. Although his voice never raised above a firm, direct tone, it *commanded*, without uncertainty, our respect.

He continued. *"IF YOU BROUGHT WITH YOU TODAY ANY GUNS, AMMUNITION, KNIVES, SWORDS—WEAPONS OF ANY KIND—DRUGS, ALCOHOL, CIGARETTES, SNUFF, DIP, PORNOGRAPHIC MAGAZINES, ANYTHING AT ALL THAT YOU ARE NOT SUPPOSED TO HAVE, THIS IS YOUR ONE AND ONLY MOMENT OF AMNESTY TO GET RID OF IT WITHOUT CONSEQUENCE. MYSELF AND THE OTHER DSs WILL LEAVE THE ROOM AND GIVE YOU EXACTLY TWO MINUTES TO CLEAR THE ROOM VIA THE BACK DOOR. THERE IS A BOX CLEARLY MARKED 'AMNESTY' IN THE HALLWAY. I SUGGEST YOU USE IT. IF IN DOUBT, THROW THAT SHIT OUT. THIS IS YOUR ONE CHANCE, LADIES. MAKE IT COUNT, BECAUSE WE WILL FIND IT, AND THEN WE WILL HAVE YOUR ASS IN A WORLD OF HURT."*

He proceeded out the door, with his cronies in tow. *"STAND,"* his voice boomed while he walked out. We formed a gaggle of a line and made our way out. I observed some guys going through their bags, others through their pockets, taking full advantage of the opportunity. I had nothing to dispose of; therefore, I didn't see anything the others were tossing out. As the last man exited the building, the real fun factor for the DSs kicked into overdrive. It seems after all, my father, brother, and uncles were not so full of shit, because the party did *indeed* get started.

With a commanding and bigger than life voice, the lead DS sounded off. *"GET THE FUCK OUT OF MY BUILDING, YOU SORRY,*

NO-GOOD SONS-A-BITCHES. GET THE FUCK OUT, NOW. MOVE, MOTHER-FUCKERS. LOTTY DOTTY, EVERY FUCKIN' BODY." It was not the pleasant voice we'd heard a few minutes prior. He was seemingly pissed right off. Shit got real, *real quick*! It was like an explosion of hatred had fallen into our laps. Our assholes puckered up so tight, you'd have struggled to stick a needle in it. It was a multitude of DSs screaming and cussing at top-level shrieks designed to instill fear to the *nth* degree. Knife-hands were circling us like a pack of wolves on fresh prey.

As I understand it, knife-handing has all but been removed from the military experience. I presume it was outlawed because it was effective and intimidating. I still use it to this day. Extend all of your fingers together in a tight group in line with the back of your hand. Your thumb should be in parallel with your fingers and slightly bent inward toward your palm. It is a method used to instruct, teach, discipline, and intimidate. Upper arm/ elbow is raised to near shoulder height and parallel with chest, lower arm at a 90 degree angle from the chest. Range of motion in this position is generally up-and-down while bending at the wrist to accentuate and drive home a particular point of instruction. Back then, a knife-hand was usually in your face or poking your chest. Poking, pushing, and other forms of physical contact from a DS is probably another practice long-outlawed in the military by now, presumably due to its effectiveness—not in my day. These were teaching tools, and they worked. We were not selling cookies; we were training for warfare.

After the lower halves of our anatomies were properly puckered-up, they formed us into a couple of columns and proceeded to march us to our temporary lodging. Thankfully, I hadn't packed much for the trip. That would soon change.

3

WELCOME TO HELL

From the outside, it appeared to be another non-descript, white-washed building. Growing up as a fourth-generation carpenter, I knew it was an old, but well-built structure. I learned that it was used to house soldiers in-processing during WWII. Oh, to have been a fly on the wall over the years. We made our bunks, brushed our teeth, cleaned the barracks, and tried to settle our nerves for what awaited us the next day.

Early the next morning around 0400, or 4 A.M. for you civilian types, we were alarmed to find a loud, empty trashcan being forcibly thrown into our building. *Cock-a-doodle-doo*, assholes! I had functioned at this hour, but never much cared for it. I was little more than a week into being eighteen years old, and so far, *adulting* sucked. We had to wake up, *brush our faces* and *wash our teeth,* use the latrine, or the head (that's the bathroom for you civilians), get dressed, make our bunk, and then clean the barracks we'd just cleaned the night before—all this before breakfast. You'd be surprised how weird people are during their morning routine. A building full of men was far worse than anything I could have imagined. Grumpy, loud, hateful, mean, nasty, and rude *almost* sums it up.

But, before chow (any meal in the Army), we had to learn valuable lesson number one: hurry up and wait! We stood and waited, then waited some more before the DSs made rollcall. Finally they marched us to our first hot meal in the Army. *What the hell?* was my first thought. This was a cruel, twisted joke, right? *Green eggs?* Toast with this white, gravy-*ish* coagulation slathered on top, and what looked like some weird form of pink-tinted sausage mixed in with said gravy. I thought it was under-cooked pork and I would die later that day. I hadn't even been issued a uniform yet. Some legacy I was going to have in the Army, combating salmonella. I would later learn that this white liquid and pink meat concoction was aptly named SOS, or Shit-On-a-Shingle.

The cook slapped all manner of oddities on my plate: SOS, green eggs, a couple strips of ultra-fatty bacon, and a small sausage log that looked like sundried dog dick. I moved along, thoroughly unsure as to where to sit. I didn't know a soul in the room. I slumbered to the drink dispenser and was trying to get some ice when this booming voice behind me said, *"LET'S GET A FUCKING MOVE-ON, PRIVATE!"* Translation: *hurry the fuck up, asshole!* Ice seemingly lost its firm grip at the bottom of my glass as it shot out of the glass and onto the floor.

"WHAT THE FUCK IS YOUR PROBLEM, PRIVATE? PICK THAT FUCKIN' ICE UP! NOWWWWWWW!" This is where, as a young pri-vate, your career begins with the internal dialog of stupid questions, because you are Lima Lima Mike Foxtrot, or *Lost Like a Mother Fucker* (LLMF). Your ass puckers harder as the questions race through your blank mind. *What ice? Where do I set my tray? Do I set it on the floor? Do I set it down where I want to eat? What do I do? Do I scream YES, SIR, like I saw in the movies? Salute him? No, your hands are full. You, dumbass… your hands are full. Oh yeah, I forgot. What did he just scream? He needs to get laid, he is uptight. I bet his kids love him. No, he's an asshole. That is a face only a mother could love…*

He continued. *"PRIVATE FUCKHEAD, WHAT IS YOUR MALFUNCTION? PICK THAT FUCKING ICE UP!!!"*

Yeah, I pretty much stood there with a dumb look on my face in a full-on, full-fledged LLMF position. Hour number six in the Army and I'm killing it. I haven't even had breakfast and this camouflaged asshole is calling me out in front of the entire mess hall (the place where you eat Army chow). I'm getting yelled at by a monster in a green uniform for frozen water, yet, I feel like the jerk.

I mustered up the strength to move. I set my tray down on the counter and retrieved the ice. I rose up and turned to show my new friend, Sunshine (because he certainly doled out sunshine), my great accomplishment, but Sunshine had positioned himself at a table full of other sunshine dealers. I wanted to throw it back down, but I opted out. I figured I had plenty of sunshine heading my way during the next 16½ weeks.

I sat down and gave my food a once-over and decided that it looked like shit, but I was starving so I scarfed it down. Lesson number two in the Army: don't do dumb shit at breakfast, food is only hot once in the Army—sometimes it's food, sometimes it's hot. I managed to get it all down, even the pickled dog dick. It tasted as awful as I'd imagined. It was a new question in life upon which to ponder: *How the fuck do they make food devoid of any and all taste?* Salt and pepper, people; it's called salt and pepper. It has been traded for thousands of years. The Silk Road, hands-down the most famous of trade routes, had salt and fucking pepper. Not us, the most advanced military in the world.

After breakfast we formed up again outside. They marched us to the Central Issue Facility (CIF) to receive our Table of Allowance-50 (TA-50), or all the shit we needed to survive the next 4-½ months in Uncle Sam's Army: head covers (hats), shirts, socks, Battle Dress Uniforms (BDUs, or our camouflaged uniforms), light weather BDU tops, trousers, field jacket (heavy winter coat), combat boots, entrenching tool (shovel), shelter half (tent), stakes, poles, duffle bags, Alice pack (framed backpack), Load Bearing Equipment (LBE, gear that holds your canteens, first-aid kit, and ammunitions magazines), your

Class-As (formal dress greens), winter and summer versions of both uniforms (BDU and Class-As), mess kit (camping-style plate and utensils), poncho, etc. It was shit, and more shit. Two duffle bags stuffed to the gills and an Alice pack stuffed in every nook and cranny. TA-50 issuance was an all-day affair. It was like pulling teeth from an angry tiger. We placed our *new-old stock* collection of gear back into our formation area and did another roll call before hurrying up to wait. We did stop for lunch at some point, and thankfully, it was less eventful than breakfast had been. It was some other schmuck that had his ass chewed by a DS to aid in digestion. All said and done, I was the first, but certainly not the last.

Of course, we all wanted to try on our uniforms. Oh, the ignorance of youth. I'd waited my entire life for this moment. Our uniforms wore no nametags, no rank, and certainly no unit patch. We looked pathetic. Day one was in the bag.

Later that evening as we tried on our uniforms and learned to blouse our trousers in our boots, the DS came into the barracks and told us about barracks cleaning. This was lesson number three: *His* barracks were to be spotless come morning. We had to use a floor buffer to polish these decrepit wooden floors that seemed to have a coat of paste wax on them an inch thick. No matter how much you buffed, you could not get the swirls out of the finish. We were destined to fail. Water spots on the cast-iron faucets and whatnot were sure to result in discipline of some form. All day, these assholes were angry with us. There was no way a moment such as this would escape their attention. Rest assured, it didn't. The next morning, DS Sunshine came in to dole out our daily ration of bright and sunny, Cock-a-doodle-doos! He threw garbage cans, kicked our boots, and acted like a category-5 hurricane towards us and our gear.

To some degree, I knew this was part of the deal, as I'd had a long family history in the Army, and one uncle (Phillip) that joined the Air Force.

He's now a cardiovascular surgeon. Boy, did he screw up, or what? Just kidding. I didn't think about life like this at the time, but the monolog of *How will this job translate into the real world* should have entered my mind, but, it didn't. Between the College Fund and seeing that tank *jumping* the battlefield terrain while expending a 120mm projectile down range, complete with fireball at the end of the gun tube, I would say, I was hooked. I thought, *Um-kay, me do tank!*

After our morning visit from Sunshine, we cleaned the ever-loving-shit out of those barracks before we exited, so the next rotation would *not* enjoy them as much as we *didn't*. Looking and feeling a bit silly in our basic-as-fuck uniforms, the DSs marched us to the on-post barber for haircuts. A time-honored tradition and rite of passage in the Army. I thought I was going to be funny when I slightly turned my head to the barber and said, *"Just a little off the sides, please."* The deed was done, though, as he ripped the clippers straight down the middle of my scalp from the base of my neck all the way up to my eyeballs.

He leaned over, and said, *"Oh, the sides."* He cracked a subtle smile and went back to his business, as there were a hundred other assholes awaiting the same treatment. The floor was a hodgepodge of hair from all over America. There must've been five or six chairs, and around every one was an asshole-shaped mountain of hair. You could barely see the barber's shoes through the melee. Black, brown, red, and blonde hordes of tuft fell indiscriminately to even the odds of individualism among the trainees. It evened the playing field. We were now all equally worthless-looking dickheads. The first thing everyone did when they rose from their chair making their way towards the door, was to drag their hand across their freshly scalped head. A constant barrage of insults and cackles came from the sunshine dealers. An endless barrage of names like Cue Ball, Slick, Dickhead, Chrome Dome, and Mr. Clean were swarming us like flies at a summertime picnic.

Immediately following *happy time* at the barber, we were quickly marched to another building with that still-fresh, *what the fuck have I done with my life* feeling in our guts. We lined up outside of this tiny building, and the DSs began passing out Class-A jackets and cunt caps (head gear for our formal wear), of various sizes. To help the reader visualize the cunt cap, the author asks you to hold your hands together in a prayer-like position, then ease your thumbs apart, as if to catch water, keeping your fingertips and pinky fingers together. The cap's general shape will reveal itself as your hands slowly spread. With blank jackets and cunt caps, it was time for that time-honored tradition of having our first military pictures made. What awesome planning. Joy!

As if we weren't miserable enough with our new hairstyles, we were now going to be quickly ponied-up for pictures we had to keep for the rest of our lives, for obvious reasons. The picture looked like total shit, rather, the expression on my face did. It looks like someone just murdered my favorite dog, stole my bike, whipped my best friend's ass, screwed my girlfriend, and pissed in my cereal while I helplessly watched. That's what that picture looks like. If that ever happened to me, that is certainly the look on my face I'd have imagined.

After our mug shots, we were marched to another official-looking building to do some administrative paperwork for the G.I. Bill, paycheck allotments, etc. After that, round *nine-hundred seventy-three* of the glorious *1992 Hurry Up and Wait Festival* continued. *Yeah, baby*!

We stood again in the formation area. Did I mention how much I wanted to try on that uniform? Yeah. Can we say, dumbass? My feet were killing me in those black leather monstrosities known as combat boots. It had only been a mere 3 to 4 hours and already it was like Dante himself was torturing my soul via my aching, swollen, itching, burning, throbbing feet that were, you guessed it, forming humongous blisters. It [the blistering] happened so fast. I wondered if they were too small. Day one and they were the bane of my existence. We staged our rucksacks and duffle bags in the formation area around 1700 hours. A Deuce-and-a-Half (three-axled, 2½ ton cargo truck, also called a Deuce.), backed up to our formation. It sounded awesome with the turbo charger whirring up to speed. This was going to carry us to our permanent barracks. Initial indoctrination was now behind us.

4

"BETTER SEND THE MEAT WAGON!"

The DS lowered the tailgate and instructed us to grab our rucksacks and load them into the truck. Sweet mother of mercy! We were about to ride in our first *real* military vehicle. How exciting! *I wonder how far we're going. I wonder who my DSs are going to be. Shit, what if it's DS Sunshine? Does that guy hate me, or does he hate everyone? Are my barracks as shitty as these old ones? When do we fire the weaponry?*

"ALL RIGHT, LADIES, LISTEN THE FUCK UP. I HOPE YOU PECKERHEADS PACKED ALL YOUR HEAVY SHIT IN YOUR RUCKSACKS, BECAUSE PLAY TIME IS OVER. NOW THE FUN REALLY BEGINS," he shouted.

I had a sneaky feeling fun wasn't on Uncle Sam's agenda. He continued. *"PICK THOSE FUCKING BAGS UP AND FOLLOW THAT MEAN-LOOKING MOTHER-FUCKER, RIGHT THERE."*

As his fingers extended into a knife-hand, our eyes followed to what was in fact, a mean-looking mother-fucker. He was big, and I mean big. He didn't look happy, either. He had a strained, grumbly voice. He spoke slow and deliberate, but could still scare the shit out of you. He sounded battle-hardened, like he ate rebar and gargled with concrete before his coffee each morning. We shall call him DS Guts-N-Gravel.

It spoke. *"ALL RIGHT, MAGGOTS, GET THOSE FUCKING BAGS OFF THE DECK AND ONTO THOSE WORTHLESS SHOULDERS. HURRY THE FUCK UP. LOTTY DOTTY, EVERYFUCKIN' BODY!"* Lotty Dotty, is a phrase meaning *everyone* should join in on this fun event.

We stood there thinking, *Wait, there are two bags here and only one set of shoulders!* You are obviously confused, DS, said not a single soul. We just stood there and looked like idiots fumbling with our bags.

Again, a booming voice came over us like a speeding train bearing down on a stalled automobile. *"REAL EINSTEINS WE HAVE HERE. PICK THOSE FUCKING BAGS UP; ONE ON THE FRONT AND ONE ON THE BACK, YOU MAGGOTS. HELP YOUR BOYFRIEND IF HE NEEDS IT. FUCKING MOVE, LADIES. WE DON'T HAVE ALL DAY!"*

We saddled up for our pleasure cruise in our first *real* Army vehicle, also known as our feet, with *real* military tires in the form of *combat boots.* We were formed, two-by-two, in a long column that seemed to never end. Because my last name begins with a 'T', it meant I was near the end of the column. Thus began the first of many marches in my black leather monstrosities. Lucky me, I had another pair on my back in my duffle bag. Day two in the United States Army.

Slowly we began our trek across the hot asphalt of Kentucky. It was the second day of September, and summer had no end in sight. Hot boots, hot socks, and a screaming hot BDU top...*Why am I wearing a fucking jacket under two duffle bags in the dead heat of summer? Why are any of us?* After a few minutes of marching around with two duffle bags strapped to our bodies, rule number one regarding hurry up and wait sounded awesome. Finally we turned off the asphalt and into the woods. Great, we're taking a shortcut. Less than 48 hours in the Army, I should have known better, but your mind works in mysterious ways when you're tired. This nature walk from Sunshine's brother was a guise to lure us into a false sense of time, place, and comfort. We marched, then marched some more. We marched through the woods, through bushes, through creeks, over rocky formations, and up-and-over hills before finding our way *back* to the hot asphalt. It seemed the farther we marched, the farther away from our destination we were; which, by all accounts, was the most logical thinking I had done inside of the last two days. In a few weeks, I would learn just how close we really were to our destination as well as the numerous *shortcuts* we repeatedly didn't utilize.

That portion aside, we were all quickly reaching exhaustion. The DS marching back and forth over the length of the column gave us verbal motivation. *"PICK 'EM UP AND PUT 'EM DOWN, MAGGOTS."* Real motivational shit it was. About two or three positions behind me was this black dude getting really worn-out. It got to the point that he was being helped along by a couple of other trainees. His speech started to get slurred as beads of sweat formed across his brow. He became disoriented. He complained to the DS, but there was no love for this dude. Our motivational speaker continued. *"YOU FUCKING PANSY. MY DAUGHTER COULD DO THIS ROAD MARCH."* A road march is one of two things: either a march by foot or columned travel by multiple vehicles. The DS got to the point where he was almost taunting this poor guy. He was really struggling and hitting his proverbial brick wall. It seemed like three hours had passed, but in reality, it was more like an hour and a half or so. We were tired as hell.

As the DS passed our position, the guy clinging to some merciful outcome expressed that he couldn't go any farther—that he was quitting. Those of us around him encouraged him to hang in there, we were almost to the barracks. He struggled on a little farther. The DS made another pass to our place in the column and gave the trainee more shit. *"YOU NEED AN AMBULANCE, NANCY?"* He passed us by and headed forward with a final note of encouragement. *"ONLY A FEW MORE MILES, YOU MAGGOTS."*

You've heard the expression, *the straw that broke the camel's back*. The look in that guy's eyes said it all. When the DS was far enough away from us, this guy came unglued. He threw his bags down and said, *"FUCK THIS SHIT. I QUIT. I CANNOT DO IT. FUCK THIS, I'M OUTTA HERE."* He broke into a full-on sprint to the left of our column, up a long, gradual hill and towards the setting sun.

The DS screamed, *"HEY, PRIVATE, STOP. RIGHT FUCKING NOW."* He ran towards the rear of the Deuce-and-a-Half, grabbed a radio, and screamed, *"WE GOTTA RUNNER AT GRID COORDINATES… BLAH, BLAH."* He grabbed an M16 rifle and fired off a single round into the air. He began his tirade. *"PRIVATE. YOU ARE IN VIOLATION OF ARMY REGULATION SO-AND-SO. YOU WILL STOP NOW, OR I WILL BE AUTHORIZED TO PUT YOU DOWN FOR BEING AWOL,"* or Absent With-Out Leave.

Holy fucking shit, I thought, *that escalated quickly*. This runner was nearing the top of a hill when he did a little half-turn and gave the DS a big right-handed middle finger. Remember Ed W, the Korean War veteran I mentioned? Well, Ed had this shirt that he loved to wear to work. It depicted a mouse extending its middle finger up to a hawk, swooping in for the kill. It read, *Last act of defiance*. I thought of dear old Ed's shirt as that guy flipped off the DS.

He then proceeded to pick up speed as he crested the hilltop. The DS continued. *"LAST FUCKING WARNING, PRIVATE NUMBNUTS. STOP IN THE NAME OF THE US ARMY, OR I WILL BE FORCED TO TAKE YOU DOWN."* He held up the rifle and stared down the sights towards the runner. He was controlled, adept, and comfortable as he squeezed off a single round at his target. Before the echo could even reverberate off the surroundings, that guy hit the dirt like a raw burger patty hitting the kitchen tile. Grass, dust, spit, and ass flipped up into the air and twinkled in the evening's golden light. His body lay there, nearly out of our sight. The sun eerily reflected its rays off his sweaty skin and uniform.

I remember thinking, *What the fuck have I signed up for? What have I gotten myself into?* That was the third time in less than 48 hours my ass had puckered up and the urge to piss was upon me in straight-up fear. I was thinking, *My family never told me about this shit.* Dumbfounded, we simply looked at one another with fresh, wide eyes; brand-new sweat and age-old instinctual fear grimaced our faces and hung in the air like a foul stench. No one spoke directly to one another. We just sort of mumbled triggered responses like *shit* and *what the fuck?* We were in utter disbelief.

DS Guts-N-Gravel started barking out commands, as he returned the weapon into the Deuce. *"EVERYONE REMAIN CALM AND GET THE FUCK BACK IN FORMATION."* He keyed the microphone on the radio and nonchalantly reported the events that unbelievably un-folded before our eyes. *"BETTER SEND A MEAT WAGON 'ROUND TO GET HIM! ALL RIGHT, YOU MAGGOTS, PREPARE TO MOVE OUT."* I felt like a worthless slab of beef, as did everyone. He was going to callously leave that guy in the dirt. I was in the beginning stages of shock, as we all were.

Needless to say, we had mustered a newfound energy to march with our duffle bags. The *now-deceased* trainee's duffle bags were thrown into the back of the Deuce, near the still-warm rifle. The DSs arm moved in a large arching motion over his shoulder as he delivered his orders. *"OKAY, RECRUITS, LET'S MOVE IT OUT."* And so it was, we began our march around Kentucky, yet again, though, with a new vigor and enthusiasm we'd not known before. Mutters of whispered sentences could be heard under the heavy breathing of physical exertion, shock, and fear. Heads were shaking back and forth in disbelief as we shared wide-eyed glances with one another, as if to confirm it wasn't a dream, but rather, a nightmare.

The scenery of his lifeless body still flashed through my mind. Undoubtedly, we all had the same visions and thoughts. I knew right then and there, we trainees were in this shit together. It was *us* and *them,* the *soldiers* and the *drill sergeants*. I reckon we marched for another forty-five minutes to an hour. Exhaustion helped remove the images from my head, but the thoughts were still ever-present. It's strange how fear and shock make you forget that your feet are burning, your back is aching, and that salted perspiration is continually running into your eyes. Everything melted away in those moments—family, friends, pain, homesickness—moments happened in slow-motion and surreal-like as my mind began to compartmentalize the gruesome event I'd witnessed. Another recruit was, moments ago, marching near me, and now he lay dead for disobeying an order. I began to understand how trained men could go to war and survive its horrors.

Finally, semblances of civilization began to appear around us. It seemed like the light at the end of the tunnel. Before we knew it, we were surrounded by buildings. There read the name of my new home, *DISNEY BARRACKS*. Much to our relief, the road march was nearing its completion. We passed several long, red-bricked buildings, one after another. After our road march, they looked beautiful as we'd hoped one would be ours. Finally, we turned to the right, in between two of them, transitioning from asphalt to wide, concrete sidewalks. It was a great feeling.

As we turned between the buildings, the sun disappeared behind them. Shadows were long stretched across the wide sidewalks and green grass beside our formation. A figure could be seen as we started to round the next corner. Our bodies and each of their quivering muscles began to sense that the journey had been completed; therefore, they began to shut down as we inched towards the shadowy figure. Then the distinctive head gear of a DS could be made out. As wonderful as it was to have completed the road march, it also meant the real journey to becoming a soldier would inevitably begin. As we stood in formation catching our breath, it dawned on us exactly who was standing there in that DS uniform—it was the runner, the unknown corpse that had flashed through our heads for the last hour. It was an *Aha!* moment for sure.

We knew we'd been royally duped by the best of them. These DSs had nothing but time on their hands to devise ways to toy with our ignorant and naïve little heads. They were masters of their domain. They truly owned our minds, bodies, and spirits in that moment. Our souls even. Of course they smiled, we smiled, and we all laughed. It would be the last laugh we would all share for quite some time after that evening. My DS, the runner, spoke…"WELCOME TO HELL, GENTLEMEN!"

5

LET THE GAMES BEGIN

They organized and formed us into three platoons. Rollcall ensued as rule number one was exercised, yet again: hurry up and wait. I was in Second Platoon, Echo Company, 2nd Battalion, 13th Armored Training Brigade, Disney Barracks, Fort Knox, Kentucky. It was well after dark before we were allowed into the three-storied building. First Platoon (PLT) was assigned to floor *one,* Second PLT and *yours truly* were on floor *two,* and Third PLT, naturally, were on floor *three.* We occupied one-half of the entire building. The building was long, rectangular, and had one door on each side that was center-mass of our half. It was the building we would face while in formation as we looked upon the DS, while also getting smoked. What's getting smoked, you might ask? That's when we in the Army learn through pain. More about that later.

The first few days were the toughest. Every single thing you do in the first days and weeks in the service is inherently wrong. Seemingly, eighteen years with my parents hadn't prepared me for this in the least. Trainees couldn't breathe, eat, shit, walk, sleep, or fart without making a mistake. We all had shaved heads, crisp new uniforms, and absolutely no clue what the hell was happening. Everything we did had better be with a purpose—a military purpose—not our own.

We also learned rule number four in the Army: if you were going somewhere, you were to be running and screaming. Yes, you read that correctly, every single place you went, unless you were in formation, you were expected to run and scream at the top of your lungs while in route. After all these years, I have still wondered what the hell that was all about. Motivation? Maybe. I kid you not, if you were going to the mess hall, you'd better be running and screaming. If you were going to deliver a message to another building, you'd better be running and screaming. If you were going to formation to then go running, you'd better scream while running to that formation. It's so comical to look back on it now. It sounds preposterous, but it did serve a sadistic purpose. If you didn't, you'd certainly pay for it.

I can only imagine what first-time visiting dignitaries, families, and friends must have thought when they observed masses of bald, green monsters running and screaming like madmen. *This* is the greatest Army in the world? You better fucking believe it, folks.

6

"IN CADENCE. EXERCISE."

For every mistake in the military, there is some form of military re-habilitation. What exactly that discipline is will be determined by the disciplinarian. The Army has ways of punishing your mind and body you could never have imagined. The push-up (PU) is an Army favor-ite. The Army has several variations, too: standard PU, inclined PU, diamond PU, wide-armed PU, wide-leg PU. They're also known as the front leaning rest position, though there is no real *resting* actually hap-pening. Mysteriously, the Army doesn't have jumping jacks. No, no, no. They have the side-straddle hop. Everyone performs these exercises as a group, as a team and in unison, unless you are singled-out for *in-dividual rehabilitative training*. It's real fun stuff.

The Army also single-handedly revamped the entire known mathemat-ical system. It's a fun game they like to call a four-count exercise. With each action in an exercise, such as the up or the down movement in a PU, the Army will call *one* for that movement, then call *two* for the counter-movement. In the civilian world that would complete one rep-etition, but not in the Army. It goes something like this: *"ONE, TWO, THREE, <u>ONE</u>; ONE, TWO, THREE, <u>TWO</u>; ONE, TWO, THREE, <u>THREE</u>."* They were effectively getting twice as much bang-for-the-buck. *Amazing!* My high school algebra teacher was so full of shit when she told me I'd need math in the real world. She hadn't a clue the Army had it covered. To add insult to injury, we had to scream out this Army-specific math in unison with the DS during the exercise. *René Descartes* would roll over in his grave.

The fun didn't stop there. They had other remedial forms of exercise like flutter kicks, hello Dolly's, the dying cockroach, chair backs, mountain climbers, and wall-ups. Wall-ups are a form of PU where you face a wall in the PU position, then kick your feet up and over your head so that you're in a hand-stand position with your heels backed to the wall, then mimic an upside-down overhead press. Those are super fucking fun. There was also the low crawl, crab walk, bicycle, rifles overhead, rifles out front, and even squats rifles out front. If you want to understand what the *out front* is, simply hold an 8-pound weight out in front of you at shoulder level for minutes (seemingly, days) on end. Just when you thought you were tired, they would torture you with *up 'n downs*. It's where you are in the position of attention, drop down to a PU position without performing a PU, then recover back to the position of attention. You simply go back-and-forth from one position to the other, *over* and *over* and *over*!

If you are a morning person, then Army training is for you. Every single day, we were up no later than 0430. If you are an outdoors type of person, then the Army is also for you. We were getting fresh air every morning by 0630. First, we had to wake up, *brush our faces* and *wash our teeth*, make our bunks, clean the latrine, polish the floors, and take out the trash. I remember the T.V. commercials for the Army and the announcer saying, *"THE UNITED STATES ARMY...WE DO MORE BEFORE 9 A.M. THAN MOST PEOPLE DO ALL DAY."* They were not bullshitting.

I found so many personality types those first few days and weeks. City slickers, country bumpkins, surfers, gear heads, nerds, preppies, arrogant pricks, quiet types—personalities to fit every bill. Some guys were great at being soldiers, while others had to work really hard at it. The tough guys were sometimes the weakest ones in the bunch, and the nerdy, non-typical soldier-types would surprise the hell out of everyone, themselves included. It was the single-most challenging thing any of us had ever experienced in our short lives. With the dawn of each new day, we began to see our old selves falling away and our new-and-improved selves building strength. There was a mixture of both regular Army and National Guardsmen in our group with two differing philosophies: one took it seriously and wanted to succeed, and the other wanted to just *get by*. Not all the Nasty Girls were like this, though. It was tough on the guys that took it seriously, understood the game, and learned to play it well. The Nasty Girls knew upon graduation they would return to their normal lives and (mostly) on a *weekend warrior* status.

Once we realized we were always wrong, could do no right, and would be punished for each and every infraction, everything seemed to settle down. We got into a routine and actually started learning how to care for our uniforms; thereby, earning a sense of pride in ourselves. We started going to the motor pool, or military parking lot, and getting some actual tank time with a non-drill sergeant tank commander (TC). While training on the tanks, it was myself, my Battle Buddy, whom we will call *The Real Deal*, and the TC. The Real Deal was a National Guardsman from Texas. Down inside the tank, away from prying eyes, the TC would let us smoke cigarettes that he kindly provided for a small, cash-only fee. It was like being a kid, sneaking out of the house to drink beer with your buddies or stealing the ole man's car. It was a much needed break from the DSs. The kind of training required to learn all the functions of the tank and how to exploit them, required a bit more finesse than the normal screaming afforded us.

7

GENERAL ORDERS, AND THE PRICE OF NOT KNOWING THEM

There is a plethora of information that the Army bestows upon you in the short time you are in training. I can only imagine what other MOSs had to endure. We had to learn the entire rank structure, a soldier's general orders, acronyms galore, names of equipment, people, military history, customs, how to walk, talk, march, and stand in formation, dress, shave, shoot rifles, pistols, machine guns, the tank's main gun, how to throw grenades, how to dress a battle wound, how to polish boots, how to buff floors, how to adorn our uniforms, maintenance on the tank, how to eat a meal in three minutes flat, and numerous other things a soldier must master in a few short months.

It is not as if you go week-after-week without a test to prove one's skills. No, no. We were tested often—constantly, in fact—several times each day, throughout the entirety of our training. In the beginning, one never knows when or where they might be tested. You could be tested immediately *after* being tested in a classroom setting. You could be tested while exiting the shower, running in formation, while doing PUs, eating chow, or handling your business in the latrine. It was all day, every day.

Without warning, the DS would break into an on-the-spot exam. *"TURNER, WHAT IS YOUR SECOND GENERAL ORDER?" "SMITH, WHAT IS THE REASON FOR INSPECTING ONE'S RIFLE BEFORE LEAVING THE RANGE?" "ALPHABET* (his name was Plebalachezck, or something, so naturally his nickname was Alphabet)*, WHAT IS THE MAXIMUM EFFECTIVE RANGE OF AN M16 RIFLE?" "REAL DEAL, WHAT IS THE ENLISTED RANK STRUCTURE, FROM BOTTOM-TO-TOP?"* There were no exceptions. Everyone was drilled on all things Army, all the time.

These questions were very common in initial training. They could come from anyone that outranked you, DS or not. One had to be able to spout off a precise answer to an enormity of questions, or a price must be paid. Note, I said precise. Literally, we began learning our general orders on day two. It really is a testament to the military-style learning implemented during the old days. There was the Army's way, or the highway. Shape up, or ship out, as they say. You either cognitively absorbed the DSs' lesson, or they improved your memory by way of physical rehabilitation. That was their way of motivating your brain to retain the information. Learn, or feel the pain and agony of stupidity.

Every soldier, regardless of race, age, political view, religion, height, or intelligence, was expected to know their general orders. We were expected to recite them as quickly as we could recite our own names. If you were to pass judgement without punitive damages, you'd better be able to belt out your general orders with the confidence and exuberance of a *fire-and-brimstone* reverend at an all-night revival.

Oh, the cunning of some of our DSs; for they could punish a man in ways you'd never imagined. On the mornings before our PT training *even* began, but after an overnight fuck-up had occurred, we would hear that famous command echoing off the hallway walls, *In-ca-dence...Ex-er-cise.* It meant we were in for a long day. It's funny how the mind can connect the dots of cognition and retaining information when motivated by pain of the body. It taught us to dig deep, though. Deep into ourselves…

From memory, I give you, General Order Number One: I will guard everything within the limits of my post and quit my post only when properly relieved.

8

MICKEY D'S READY-TO-EAT

"DUDE, I'LL GIVE YOU $20.00 IF YOU CAN EAT THAT PACK OF CRACKERS IN UNDER A MINUTE, WITHOUT A DRINK OF WATER." The gauntlet had been hammered down, the stakes were high, and the rewards were exponential. Bragging rights would have run rampant through the barracks like wild fire if someone could do it with crackers from an MRE (Meal-Ready-to-Eat, or prepackaged Army food). The challenge went unanswered, as no normal human being could do it. You'd have greater success in picking up two handfuls of sand from the Mojave Desert and swallowing them. It was an awful challenge. An MRE is a freeze-dried meal the Army serves a soldier when on the move or inaccessible to a normal dining facility. It packs about 2,000 calories into a single meal.

If you mixed your sugar and creamer packet up with a little water, then heated it to caramelize the sugars, you had yourself a field-made Ranger Cookie. It didn't taste like a real cookie; it was probably closer in taste to a Ranger's sock after a 25-mile hike in South America. It got the job done, though.

This is another one of those things that have assuredly changed since my time in the service: the quality of dehydrated meals. We had

Chicken-A-La-King, Spaghetti and Meatballs, and my personal loathsome champion, Corned Beef Hash. It usually came with a main meal, a side item, Potatoes Au-Gratin, or Potatoes *All-Rotten* as we affectionately renamed them, a cookie or cake, crackers, and peanut butter, again, with maturity, we quickly named it *Penis* Butter, because we were disgusting male chauvinists. It included a smaller packet of sugar, coffee creamer, salt, pepper, and a tiny bottle of hot sauce that you put on everything, because it helped with the taste of, literally, everything.

If you were in a large group, you could do some horse trading, like a dessert for a main course. Remember the fruit cakes your grandmother would send the family a month before Christmas? The cakes that tasted awful and never got hard due to being loaded with preservatives from every corner of the earth? The MREs were worse than that. I wish I were stretching the truth on this matter, but some of those meal combinations were terrible. Most of them would disgust a Billy goat.

What they didn't tell you when they passed them out, was exactly how backed-up your entire digestive system was going to be. It's as if you'd eaten a clump of cheese the size of Detroit. You were not going to have to worry about shitting for a month, maybe two. Your bowel movements turned into a concoction of toothpaste, concrete, plaster, and 5-minute epoxy rolled into one petrified log.

Another running joke in the Army was, *SOFT PETER.* It was a supposed magical potion the Army instituted into all of its food. We were to believe that the same people that brought us push-ups and Military Intelligence, were the same ones that had scientists introduce *Soft Peter* into our diets. It was specifically designed to keep your dick from getting hard in training; so a trainee could focus on training and not pussy. Given there were no women amongst our group and none to be seen in our area, trust me when I say, all it took was the right breeze to make our peckers harder than Japanese arithmetic.

9

THE DEVIL IS IN THE DETAILS

Inspections were a tedious affair. It wasn't your mom and dad looking beneath your mattress for dirty mags or laundry in your basket. Inspections neared microscopic proportions. They inspected whether your boots were shined, your socks were rolled correctly, your toothbrush faced the correct way, your soap box oriented correctly, and your TA-50 was stowed and stocked exactly like every other man in the PLT. I cannot stress enough how inspections became the bane of our existence.

If anything was out of place, the entire room was ripped apart and everything in it was thrown about like a wild Tasmanian devil had torn through. Unless you have been through it, you can only imagine the hell it truly was for us. Sometimes, it would last all day and into the night, even into the next day in some rare cases.

You have to imagine the complexity of trying to get *every single man* to do *exactly* the same thing as the other thirty-some-odd swinging dicks in the PLT. Sounds impossible, right? Well, let me be the first to tell you that it damn near was. I can only imagine if we'd had women in the barracks with us. My apologies, ladies, but you know who you are. I mean every pair of boots, every shoeshine box, every uniform for every single man, which averages out to about two-hundred and fifty coat hangers of clothing, every pair of socks, every set of drawers, every single picture and, albeit few, remnants from home, every tube of toothpaste, entrenching tool, foot powder container, *every single item* oriented in the same exact way in every wall locker and bunk area. Every laundry bag had better be oriented and tied the same damn way. Every single bunk fashioned to Army standards. Every single boot polished to Army standards and uniform up to snuff, or it was tossed on the floor without prejudice alongside the next guy's possessions. It was absolute pandemonium where an infraction occurred. Mattresses were tossed around like plush dolls, bunks were rearranged, drawers pulled from lockers and their contents dumped on the floor before the drawer was thrown on top of your belongings to add insult to injury. During those first few weeks in the Army, I would liken our inspection regiments to assembling a thousand-piece jigsaw puzzle. Then, we stood tall for re-inspection. Failure. Jigsaw…Failure. Jigsaw. It was like a bad dream, until we got it right. Then pride set in. Life sucked on those days, but I would gladly do it again, and again, knowing now what I didn't know then.

It wasn't like we had all day to prepare for these inspections, either. Anyone, at any time, was subject to an inspection. Some were coordinated, but most were on-the-spot inspections. Sometimes we were punished for personal infractions, and other times we were punished as a team. The idea was, we had let our PLT down by not ensuring PVT SO-AND-SO was squared away. Squared away meant having yourself and all your shit in good military order. It meant you'd better keep your shit in the best possible military presentation. Squared away could mean your weapon, the barracks, the latrine, you, or anything else that needed attention.

God help you if they found contraband in your wall locker or on your person. Contraband could be left-over snacks from care packages, pornography, cigarettes, drugs, live ammunition, soda cans, newspapers, magazines—a plethora of things were absolutely forbidden. Smoking was a big one that caused untold thousands of PUs. It could even lead to a stain on your permanent military record and a possible recycle to the next rotation of recruits. Recycling meant you repeated your training from the beginning. Brutal, I know. They would probably place you on suicide watch as well; you couldn't wipe your ass without supervision.

Speaking of smoking…some of us did it anyway, like yours truly. The bad part was, I was the Platoon Guide and knew better, but opted for my own personal form of youthful rebellion. I was chosen by the DS to lead the men as an acting corporal. I held it from just before the halfway point through the completion of training. I was supposed to be the example. The DSs knew I was smoking because they had noses and they undoubtedly worked. I was never physically caught by *my* DSs, though, as you'll read in a subsequent chapter. They would tear my wall locker, bunk, and all my possessions to shreds in the hopes of finding my smokes, but they didn't outsmart yours truly on this one. They tried several times before they gave up, so I remained the PLT guide. I guess it doesn't matter now, because the uniforms have completely changed, so it's safe to let the secret out of the bag.

Behind the collar of our field jacket was a zippered compartment for a rinky-dink rain hood that we never used. Sewn into the outer rim of the hood was a bungee type string to tighten the hood over your head and face. Care packages from home were always inspected, so a plastic zippy bag to keep cookies fresh was never given a second thought. I poked two holes at the top of the bag and laced the bungee strings through it and knotted them off. I formed the holes far enough apart that a pack of smokes would just slide into the opening. Viola! They knew I was smoking, but they could never catch me. It was normal to have lighters in training because we had to either cut or burn off the loose sewing strings from the manufacturing of our uniforms. Failure to keep these trimmed from your uniform meant you were beating your face in the front-leaning rest position. Plus, we needed lighters to spit-shine our boots. Speaking of which…

10

SPIT-SHINED BOOTS

Long before I ever stepped off that bus in Kentucky, the art of spit-shining was imparted to me via my Airborne Ranger sister, I mean brother. Your little brother had the last laugh on that joke! Every man would develop his own style as we mastered this lifelong skill. Over the last few years as the uniforms have changed, I've seen soldiers walking through the airport that may never understand the struggle of training in boots all day, then polishing them to a shave-worthy reflection later that night.

First, you had to clean all the shit, filth, and ass off your boots. Then you'd do a once-over with polish, let it dry, and buff it out with a horsehair brush. Then you'd get an old t-shirt or sock, and using small, tight circles, you would slowly start embedding the polish deep into the leather. You'd have to rub the whole boot over and make sure there was a nice, even coat. After a nice coat on boot number two, you'd be ready to start back on boot number one. I would take another finger swipe into the polish, and then spit on the boot while I rubbed it in. Then as the polish and spit were gleaming in the fluorescent light, I'd use my lighter to *cook* the concoction until it reflected like glass. You couldn't do it too long or you'd burn the shit out of the leather. Too little and you'd not have that deep shine. It took practice to time it *just* right. While it was warm, I'd take another dab of polish and, again, spit and rub (insert immature masturbation joke here) the ever-loving shit out of it. It would really look like someone used high-gloss paint on the boot. The heel and toe were areas of special concern, as they held the best shine.

Your finger would get so flat and depressed-in after the first few nights, but after a while you were simply numb to the pain. Other days, you said, *fuck it*, and just did a normal polish with a brush. Polished boots showed the difference in the amount of time a soldier took, or didn't take, to present himself to his peers, the DS, the unit, and the Army as a whole. It was *very much* a matter of pride. You could go out-and-about performing your duties in the mud, dirt, rain, snow, getting your boots beat up against steel and rough surfaced areas in and on the tank, yet still *make* the time to polish your boots to a highly reflective shine. I polished mine with pride, and the DSs noticed.

Sitting around polishing our boots was the time when we really grew together as a platoon. It was when the DSs were usually away that we could relax with one another around the barracks. We would talk about home, our girlfriends or wives, and our buddies back home…all the shit we were before we decided to join the Army. It was good, though. We learned more about each other. We learned about our strengths and weaknesses. We learned who could do more PUs than the next bad-ass. It was a time when we got to teach one another trainee-level shit. So, I got to teach the boys about the infamous *impossible sit-up*. What is the impossible sit-up, you might ask?

11

THE IMPOSSIBLE SIT-UP

We had this guy, I forget his name, but we shall call him PVT Smoking-Dope. He was thrown out of the Army for failing a drug screen after Family Day, for, you guessed it, smoking marijuana. Family Day is when your family gets to visit you about halfway through training, but more about that later.

My brother, father, grandfather, and countless uncles clued me in to most of the DSs' tricks, less the shooting incident on day two. One trick, in particular, my brother taught me was the *impossible sit-up*. One night while the DSs were away and we were left to our own devices, PVT Dope was feeling rather uppity and bad-ass and told us that OSUT was bullshit, the training wasn't hard. He said he could do any challenge that any of us could offer. Oh, really? I asked him if he could do the impossible sit-up. Foolishly, he accepted my challenge… Dumbass.

I told him to lay down in a slightly modified sit-up position: back flat on the floor, knees slightly bent, and hands at his side and tucked under his buttocks, versus the normal hand position behind one's head. Length-wise, I rolled up a towel and explained that I was going to place the center of the roll over his eyes and hold it down on either side of his head. His job was to perform a sit-up against the resistance of said towel. I explained that he could use his arms and hands, but only at his side; he could pull on his legs and buttocks, so long as his arms remained at his side.

"I FUCKING GOT THIS, TURNER. LET'S GO. THIS IS GOING TO BE SO EASY," he confidently muttered.

"OK, HERE GOES. ARE YOU READY?" I asked.

"LET'S DO IT! HOO-RA," he asserted with verve.

I placed the towel over his eyes, and, unbeknownst to PVT Dope, I switched and had another guy hold it down in my stead. Another man was placed to secure his feet to the floor during his struggle. So PVT Dope was, by all accounts, blindfolded.

"ARE YOU READY, DUDE?" I asked.

"THIS IS STUPID, TURNER. LET'S GO," he replied.

I started my countdown. *"THREE, TWO, ONE. GO!"* He started struggling, pulling and straining to do just *one* sit-up. All the guys started cheering him on. Instantly, the room went loud with encouragements. He kept struggling to pull his body toward his knees, much like a normal sit-up. The room got louder and louder as PVT Dope dug deeper and deeper into his strained grunts and groans. He was losing, but nonetheless, desperately trying.

I made eye contact with the towel guy and lip-synced instructions to him upon my count to three. He nodded in agreement. I extended my thumb and nodded as I quietly started with a one-count. The towel holder readied himself.

The room was in a riotous, but dull roar, as we certainly didn't want the attention of the DSs. PVT Dope was seemingly gaining ground on the towel, so I knew it was time to make my move. I looked around the room and held my finger to my lips to signify a hushed-operation, then I dropped my exercise shorts and boxers down to expose my hairy ass and balls. The room looked at me in disbelief. I faced away from PVT Dope while positioning my hairy ass near the tops of his knees. The countdown continued as I extended a second finger and lip-synced the number *two*, all while trying not to laugh out loud. I adjusted my position and gave the final finger to the towel guy to quickly release the towel from PVT Dope's head and eyes. The tension he had in reserve was like a loosed catapult as his face arched up to directly meet my hairy ass. It was at the perfect angle to make a loud *SMACK* when his face hit home. The room exploded into uncontrolled laughter. PVT Dope sat there a second or two in wonderment, all the while a sash of imprinted towel marks lay across his pocked red face. He was blushed red from straining, but especially so when the red of anger washed over him. Dumbstruck wonder soon turned to untamed fury.

I think he jumped straight up from the floor, and in a single movement, landed in a poised fighting stance much like a recoiled cat. He came at me with pure ire in his eyes. It took an unusual amount of guys to hold him back due to the uncontrollable laughter that had overcome their motor functions. Damn near the whole platoon was in there for that event. He soon calmed, and I apologized. I made him realize that the situation presented itself and I'd simply opened the door as, no doubt, he'd have done the same in my shoes. He agreed and was a decent sport about it, after the fact.

I guess these days if I did such a thing, it would probably warrant UCMJ (Uniformed Code of Military Justice, A.K.A. Army law) action on yours truly. It would probably earn me an Article 15 (disciplinary action at the unit level), or even a Court Martial, who knows? Depending on the severity, they can take half of your pay each month for an indeterminate amount of time. You also have to perform extra duty like buffing the 1SG's office or cleaning HQs building, anything that leadership can think of to punish you. Hell, I would suffice it to say that with the way things have changed over the years, I would almost certainly face a sexual harassment charge.

I look back and think *what if* I'd played by all the rules and was the face on a U.S. ARMY poster, but what fun would that have been? You can no longer get away with the things that we did back then. I am certainly glad I hammed it up and lived in a world that wasn't so intent on being offended by every misdeed or filthy uttering. Thank you, 1970s-to-1990s America. Come to think of it, these days they would probably reinstitute the practice of having me drawn-and-quartered were I caught doing that trick.

12

AMBIDEXTROUS RIFLEMAN

Naturally, a soldier's basic characteristic is to know how to handle military-grade hardware: pistols, rifles, fully-automatic machine guns, grenades, and the like. The rationale was that if our tank ever broke down on the battlefield, we were to become grunts, or basic infantrymen, and have the competence to fight while dismounted from the tank. Logical thinking.

On the tank we, naturally, had the 120mm smooth-bore main gun, Browning M2 Heavy Barrel .50 caliber MG, the coax and loaders M240 MGs. Off the tank, we had one M16 rifle and our 9s, our personal pistols, the M9 Berretta 9mm. If we had a serviceable M240 at that point, we'd carry it to defend ourselves from an enemy infantry squad.

After weeks of training on how to disassemble, re-assemble, and function check our weapons, we finally made it to the range to qualify on the M16. I am right-handed, but had never fired a rifle before, and the Army taught us to use our dominant hand, though I'd always shot my pellet gun with my left. Dad always taught us boys to use both hands while learning the various construction trades; we had to know how to set a nail with either hand. It was something I'm thankful for to this day. Night after night, we practiced with our M16s; only not on the range and without ammunition. We placed a dime on the end of the barrel as we *squeezed*, not yanked, the trigger. We had to train our minds and bodies to be steady as we squeezed off imaginary rounds. We did all of this before ever expending brass, ammo, and cordite at the range.

Per usual, the rifle range was miles away, and for us, only accessible by foot. We arrived and went through this mockup formation while seated on these screaming hot, aluminum bleachers. Thankfully, they had some cover from the sun. After a short, but thorough, safety briefing, we were divided into smaller groups and tasked with one of three DSs. I was thankful that I was with my DS. Eventually, I found myself lying on the dusty earth with a rifle in my hand and fifty rounds of live ammunition. They were training rounds, but still enough to kill a man, or fifty men if you were a crack-shot.

I established my target, three-hundred yards down range. I was thankful for my 20/15 vision that day, and now I'm thankful to read road signs at night. My DS came by and momentarily observed my awkward body positioning, before asking me what the hell I was doing. I tried to explain to him that I was unsure as to which arm to fire from: my right, per Army training, or my left and what felt natural. Of course, he asked me which was my dominant hand. I explained that I was right-handed, but felt more comfortable with the rifle in a left-hand/ left-eye configuration. We had ten rounds to zero our weapon and forty to qualify. He asked if I was fucking with him to get more lead down range. No way, I was dead serious, as it felt better with my left. He said to go ahead and try my dominant hand first. If I sucked, he would let me restart and attempt with my left. Right-handed, I wound up hitting 36 out of 40. Not great, but an expert qualification, nonetheless. He called bullshit and asked if I was really more comfortable with my left. I assured him I was.

To satisfy his curiosity, he allowed me to attempt qualification with my left, but not before calling me out to the PLT to raise the stakes of if I would even qualify at all. I hit 39 out of 40—a near perfect score. He gave me a look that said, *I know damn well you've fired a rifle before, Turner.* Truth of the matter was, I hadn't fired an actual rifle in my life, but my left always *felt* the stronger eye for rifling. I guess my pellet gun did something for me. Contrary to that holiday movie, I never shot my eye out!

To this day, I fire a rifle better left-handed and a pistol right-handed. I still get those same crazy looks from people once they notice the difference.

A few weeks later, we were allowed to throw actual hand-grenades. Oh my sweet lord, was that ever awesome and scary all at the same time. A few months earlier, I was in high school, chasing girls and that ever-popular weekend beer-buzz with my buddies, and then I was throwing fucking hand-grenades in the hills of Kentucky. It was pretty bad-ass! The movies do hand-grenades no justice, whatsoever. The concussion from a grenade is an awe-inspiring event. It is, in no shape or form, anything you can describe to anyone that hasn't felt it. It lets you know just how puny and fragile humans really are. I didn't take any chances on this, though, I threw all of them with my right hand, as that was and is my throwing hand. I know, I'm a weirdo. What can I say? I qualified expert on grenade, so I'm an accurate fucking weirdo!

We were behind this huge bunker of sandbags several feet thick. There were, maybe, three of these bunkers all lined out at the range. I remember thinking that I hope the asshole in the next one didn't have a grudge to settle. The DS was right there with each man as he pulled the pin, performed a short-count, and threw that bad boy as far as our arms and shoulders allowed. I think we threw three live grenades. I was fortunate enough to be the first one to throw from our bunker. There are no words to describe the concussion, the brute force and strength you feel from the real ones versus the training ones. They rock you to your core. Your brain stays on high for a couple of hours after that experience.

If you ever get the chance to throw a real grenade, I highly recommend it, *it's so choice*. My current career has me travelling a lot, so coming into my local airport, I get to meet a lot of the guys just joining the Army, and they have informed me that they do not get to throw grenades these days. I feel so bad for these guys. Getting to throw a big chunk of metal that goes, *BOOOOM*! What's not to like about it?

Firing weapons at non-vital targets was fun, but there was another dynamic to that…we were required to low-crawl through a live-fire exercise. Yes, back then, we had to low-crawl on our bellies through a cold, muddy field, while the DSs fired live rounds from M240s above our heads. Meanwhile, small bunkers of munitions exploded all around us. It tested, to a small degree, how we would react in combat. It was amazing to see how many people actually feared for their lives, especially in a controlled setting. I remember motivating some of the guys to push forward to reach the objective, reminding them that it was only another test to graduation. Watching tracers close overhead was definitely a thrill-seeker's delight. It opened a very real dialogue in one's head about what he'd signed up for when he took that oath.

13

DEAR JOHN, IT'S JODY.
SIGNED, MARY.

Another fun time was mail call. We would form a line on both sides of the hall from the DS's office, clear down to the latrine. He would then proceed to call out the names of those who'd received mail. Letters from home were always so welcomed during training. It was a momentary lapse in the insanity that consumed our lives. Now, recruits all have phones, and training is recorded and posted to social media pages. Seriously, they do this now.

I doubt they even do mail call anymore, except for care packages. It was so nice getting mail from your folks, your friends, and especially from wives or girlfriends. If the mail smelled like perfume, you might have to do extra PUs, but it was worth every one. It was always nice to see someone get mail when they hadn't received any in a while. About once every few weeks, I would get a letter that was assuredly resulting in an untold number of PUs. Remember that Airborne Ranger I spoke of? Yeah, the one I call my own flesh-and-blood brother. Let me tell you a story...

The DS would call out our names and dole out each soldier's mail, all while reading the notes that loved ones had adorned to the exterior of the envelope. No one had control over what they received, and Kevin took full advantage of that fact. He would send me letters of varying colors and design. One was from a fictitious clinic and read, in large, bold-type letters, *"HERPES TEST RESULTS."* That went over like a wet newspaper. *"DROP, TURNER,"* the DS would command.

I would be remiss if I didn't include my own personal favorite gag mail from *SMALL CONDOMS, INC.* Also in large, bold letters it read, *"SAMPLE ENCLOSED."* So, naturally, the envelope included a tiny O-ring a little bigger than the diameter of a first-grader's pencil. These elicited a lot of laughter from my fellow trainees and the DS. For me, it meant a lot of PUs. It was all in jest, though. I wouldn't trade anything for the PUs I did then.

The ones I paid dearly for were the ones marked, *RANGERS LEAD THE WAY, TANKERS AREN'T REAL MEN,* and *TANKERS ARE SISSIES!* It was a plethora of Ranger-inspired Tanker haranguing upon which my arms and chest paid for in the worst way. *"TURNER,"* the DS would call out. I would, of course, run down to him and stand at attention awaiting my penance. *"DROP, TURNER, BEAT YOUR FACE,"* as he would read my brother's choice words regarding Tankers. It made it fun, though. There were no spared feelings. We were all open to ridicule, as it was character building, Army style.

Of course, there was always the chance of getting a Dear John letter from home. This is where it may get confusing. A Dear John letter was about Jody, and it also meant you were getting dumped at the worst possible time. Jody was the name given to any guy back home that was making time with your girl, or who had taken your girl while you were away in the Army. Everyone fucking hated Jody. He was an even bigger asshole than the DSs. The DSs weren't polishing their knobs with your girlfriend or wife; they were just making you stay awake all night polishing bathroom fixtures and rifles. If it was learned that your girl had broken up with you or was seeing someone else, well, she was affectionately named, Mary Jane, or Mary Jane Rotten-Crotch.

I mean, come on, here it was, America was engulfed in a war in the Middle East and we were going into the service, and your girl shills you out for some punk back home because you are unable to call or write often enough. It was the only logical choice for nicknames. Besides, we were the life-takers and heart-breakers. We could shoot 'em full of holes and fill 'em full of lead. It was okay for us to break their hearts, but not the other way around.

You could see the hurt, the anger, the frustration, and the helplessness in the eyes of those with trouble back home. It's not like we could text or call any time we wanted. No, we had to wait until we could get to the phone and hope they were home. Caller ID? No such thing in those days. We had to call collect, too. Otherwise, we wrote a letter the old-fashioned way and waited for a response. When bad news came, it stuck with you. You dealt with it and moved on like a good soldier. You learned to rely on your buddies, on your squad, on your PLT; hence, the brotherhood was locked-in, earned. That's where it was tattooed onto your soul and crept into your blood.

In the quiet of the night, you also learned to rely on yourself. You learned to channel the anger and pain into a different place within your mind and heart. You had to deal with the inner voices, the feelings, and everything into being a soldier. It was almost bliss in the face of utter turmoil. You had an out, if you knew how to use it. The wonderful thing about the cussing, the name calling, the pain, and the punishment was that it took your mind off the turmoil. Rather, it channeled that energy into something else. It's hard *not* to channel anger into a PU or a flutter kick. It was an outlet for pain, inside the very feelings you were experiencing.

I still felt bad for the other guys that had bigger issues: sick parents, medical problems, losing friends or lovers back home. It's hard not to feel, even at a basic human level, some compassion for them and their plight. These problems were only part of the things we faced every day in training. The Army did so much for us, and most didn't even know it. We did always find some humor in things, and, believe it or not, the DSs were actually there to help us in more ways than just how to be a soldier and shoot things. I had my moments, just like anyone else. Mail call could be a wonderful thing, and most of the time it was, but it had a dark side, too. To all the Jody's and Mary Jane's of the military world…I say to you, *"Eat shit and die!"*

14

THE ULTIMATE PUNISHMENT

Punishments were not always an individual affair. Sometimes, we suffered together, as a team. If one guy made a mistake, we all made a mistake. We had, in essence, *allowed* him to err. We didn't train him enough at the PLT or individual level. Sometimes it was a squad mistake; thus the entire squad would pay. Sometimes the PLT would be at fault; therefore, the entire PLT paid the price.

The most memorable time was when Third PLT screwed up. I've forgotten now what they did, but oh, boy, did they ever shit the bed. I didn't feel bad for our PLT during training for our mistakes. We suffered the punishments that were earned and accepted what the DSs doled out, but these guys…I truly felt bad for these poor bastards. My heart truly ached the entire time I was laughing and looking down on their plight. Their lead DS was one tough mother. These guys had inspection after inspection after inspection. But this was the MOAI, or mother of all inspections.

Now mind you, every time one of us exited our building, we were screaming and sprinting at a break-neck speed. We could have simply ran out the front door to the formation area, but no, we had to go out the back door and run around the building. Usually, we had to race the

DS down a flight of stairs, around the building and form up before the DS made it out the front door. Ah, good times. But, for these boys, it was the epitome of *BOHICA* (Bend Over, Here It Comes Again).

These guys had to remove everything from the third story that wasn't bolted to the floor or wall. Now, when I say everything, I mean ev-ery-single-fucking-thing was moved down two flights, had to be run around the scenic route to the PLT formation area, all while scream-ing like banshees. Every single bed, mattress, washer & dryer, pedestal fan, trash can, cleaning closet supply, shoe shine box, rolls of toilet paper, pictures of girlfriends, tubes of toothpaste, socks, every let-ter from home, all of it brought down, set up dress-right-dress, and then inspected. And every time something was out of place, it was strewn about recklessly by the DS. It was bad. After the tornado ripped through, their boots were to be polished again, every bunk was to be made to Army standards, and every laundry bag was to be tied to their bunk in a uniform fashion. If one swinging dick had his toothpaste sit-ting atop of his bunk to the left of his toothbrush, then every swinging dick had better have the same.

The bad part was, this all started around 1500 hours on a Sunday. Once or twice a month on Sundays, we were allowed to go to church, or visit the PX (Post Exchange, an Army store) for hygiene items, boot polish, stamps, and stationary. It gave us a little time to write home and decompress. We were good little angels…that Sunday. Third PLT was not. Whatever these guys did, they paid dearly for it. I am sure they took for granted some liberty the DS extended, or rather, didn't extend. These poor SOBs were out there long after we went to sleep, because Monday *always* meant back to business.

It must have been 2300 hours, damn near midnight when they fi-nally passed inspection. Then, the daunting task of taking every single-fucking-thing back upstairs to its rightful place began. Then it was painstakingly re-inspected, wrecked, and inspected again umpteen times before they got it right. I don't think they even slept that night. All-in-all, I think those boys paid for their screw-up until the following Sunday. Other than that instance, I knew we all signed up for this shit.

That night as I lay in my bunk, I thought about those poor boys and the hell they just suffered. Alone time could be especially hard on a young soldier. It was the time of reflection for that day; on your strengths, your failures, was all this worth it, why did I do that dumb thing, or why did my buddy do that dumb thing? Sometimes we would get in bed early enough to hear *TAPS* playing through the loudspeaker on post. It was to signal lights out. Now that I have served and lost some brothers along the way, that tune has a new meaning. I can barely listen to it without tearing up and crying. It's only because I served and had these experiences that I appreciate it so much, the significance of the many soldiers that have made the *ultimate* sacrifice to make this nation great. I am thankful for the people that endured these same punishments to make possible the freedoms we so comfortably live, work, and make memories in…these United States of America.

15

NO MATTER WHAT
THEY TELL YOU,
SIZE DOES MATTER

We did a lot of wild and crazy things during our time at Fort Knox. Before continuing into this chapter, the reader should understand that it was a different time, era, if you will. The world hummed to a different rhythm. It was an amazing time to be young, to be a soldier, to be a man, to be an American in the United States Army. The world, it seemed, was not so grown-up, or should I say, so sensitive. As mentioned in the preface, it was a time of innocence, of not being so hung on ourselves (pun not intended, as you will see in this next segment). Men were men, and women were women. Training to be a Tanker back in those days didn't include women. Furthermore, there were only two genders—women and men. I may lose some readers by this brilliant observation, but oh, fucking well. Simply said, life was different back then and so were we.

Life for a recruit wasn't always running, screaming, and PUs. It did actually consist of classes, tank simulators, and actual courses on maneuvering and tactics. One day, while seated in an auditorium-like classroom, with a few extra minutes to spare, the DS started making small talk with us. To our front was a small stage from whence the DS instructed and operated a projector. It was the more traditional form of learning, as opposed to memory by muscle failure. I debated as to whether I would include this story, but as they say, you only live once. Besides, once you're dead, they stop referring to you by your name; you are then referred to as *the body*. The mortician doesn't say, *"MOVE MR. TURNER ONTO THE TABLE,"* or *"MOVE MR. TURNER INTO THE CASKET."* It's move *the body*. In any case, there are far more horrible legacies a man could leave behind him in this world, and this certainly isn't the best (arguable, though), nor the worst I have to offer.

The DS started some friendly banter. He would ask where someone was from, even though he knew our profiles. He simply wanted to engage us in conversation; a little fun to ease the tension of training. He would pick on one guy about being from Texas (insert the old joke about only steers and queers come from Texas and there being no horns on whomever the joke was intended, so they were the latter…assuredly, another punishable offense by today's standards), or another fella for being from Georgia, or wherever; hence, it didn't matter your color or creed, it was all in good fun. Get a group of machismo guys in a room, and it doesn't take long for a dick joke to make its way into the conversation. Of course, the DS being the one in charge, nobody's dick was bigger than his, and by proxy and experience, he also had the best one-liners out of any of us. It didn't hurt that he was black, either. Nobody was going to crack jokes on the DS, but it was sure open season on the rest of us in every shape and form.

I don't remember exactly how it came about, but I remember the joke included the DS holding up his pinky finger. It spurred a good laugh from his audience. I have a hardy, loud laugh anyway, but the joke caught my funny bone and I laughed a little too boisterously. Of course, the DS immediately turned his attention to me and started his barrage of wise-cracks on his new target, which incited more laughter from the group. The DS was on a roll, cracking jokes on me, as he was extremely experienced, given the untold number of recruits he'd churned out from underneath that brown-n-round hat. There was no doubt, he was funny.

Before I continue, I feel it necessary to back up several months to my high school days…A friend of mine, Jacob, and I were hanging out with our usual group of miscreants and daredevils. At some point, one drunken evening, he informed us that a man's penis was supposed to be, when erect, as long as his hand. Yes, from the tip of his middle finger to the crease in his wrist; it all sounded very scientific and mat-ter-of-fact at the time. Jacob was, after all, hyper-intelligent and had a full scholarship to college, the whole enchilada. I'll pause writing so you can check it out for yourself, guys…I wouldn't lie to you.

Of course, we didn't whip our dicks out right then and there to check, but, even in our drunken stupor, it resonated in our adolescent brains amidst all the barley and hops. I could hardly wait to *get it up* and verify for myself if this was indeed a scientific fact, or myth. To both my amazement and delight, it was true. I thank my dad every sin-gle day for his endowing contributions to my life with the opposite sex. Thank you again, dad. To my audience, you're welcome for the information.

… Back to Fort Knox. The DS started making fun of me. So, just as Jacob did that drunken night so many months ago, I, matter-of-factly, cued in our DS to this information regarding one's *size*. As I did, I held up my hand to infer confidence and truth. Of course, this incited even more laughter and gusto into his comedic assaults, to which the DS called bullshit. Boy, oh boy, I had dug the hole now.

"NO, REALLY. IT IS, DRILL SERGEANT," I said, ever so confidently. *"IT'S A SCIENTIFIC FACT. THE SAME WAY YOUR FOOT IS THE SAME LENGTH AS YOUR FOREARM."*

"BULLSHIT, TURNER," he started. *"I SEE YOUR HANDS, AND THERE AIN'T NO WAY THAT YOUR SHIT IS THAT BIG."* More laughter followed.

"WHEN IT'S HARD, IT'S EIGHT INCHES, DRILL SERGEANT," I said.

Then he slammed down the gauntlet. *"THEN WHIP IT OUT, TURNER. BE A MAN, SINCE YOUR PACKAGE IS SO BIG."*

This is one of those moments that I begin to question *every-single-thing* I ever did as a young man.

"WELL, DRILL SERGEANT. I'M CERTAINLY NOT SITTING AROUND WITH A HARD-ON IN A ROOM FULL OF MEN," I retreated.

He pounced with, *"SEE, BECAUSE YOU KNOW IT'S NOT THAT BIG. YOU AIN'T GOT A HAIR ACROSS YOUR ASS, TURNER, IF YOU DON'T PROVE SOME SHIT LIKE THAT,"* again holding up his pinky to reiterate his point.

I couldn't believe what I said next. *"I'LL WHIP IT OUT, BUT IT'S NOT THE SIZE OF MY HAND AT THE MOMENT."*

"BULL-SHIT, TUR-NER." Again, with that pause between each syllable; a skill expertly employed by drill sergeants.

This is where you, the reader, may start to question your choice of reading material, because now you are asking yourself, Does he do it? Does he chicken out? Fuck no. Table in front of me, I stood up out of my chair and started unbuckling my belt.

"YOU ARE FULL OF SHIT, TURNER," the DS belted out. *"WATCH YA'LL, HE'LL BACK OUT. PEE-WEE IS NOT ABOUT TO WHIP HIS DICK OUT,"* he spoke with such arrogant bravado.

I unclasped my three buttons from my BDU bottom, slipped the fly on my boxers, and whipped it out, right there in front of the whole PLT. Shock and doubled-over laughter erupted from the room. So much so, that another DS from another class ducked in to see what the ruckus was about.

"THAT IS NOT EIGHT INCHES, TURNER. THAT IS A BUNCH OF BULLSHIT," he yelled out above the laughter.

"I TOLD YOU THAT SITTING IN A ROOM WITH YA'LL IS CERTAINLY NOT GOING TO GET ME HARD, DRILL SERGEANT," I defended. It was a soft, but respectable healthy 4½ to 5 inches, though.

Trust me when I say that, several weeks and months of not seeing another woman, with the exception of Family Day, definitely made it hard to stifle a woody when the wind blew right. I was stroking that thing so much during training, it was as if masturbating was about to be outlawed in all fifty states.

After the laughter and shock wore off, the DS said, *"TURNER, THAT'S NOT EIGHT INCHES, BUT MAN DO YOU EVER HAVE BIG BRASS BALLS. YOU ARE ONE CRAZY WHITE BOY."*

I had the last laugh, though. I had more than a couple of the guys say to me, *"NO KIDDING, TURNER. YOU WERE RIGHT. THEY ARE THE SAME SIZE. THAT WASN'T BULLSHIT, DUDE."*

This was normal behavior for us at the time. It wasn't grotesque, it wasn't disgusting, and it didn't offend anyone. We were recruits in the

U.S. Army, not the local troop selling coconut cookies. We were training for war. We understood that should the need arise and our country called upon us to defend the constitution we swore to uphold, we would go and do our duty with few hang-ups.

Our showers were not partitioned, so we'd all seen one another, hell, we took shits beside one another, we ran together, we ate together, we suffered together, we failed together, but most of all, we *succeeded* together. A few short weeks before, we were perfect strangers, and then through it all we became a team, a unit, a well-oiled machine. We all started off as civilians, but had defined our existence through suffering, learning, hardship, and teamwork to become a band of brothers.

16

GAS, GAS, GAS...CHAMBER!

In the Army, we received all kinds of high-speed, low-drag training. One of them was our NBC (Nuclear, Biological, and Chemical) training. It is designed to give a soldier a better chance of survival, should any of these events occur, when donned in the right equipment. As a rule of thumb, we always had with us our protective mask (pro-mask), or what most of the world calls a *gas mask*. When we did road marches or went full *battle-rattle* (with battle ready equipment), we always had our masks with us. We would be marching along, covered in sweat and blisters, or freezing our asses off, and the DS would turn and scream, *"GAS, GAS, GAS!"* We would then have, I believe, seven or eight seconds to don our M40 pro-masks. Sounds easy, eh? Not so much. If we were marching along in full battle-rattle, we were also wearing our Kevlar helmet with chin strap and carrying an M16 rifle.

We would have to lay down our weapon, doff our helmet, rip open the pouch flap, don the mask, clear it of any contaminated air that could possibly be ingested, then complete the process with the additional hood and straps. It took a hell-of-a-lot of practice to perform correctly and in time. Like so many other tasks in the Army, we eventually mastered it and became the model of efficiency.

We also had MOPP (Mission Oriented Protective Posture) training. That's a fancy way of saying we wore a suit to protect us in a biological or extreme chemical warfare attack. It included a set of trousers, jacket, gloves, boots, protective mask, and a canister of M9 Detector Paper. I believe we had eight minutes to don the entire suit, maybe seven? Either way, it was another timed event. How hard can it be to don a set of trousers, jacket, gloves, and some floppy boots? I'll be the first to tell you, it was fucking tough.

The first thing that happens in a gas attack is you have to don your pro-mask, which makes all practical exercises thereafter, extremely cumbersome. You now have this mask over your face that hinders breathing, hearing, seeing, and all normal reality as you know it. Sight being the largest dose of *this is going to fuck-with-you*. Hand-eye coordination skills were a must. Once your mask is on properly, you now have to don these old, ratty pants and jacket over your uniform and then over your combat boots. It's not like you're going to take off your combat boots in a chemical attack, but you can only do this after you remove the pouch strapped to your leg and waist. The jacket is the same shitty-fitting, ratty wares that now adorn your lower extremities. Then you put on these floppy, lace-up boots. I would liken this experience to walking a wildcat on a leash, through a wading pool.

I remember it was hot and humid that day, early in the cycle of our training. It, like every other place at Fort Knox, was miles away, albeit, that day fortuned us with a nicely paved road, but only accessible by foot.

Score for Uncle Sam:

Privates—0: Army—1

Completing the gas chamber is when a young recruit learns to *trust* his or her equipment. It was great training. Seriously, all bullshit aside, it allowed you to overcome the instinctive desire to run away from a chemical attack.

I cannot attest to the facilities of other posts, but I can tell you all about the gas chamber at Fort Knox. Did I mention it was in the middle of nowhere? Only accessible by foot? They march our whole company, three PLTs, out there to this desolate, god-forsaken place in the dead heat of summer, naturally. After a short break, we were lined up at the entrance, standing like a bunch of assholes. We were about to enter a room filled with CS, or tear-gas (2-chlorobenzalmalononitrile). This is the stuff the police and other agencies worldwide use to disperse angry, riotous mobs. The difference was, they were not opening those pussy little canisters like you occasionally see on the news. No, they were about to light an indeterminate amount of it on fire in a small room full of masked assholes, thereby turning that CS gas into an incendiary.

Let's say for the sake of the story that the entrance and exit to the building were oriented east-west. If memory serves me, we were lined up at the entrance door without a clear view of the exit. We were all nervous to varying degrees. One of the DSs came out to clue in a group of five-to-seven guys before they went in to experience the chamber.

Our group entered the smoke-filled room. We witnessed the smoke bellowing from a large restaurant-sized vegetable can. We formed a line in front of the DSs. After everyone was comfortable that the mask had a good seal to one's face, and in fact, the mask worked, we were to remove them and breathe normally. Cue the chuckles from those of you that have experienced it first-hand. Here is where the DSs are inventive. After removing your mask and huffing down on this riot control gas, we were then ordered to assume the *Front Leaning Rest Position*. No shit. Push-ups. Not for disciplinary measures, not for re-tarded fuck-ups, not for forgetting one's general orders. No, this was just an old-fashioned, simply because they could fuck you. Then to place a cherry on top of your sundae, we had to perform these PUs while reciting our name, rank, D.O.B., and SS#. Nice touch, assholes! I don't know why I'm calling them assholes; hell, I'd have been doing the same damn thing to new recruits had I been in their boots.

It was corny, but in the end, it made for good fun. You see the guys entering and you think, *How bad can it be? Several thousand men and women have done it before me, right?* Right. You step into the room with your mask donned and breathe normally, no problem. Naturally, the DSs are standing there in their masks, too. Again, no problem. Everything is on the up-and-up, so far. The mask works. It really does ensure that you learn to trust your equipment. The room is smoky as all hell, the gas burning wildly inside the open-topped can. It looks brutal as the smoke bellows intensely throughout the room.

Because the masks muffle all oral and audible communications, the DSs are forced to scream all instructions. We stand facing the DSs, dress-right-dress, in a single file across the length of the room. Then comes the order to remove our masks. We are ordered not to hold our breath, as this would only serve to incite more anger and fury upon that particular individual.

It is a bit nerve-racking as you reach up to remove the one protection you have from a known irritant. They said it would disorient us, make breathing extremely difficult, and force our eyes to swell and tear uncontrollably due to the burning sensation. The DSs also told us that we could live in a CS-rich environment, but that life would suck and we would, with almost every certainty, be overrun by the enemy and die in another horrible fashion.

I reached up, grabbed my mask, and lifted it from my face. I took a normal breath while opening my eyes. It was as if at that moment someone released a poltergeist into the room. The melee that played out like a first-class comedy skit was attacking every nerve within the known human sensory spectrum. It swarmed the room like a supersonic spirit had possessed the whole lot of us. It entailed some guys having an immediate and horrific reaction to the chemical. It tore through them like a rotten Mexican burrito from a street vendor in Tijuana. They immediately doubled-over, wiped their eyes, and lost any and all situational awareness to their surroundings. These guys totally disregarded the DSs' instructions and followed their instincts and got the fuck out of Dodge.

Other guys stood there and withstood the devil's breath. Those of us that remained, immediately went into the front leaning rest position to beat our faces while screaming out our particulars. You could have belted out the national anthem like Pavarotti and no one would have known the difference. It sucked, but we didn't freak out like some guys. And then there were the guys like me, albeit just a handful of us within the entire company, that didn't really suffer from the detrimental effects of direct CS exposure. Sure, it burned, it felt like Satan had sneezed into your lungs, but it didn't seem to unleash the seven-hells on us like it did most everyone else.

What was even more interesting was the realization of how different people reacted to the gas. Those differences told you a lot about how someone would react in the face of danger, possibly in the face of death or any emergency situation for that matter. Some of those guys really thought they were going to die in that stuff. I was beside the last guy farthest from the door, so I knew the demons would have to be exorcised from the jerkoffs between myself and the door before I had any chance of exiting the room. So, I waited and tried to be a tough guy, even though the DSs all knew I was one of the few it didn't affect as harshly. Eventually, the room cleared out and I recovered after doing more than the required ten PUs. I think I did, maybe, twenty-five, just to showboat a little. I was a cocky little shit back then.

Don't get me wrong, it royally sucked in that room. My eyes burned, but they didn't tear up uncontrollably to the point of complete visual obscurity. My nose and throat also burned, but I could breathe fairly well and my nose functioned, considering what I'd seen happen to some of the others. I was the last to leave the room. I was so happy that my physiology allowed me to escape the shit part of CS exposure.

You see, just a few feet from the exit was this humongous pine tree. When exiting the door, you either took an immediate left or right, or you were running into that tree. This is what our fearless leaders failed to mention, rather, purposefully neglected to mention. Somehow, in all of their explanations of the gas chamber, this *needed-to-know* tidbit was absent in any of the dialogs pertaining to *gas, gas, gas* training.

This was where the real show began. As soon as I exited, I saw the first guy, the freak show in the gas chamber, doubled-over with a bloody nose. He ran out of that building so fast, he ran smack into that pine tree. Other guys ran out with snot dribbling from their noses, hanging clear to their knees—no bullshit. It was every seven-year-old's dream of seeing a nose-loogy so long that it actually stretched to someone's knees. It was as if eighteen years' worth of pent-up snot was let loose in one fell swoop. Their eyes were so blood-red, it really looked as if they had been possessed by a demon. Even though I was toward the end of the whole affair, I still had a *helluva* show that afternoon. Some guys hated it; others thought it was a cool experience. I thought it was making me a better soldier for having been exposed to one of the many possible dangers I could face in combat.

I understand that these days, they will actually film your OSUT or BT experience. I can only imagine the footage they would have had, had they done this back in our day. But, these days I imagine they would also ensure that there were no pine trees directly outside the exit. Those days are probably gone forever. I can imagine some girly-boy texting home to his mama, resulting in WWIII with the DSs due to hurting her *precious* baby boy. This whole sissified world where everyone is hurt or offended has truly gotten out of control. I know that not all kids today are Nancy's, but it sure seems like we are not training America's finest to win in war as much as we are for winning social status and popularity contests. I'll leave it at that, as it sure was a shit ton of fun back in our day and, quite frankly, good for us.

17

FAMILY DAY

It wasn't all bad. We had a little break in the middle of training, maybe towards the middle of October. It was a short-lived weekend, two overnights with our family. My parents, best friend Josh, and girlfriend at the time all drove up from Alabama to see me. My brother drove in from Fort Benning, Georgia, where he was stationed with the 4th RTB (Ranger Training Brigade). It lasted from Friday night until Sunday night.

My brother came up to see me in his dress uniform, his Class-As. At the time, he was a CPL (Corporal), and had approximately six or seven years of service under his belt. CPL was a little low on the totem pole considering the fruit salad, or ribbons and accolades, he wore on his uniform. He had already been to combat in South America and received several high-speed awards and decorations. He'd earned both American and Paraguayan jump wings, for jumping out of a perfectly good airplane with two different armies. He had earned the CIB (Combat Infantryman's Badge), a Ranger tab, and countless other awards. He was part of the assault forces that invaded Panama's Noriega, so he also had a combat patch and a combat (airborne) jump, which is rare these days. All-in-all, he looked pretty bad-ass for a lowly corporal. He'd have looked bad-ass even if he was an E-7 Platoon Daddy.

At the time, if you were Airborne Ranger or Airborne Infantry, and on active jump status in a unit, meaning you were regularly jumping out of airplanes, you could wear your dress uniform, or Class-As, with your pants tucked into your jump boots. This included Special Forces, too, and of course, you wore your black, green, or red beret instead of a cunt cap. He looked like a poster child for the Army. I have to admit, he looked damn good in that uniform…naturally, because we looked so much alike. He looked so good, in fact, that the DSs thought he may have been *embellishing* a little on his uniform, in an attempt to look good in front of everyone for family day. By *embellishing*, I am referring to what has, in popular culture, become known as *stolen valor*, or wearing something on your uniform that you didn't earn. This was not the case with my brother. He certainly had more fruit salad than any of the DSs, and they were jealous. You see, tankers don't require all the bells and whistles that the *Queens of Battle,* or Grunts, need. Yes, that's a friendly dig, to all my infantry brethren out there.

He looked so good, in fact, that one of the DSs pulled me aside after my brother's visit that first night and questioned me as to why he had so many decorations, yet very little rank to accompany them. He informed me they were considering opening an inquiry into whether he was the real McCoy or not, to see if his uniform displayed what he had actually earned. The term *stolen valor* didn't exist then, or if it did, few had heard of it. You either both earned it and wore it, or you hadn't earned it and didn't wear it.

I had to explain to them that he was a SSG, or staff sergeant, before he was demoted. Naturally, they asked why exactly he was demoted. I explained that he was out drinking in a bar, when he whipped some guy's ass. Unfortunately for my brother, that guy was an off-duty lieutenant in the U.S. Air Force's version of the military police. A smile cracked across the DS's face as he nodded in understanding. My answer was satisfactory. Where was he stationed, where did he get the combat patch, and other like questions followed, and the answers, of course, jived, so they let rest their suspicions for an inquiry. He did look like an Army god, so looking in from the outside, it did seem suspicious. The uniforms for Airborne Infantry, Rangers, and Special Forces were the embodiment of what every boy in America wanted to be back then… aside from the WWII era, they were damn good-looking uniforms.

I, too, was especially proud that weekend, as I'd taken first place in a little in-house competition for family day. We gathered in a huge gymnasium in front of all the families and friends in attendance. Six tables were erected in the center of the room. On three tables lay three assembled M240 Machine Guns, and on the other three tables were three assembled M9 Beretta pistols. Each pair of weapons represented each PLT. I represented Second PLT. I was the fastest to disassemble, reassemble, and functions-check both weapons. It was a satisfying moment that I'd practiced extensively for over the course of several weeks. Some of the guys would even help me with chores like doing laundry and cleaning, so I could practice and we would win. We would receive an extra phone privilege or something, if I won.

With the crowds watching and stopwatches zeroed, we were all cued to begin. I was a bit nervous in front of the crowd, but I simply did what I'd trained so hard to do… *WIN*! And win, I did. After that, I was made PLT guide and held that title until the end of our training, more than two months. My DS told me I had better not lose, as he had a beer bet with the other DSs, and he aimed to win it! I asked if there was any chance I could have one of those beers if I did win. He abruptly told me, no. I was in it for bragging rights and glory; he was in it for bragging rights and beer.

I had the disassembly, assembly, and functions-check on the M240 MG down to just under a minute, or something crazy like that. With hours and hours of practice, I was damned fast. I even scored with my girlfriend that weekend, too. It was a win-win all around, as next to no one got lucky during OSUT, which reminds me…

The DSs did issue a warning that weekend, as they were no dummies. The guys that didn't, or couldn't, have family visit had their battle-buddy's family check them out as well. The DSs didn't just give us a weekend off, no fucking way. We had to be *released* to a responsible adult. So the DSs did give those guys a heads-up warning to beware of what they'd find in the neighboring towns of [smaller] Radcliff and [larger] Elizabethtown.

They were notorious for being home to a great many strippers, pole polishers, burlesque queens, *polefessionals,* striptease artists, erotic performers, show girls, and exotic dancers, but it was also home to *other* nefarious exotica. They were warned and, subsequently, didn't listen, to the almighty and wise drill sergeants, thus, they returned with them a little parting gift from earlier mentioned town professionals. They brought back with them *Pthirus pubis*, or a condition known as *Pediculus Pubis*, A.K.A. *fucking crabs*. Yes, they returned to our midst with *pubic lice* for fuck's sake. I believe it was two, maybe three of the guys that were guilty. Naturally, they were warned with Article 15s and various other punishments, but they were idle threats, as crabs were punishment enough for those retards.

18

BOOT-TO-CHEEK INTERFACE

I made PLT guide earlier in training and was later tapped for *soldier of the rotation*, but falling a couple of points shy on my PT score, I didn't earn it. I almost lost it all, though. A little quote of my own coining is, *"Life is like a wad of toilet paper…at some point you are going to cross an asshole!"* We shall call him Pinky to protect the prick that nearly cost me everything. Pinky was your typical, run-of-the-mill pecker-head that thought he need not conform to the standards of the Army, thus enriching our lives with PLT level disciplinary actions. His fuck-ups were by proxy, *our* fuck-ups. I shall explain.

About three-and-a-half weeks before graduation, we were tasked with completing an exercise called FTX (Field Training Exercise). It was a ten-day camping trip, complete with sleeping on snow-covered earth with a group of smelly guys and no beer. We were out in the cold, beneath the open skies, in the woods of Kentucky at the end of November.

We marched out into the middle of nowhere and began to set up camp with our Army-issued shelter halves, Army-speak for tents. They are incredibly small and just-do fit two men in them. With our shelter halves, we had to form a secured perimeter for the AO (Area of

Operations), yet another Army acronym for camp. The fifteen some-odd tents were to be spread out approximately fifteen-to-twenty meters apart from one another to form a large-area circle, or perimeter, which we would guard and secure with our very lives. Security of an AO is a big deal. Naturally, the security of *everything* is a big deal in the Army. Me being the PLT guide, it was my duty to ensure the tents and men were formed up correctly. It wasn't, thanks in part to earlier-mentioned prick. Maybe PVT Prick would be more appropriate? Anyhow, the DS came to me and said there were two shelters out of formation. He named off the violators, and I quickly responded, *"ROGER THAT, DRILL SERGEANT. I'M ALL OVER IT."* I moved out smartly, gritting my choppers, because PVT Pinky was one of the offenders.

A little history on Pinky. He was someone that wanted to do *every-fucking-thing* his way, not the Army's way. He wanted to cry and whine every time something didn't go *his* way. He was a born-too-soon, *me, me, me,* millennial. It was like an act of congress, near impossible, to get him to pull his weight and stop fucking around so all of us didn't suffer for it. The PLT had done its fair share of PUs and flutter kicks for this *fuck stick*, another merited nickname for dickhead.

I first went to square things away at the tent that was not PVT Pinky's. I knew they would follow orders without any flack. As I imagined, no issues whatsoever with these guys. They were going to handle the problem and correct it ASAP. Then I range-walked (a fast-paced, deliberate, military-like movement) to where PVT Pinky and his battle buddy had set up their shelter half. I told them, politely mind you, that they were out of formation and needed to move it in about eight meters, to close-up the perimeter. As fucking expected, PVT Pinky immediately started in with, *"WHAT THE FUCK, TURNER? MAKE EVERYONE ELSE MOVE. WE ARE ALMOST SET UP. I'M FUCKING TIRED. THIS IS BULLSHIT, TURNER."* Just count to ten, I reminded myself. You expected this bullshit.

I'd had enough of PVT Pinky, as had the PLT. We were fed up with his prissy, me, me, me tactics. We had all put up with his bullshit for nearly four months. It was three-and-a-half months too many.

I dove right in. *"PINKY, JUST PICK YOUR FUCKING SHELTER HALF UP AND MOVE IT THE FUCK IN LIKE I SAID. I AM NOT IN THE MOOD FOR YOUR PANSY-ASS SHIT TODAY. WE ARE ALL TIRED. ONCE SOMEONE ELSE IS DONE SETTING UP, I'LL SEND THEM OVER TO HELP YOU GUYS OUT."*

"FUCK THAT, TURNER. I'M NOT MOVING MY SHIT. YOU FUCKING MOVE IT, IF YOU WANT IT MOVED." Bratty voice and all.

"YES, YOU MOST CERTAINLY FUCKING ARE, PINKY. YOU ARE MOVING YOUR SHIT. I WILL TEAR IT DOWN IF YOU DON'T MOVE IT RIGHT FUCKING NOW," I barked out.

"FUCK YOU, TURNER. I'M NOT FUCKING MOVING," his cock holster mouthed-off. I was keeping my cool throughout this whole exchange of verbal fodder, but my patience was about to change perspectives, as I'd reached my limit.

My knife-hand was about to come out. Nostrils flared and a stiff upper lip, I raised my voice to a cold, guttural, matter-of-fact tone. *"PINKY, I DON'T WANT TO HEAR ANOTHER WORD ABOUT IT. PICK YOUR FUCKING SHELTER HALF UP AND MOVE IT THE FUCK IN. I DON'T WANT TO HEAR ONE MORE WORD ABOUT IT, MOTHER FUCKER. NOT A FUCKING SYLLABLE, PINKY. ONE MORE WORD, AND I SWEAR I WILL WHIP YOUR ASS. UNDERSTOOD? JUST MOVE YOUR FUCKING SHELTER HALF, NOW!"*

His battle buddy fell right in line with my orders, or so I assumed by his silence and peripherally perceived movement towards their shelter half. I waited.

His downfall began. *"YOU'RE NOT GOING TO DO A THING, TURNER—" POW! THUNK!*

Pinky was to my left about 3½ feet. He was close enough that when I grabbed the small tree between us with my left hand and brought my right leg up to meet the left side of his face, he felt the brunt end of a semi-dusty, spit-polished, leather torture device known as my combat boot. He hit the dirt like a sack of boiled potatoes. I jumped on top of him, legs straddling his stomach, left hand at his throat and my right drawn back ready to commence to punching his lights out. The fear was there in his watery eyes. He tried calling my bluff, and I made good on my word. He was truly scared that night in the backwoods of Kentucky. I was about to let loose the pent-up rage of thirty-plus guys in Second PLT that night. I was going to kick his ass for every one of my soldiers. Thirty men + four months of rage = one spectacular ass-kicking. He was going to feel the wrath of every single PU that every single DS doled out for that prick during our tenure at Knox. He was going to feel it through the extension of my fist.

I quickly started in before he had a chance to react. *"PINKY, IF YOU DON'T GET OVER THERE AND PICK UP THAT FUCKING SHELTER HALF AND MOVE IT IN LIKE I TOLD YOU, I'M GOING TO REALLY FUCK YOU UP. DO YOU UNDERSTAND ME, MOTHER FUCKER?"*

"O-O-OKAY, TURNER. I'LL MOVE IT. I'M-I'M-I'M SORRY, DUDE," he said with a trembling voice.

Glaring eyes keenly focused on his soul, I leaned in, knife-hand to his nose, teeth-clenched, in a firm, controlled voice and said, *"IF YOU SAY ONE FUCKING WORD, PINKY, ONE FUCKING PEEP ABOUT THIS TO THE DS, I SWEAR TO GOD AND EVERY ONE HERE THAT I WILL MAKE IT MY MISSION IN LIFE TO HUNT YOU*

DOWN LIKE A DOG AND FUCKING END YOU, YOU PIECE OF SHIT. NOW GO FUCKING DO AS YOU'RE TOLD."

"I WON'T SAY A WORD, TURNER. I-I-I-I PROMISE. I PROMISE, DUDE. I'M-I'M SORRY, MAN," he stuttered back.

I knew I didn't have to say a word to the rest of the PLT, as they had done just as many PUs, flutter kicks, and mountain climbers as I had, all in the name of PVT Fucking Pinky. As fate would have it, his left cheek looked as if he'd put an entire grapefruit into his mouth. I thought for sure my goose was cooked, but I never heard a peep out of anyone, most importantly, the DSs. I certainly received a lot of pats on the back from the rest of the PLT after that exchange. After ten days of FTX came and went, Pinky still looked like he was trying to smuggle a golf ball inside of his mouth.

Let me pause here for a moment to step back and really take a good look at what was happening during that time and at that particular incident in my life. There are special times in your life when the gods do smile on a situation, or an individual. The Pinky debacle surely left me feeling very, very blessed in this department; hence, I spiel my wonderful experience with great pride and joy for you today. The Army wasn't trying to train soft, belly-aching whiners back then. No, they were trying to instill a tough, fighting spirit into its young defenders of freedom. We were the next generation of men that were to heed the call, should it come. We had no time for soft feelings or offences of the psyche. We were in the business of war, in order to facilitate peace on earth, but namely for the United States of America. So, albeit under duress of stress and fear of being hunted down like a dog, I will give PVT Pinky props for not ratting me out. He knew what he had coming and it was delivered in spades, so kudos to him for keeping that whiny trap shut; otherwise, it would have fared far worse for us both had he not. After that night, Pinky remained on his best behavior in my presence.

Golf ball in tow, we returned to our barracks shortly after 1500 hours for a much needed shower and some *real* food, or as close to *real* as Army food gets, especially after ten days of MREs. Once again, we had electricity, running water, and a bunk to sleep in. I never knew how awesome those barracks were until I slept in the woods far away from them.

I waited until everyone else had finished their showers before taking my own. A good leader gives to his men before thinking of himself. I had a habit of dragging all of my gear into the shower and scrubbing it down in one fell swoop. Besides, I had to properly clean my filthy defenders of righteousness, my combat boots, or Pinky Punters! Hell, I stank to high-heaven anyway. Might as well get the grunt work over with, and then really enjoy my shower. I waited until about 1900 hours, cleaned my gear, and then returned to the latrine to enjoy a nice, long, hot shower. I'm sure I probably managed to rub one out in a little peace and quiet, too. There are two kinds of men in this world: those who masturbate and those who lie about it.

After my shower, I started making my way back to my room. I had to pass a couple of the larger, bay-style rooms where ten-to-twelve guys were housed. Being the PLT guide did come with a small, but wonderful luxury of a two-man room, just me and my battle buddy, the Real Deal. In route to my room, I also had to pass the DS's office and the opening to the stairwell, located in a little *S*, or double 90-degree jog in the hallway. Now this was where the gods truly favor the good guys. As I came around the corner, I found myself at the back of both my DS and Top, or First Sergeant. On the other side of them, standing at attention, facing the three of us, was none other than PVT Pinky. With a shit grin, I remember muttering to myself, *Son-of-a-bitch, this is great.*

Sometimes, timing is everything. Whether it's good or bad, it's crucial. I had a front-row seat to the best show in town, and I was, that evening, the only VIP in attendance. Just as I rounded the corner, I heard Top finishing up an expression he had, no doubt, mastered over the years. I've not heard it before or since. In his thick, Kentucky drawl he said to Pinky, *"GODDAMN, BOY, WERE YOU SITTIN' ON YOUR ASS, RUNNING YOUR MOUTH, WHEN SOMEONE TOLD YOU TO SHUT UP, NOT STAND UP, AND THEY PUT YOUR ASS RIGHT BACK DOWN?"*

This, folks, is where the hero of the story gets to decide what to do in that, *oh, dear god*, climactic moment. I would be remiss if I didn't say that I took full advantage of this unique situation. I wore a smile on the inside of me that still shines today. I'm smiling right now writing about this moment.

Pinky had that same look of panicked terror on his face from ten nights earlier, just with a golf ball in his mouth. There it was, Top and the DS were point-blank asking Pinky what exactly happened to his face. Unbeknownst to both Top and the DS, standing directly behind them was the person that could answer that question better than anyone. He stood there, his body puckered in fear, and sweating nails as to what to do. It was so obvious, a blind man could see the possibilities were running a marathon of *what-ifs* between those half-empty ears. The most-ranking NCO in our PLT along with the man we all feared most, the DS, putting him on the spot. This was his out, his moment of inner-dialog asking, *"What the fuck should I do? Do I lie, or do I come clean?"* A conundrum, indeed.

He looked pretty pathetic standing there writhing in his own fear. I almost took pity on him…the fuck I did. That wouldn't have ended well for yours truly, or you, the reader. So, I did what any rational person would have done in that situation and acted like a responsible adult. Before Pinky's feeble mind could muster any verbal responses or involuntary ticks, I peered between the shoulders of my superiors, giving Pinky an intense, hateful look. I had my right fist balled up and thumb extended, when Pinky's eyes half-met mine. I lifted my chin and slowly drug my thumb across my throat, implying a Colombian necktie—a friendly reminder of my promise to him. Terror struck his eyes. It was beautiful…wonderful, in fact. A screen writer couldn't have written this amazing scene any better. It played out like a dream. I was vindicated in my prowess of life-threatening abilities. I wasn't really going to kill him, but he didn't know that. I simply didn't want to get busted for kicking his ugly mug.

"I-I-I-I FELL, FIRST SERGEANT. I FELL DURING FTX, T-T-TOP," Pinky stammered, exactly as he'd done that night in the woods. You do not get to the position of First Sergeant for being an idiot, and Top was no exception. I'm sure he'd both doled out and seen a few ass-kicking's in his time in service.

In a sarcastic and mistrusting tone, Top asked, *"YOU FELL, PRIVATE? IS THAT WHAT REALLY HAPPENED?"*

With a sweaty brow, Pinky said, *"Y-Y-YES, FIRST SERGEANT. I FELL ON A R-ROCK."*

"WELL, THAT ROCK WHIPPED YOUR ASS GOOD, BOY," Top said with a chuckle.

I gave him a nod of approval to reassure him that he was safe…for now. The DS dismissed him from further inquiry, as well as from their presence.

At this point, we only had a couple of weeks or so remaining before we graduated. I felt fairly comfortable after this small, but ever so sweet interlude. It was great. It wouldn't have been such a sweet victory had he not deserved it so and everyone in the PLT appreciated my disciplinary actions. Unbeknownst to me, the deal would be even sweeter at graduation. I know, I didn't think it could either, but it happened.

It was finally upon us. After all the hard work, after all the PUs and the bullshit, it had arrived…Graduation Day. The day we no longer had to listen to the DSs' every syllable in fear of reprisal. We were men. Soldiers. We were officially Tankers in the United States Army. The platoon formed a single-column line, shoulder-to-shoulder. The DS walked along giving us each a handshake and the occasional pat on the shoulder. He muttered a few words to each soldier as he passed. When he got to me, he extended his hand and said something that the guys to my left and right could hear about great job, congratulations, etc. He looked at me with a tipped-down head and a stifled smile on his face, then he leaned in and said, *"IF YOU'RE GOING TO KICK PEOPLE'S ASSES, TURNER? DON'T GET CAUGHT LIKE YOUR BROTHER DID, YA HEAR?!"* I knew right then that he was full aware of what happened at FTX. But, I was a good soldier and had taught PVT Pinky a great lesson in life…*Don't fuck with Turner!*

19

"FILTHADELPHIA, DRILL SERGEANT"

I wasn't always so lucky, though, as just a few days later, I really did almost get in serious trouble…Again. It was an amazing night, of sorts. After FTX, we entered a very special time in our training: Red Phase, or the last of our four phases. We wore earplug canisters from one of the breast pocket buttons of our uniform. Adorning these canisters were colored tape: green, yellow, black, or red. The color indicated which particular phase a recruit was suffering through. It made it easier for the DSs to identify us as we made our way around Fort Knox running and screaming like packs of idiots.

In this last phase, they started easing up on us a little, as most of our *basic* soldiering was mastered and we were fairly comfortable as soon-to-be newly minted soldiers. Our confidence was high, as was our physical and mental abilities. We were, more or less, starting to hone our actual tanking skills, as we were now comfortable in and around the most lethal tank on the planet. As such, we were afforded some extra privileges, too.

One important privilege was the few extra minutes afforded us to talk on the phone Sunday evenings. No doubt, we all took full advantage of it. We may never see them again, and some of you may never have seen them, but we called them phone booths. There were a row of nine of them, attached to one another and complete with folding doors to block out some of the noise from the animals just outside. It was hard to woo your girl with loud, adrenaline-filled Tankers waiting in line. All stood at the ready to assault you during the delivery of sweet-nothings to her. We were one hard-core pack of animals. Sometimes you just wanted to cry, and other times you wanted to tell all the wonderful stories that were, often, too gruesome for mom or your girlfriend, but, on-the-other-hand, they understood you were transforming into a soldier, a man. A collect call home could last anywhere from fifteen to twenty minutes, then it was time for the next swinging dick to make his call. I happened to call my folks that evening.

Before continuing, I feel I should give you a little history on my father. My father rarely ever spoke with me regarding his time in Viet-Nam. I knew he enlisted in the Army before he could be drafted into whatever service the government decided, so he was able to choose instead of being chosen. He wanted the Army. I knew he was trained as a machinist, the same job he was doing before he was in the Army, and I knew he did some of his training at Fort Benning, Georgia. I had seen all the pictures he had from Viet-Nam, as I used to sneak into the attic boxes when he and my mother weren't around. Some photos were extremely gruesome, especially in 8x10 black and whites; guys that had been ripped apart by the Ma-Deuce .50 Caliber MG. It was through this that I became enthralled with warfare.

After one memorable incident, I then knew better than to ask him about his time in the war. For years, whenever movies aired regarding Viet-Nam, he was always very, very quiet. My mother used to tell me stories about being pregnant with my brother, and going to watch the airborne guys jump from the famous training towers at Benning. She said she always wanted to jump out of a fully functioning airplane; so on my fortieth birthday, that's exactly what we did. It was one of, if not *the*, most awesome thing I ever did with my sweet mother. I also knew that he was at Fort Knox for some time, too. I never knew what he did at each station though, as I rarely was able to speak with him about it.

That night, as I neared the end of my training, my dad said something to me that I thought so profound. I can still see the position of my body and how I was standing in that cramped phone booth on that cold night in Kentucky. It was as if I was on the outside of a surreal dream looking in on myself.

During the conversation regarding my approaching graduation, he said, *"HAVE YOU MARCHED UP-AND-DOWN MISERY, AGONY, AND HEARTBREAK YET?"* I could hardly believe my ears.

I asked him, *"WHAT? HOW DO YOU KNOW ABOUT THOSE HILLS?"*

He answered, *"I USED TO MARCH THOSE SAME HILLS BEFORE I WENT TO VIET-NAM, SON!"*

After eighteen long years of knowing very little of what my dad did in the war, here it was. He approached me with a conversation about his time at Fort Knox, twenty-four years earlier in 1968. That night would prove to be the beginning of so many more conversations about his thirteen months in Cha-rang, or Death Valley, Viet-Nam in 1969–70.

It took a few more years for the reality of that moment to truly sink in and develop, as I finally understood why he never spoke to me about his time in the Army; it was because I didn't yet speak the language of a soldier or have the understanding of one, either. As a kid, I hadn't marched umpteen miles in combat boots, I had yet to do so many of the things that make a soldier, *a soldier*. It truly is a special club, whether you were in combat or not. It is a club that you are potentially willing to die to be a member of, should the call come. If your country needed you, you were there. You signed the dotted line and gave an oath to defend the constitution and the people of this great nation. I know that guys that served in combat are, in most cases, tighter than those that didn't. Either way, the brotherhood of being a soldier spans beyond time, experiences, race, creed, background, everything.

I had intended to finish the call with my folks, exit the phone booth, and get right back in line to call my girlfriend with the extra time we'd earned. What I failed to mention during the first half of this story was that while I and a couple of other guys were blabbing away on the phone, we were also trying to be stealthy cigarette smokers, too. We were, obviously, not as tactical or cloak and dagger as we regarded ourselves, thus our phone calls were abruptly interrupted. An unknown NCO came over and said, *"YOU, YOU, AND YOU! FOLLOW ME, FUCKSTICKS."* I immediately had to cut my phone call short as I had, once again, a puckered asshole from fear. Here it was: less than two weeks from graduating and I was finally caught. I can hear that old song about the boys' room, just worded differently. *"SMOKIN' IN THE PHONE BOOTH!"*

All three of us were from Second PLT, which meant I knew my partners in crime all too well. I wondered to myself just exactly how fucked we were. He marched us to a building we'd never been inside before, but had run by countless times, screaming no doubt. We marched in and made an immediate right turn, following him down a dark hallway. He [sergeant] knew our names, our faces. There was no point in running, though we were probably in better shape than he. It was a probability we were not willing to chance. He ordered us to wait outside this partially closed office door. We could see a figure sitting at the desk inside, no doubt his superior. Neither were DSs, but that didn't stop us from calling them drill sergeants, because, as recruits, we knew we were not allowed to smoke, and in our world, everyone was a fucking drill sergeant. We could hear him explaining the situation while we awaited our fate with puckered assholes and sweaty brows.

Finally, he responded, *"WELL, LET'S MEET THESE MARLBORO MEN OF YOURS!"* He marched us into his office where we stood at attention. He immediately started grilling us individually as to what company we were in and to whom we belonged. He paused, for effect no doubt, in between his questions. He soon came to realize we were all in Second Platoon of Echo, 2-13.

"WHERE ARE YOU FROM IN THE WORLD, PRIVATES?" he asked the guy to my left. I could hear that he wasn't from the South, so today I was from my hometown of Detroit, not my Home of Record in Alabama. Home of Record is where one is living when they join the military.

"TEXAS, DRILL SERGEANT," was his response. We waited for the *steers and queers* joke to come, but it never came. I'm sure he figured that we'd heard it before, judging from the red tape on our earplugs.

He then focused his attention to me and asked, *"AND YOU, PRIVATE?"*

"DETROIT, DRILL SERGEANT," I responded.

Emphatically, he points to the last guy, waiting for his response. He then calls out, *"FILTHADELPHIA, DRILL SERGEANT!"* *Filthadelphia* is a common nickname for Philadelphia.

"BULLSHIT, PRIVATE. WHERE IN PHILLY YOU FROM?" he fired back.

My buddy, PVT Tattoo (he was covered in them), named off the section of streets he claimed as his home turf. The sergeant then asked him if he knew of a certain deli, presumably in that same area. They were in their own world for a few while they spoke about the menu and their favorites from it.

PVT Tattoo answered, *"I DON'T GET MY PHILLY'S (Philly Cheesesteaks) THERE, DRILL SERGEANT, BUT I LOVE THEIR PASTRAMIES."*

"NO SHIT, PRIVATE, YOU ARE FROM PHILLY," the sergeant said with a little wry smile. He looked us over very carefully, letting us sweat it out in what seemed like hours in those few strained seconds.

"YOU BOYS GET THE FUCK OUT OF HERE AND DON'T LET ME CATCH YOU SMOKING AGAIN," came his shocking decree.

"ROGER THAT, DRILL SERGEANT. THANK YOU, DRILL SERGEANT," was our unanimous response as we high-tailed it out of the building as fast as possible.

We achieved a safe distance before we busted out in a riotous, but nervous laughter. *They didn't even confiscate our cigarettes!* I threw my arm around PVT Tattoo's shoulder and told him how thankful I was that he was from *Filthadelphia*. I knew I was extremely lucky at that moment. My sweet spot in the field jacket never failed me.

20

MISERY, AGONY, AND HEARTBREAK

There are three famous hills at Fort Knox, and they carry with them befitting names: MISERY, AGONY, & HEARTBREAK. Assumingly, anyone that has completed Basic Training, Advanced Individual Training, or One-Station Unit Training at Fort Knox knows full-well to what I am referring. They are the challenging hills that every recruit must conquer in order to pass training there. It's hard to articulate into words what exactly this experience means to a group of men, women, or the individual soldier. It's even more difficult to explain the full immensity of these plods of earth and how huge they truly are when you have to march up and over them on foot, especially in full battle-rattle. Pride and joy comes from conquering such a behemoth of earth in full gear.

Misery and Agony we did quite regularly. Each week we did a forced road march on foot. During this road march, we carried along a few items the Army issued to us, that they thought we should take along for the ride. Remember the *TA-50* mentioned in Chapter Three? Well, this is a basic rundown of what we carried with us on these road marches: *full* Battle Dress Uniform, t-shirt, socks, BDU top and trousers,

Kevlar helmet, M16A2 rifle, LBE (consisted of two canteens of water, four magazines of [dummy] ammunition, and first-aid kit), our NBC mask, and a rucksack full of roughly 60 lbs. of useless shit, including extra socks, shelter half, poncho, spare uniform, an entrenching tool (shovel), and a horde of other goodies. It equated to nearly seventy-five pounds of shit to carry up and over the hills of Kentucky. Water and extra socks were truly the only thing we required, but what fun would that have been? No challenge there, right?

At the beginning of training, I believe we started our regiment of road marches at 2½ to 3 miles, increasing them as much with each road march. Before graduation we had to do the Holy Grail of Tanker road marches in order to be named in the hallowed halls of Fort Knox lore and glory: *25 miles to Hell*, which included the most famous of hills, perhaps in the U.S. Army in terms of stateside duty, the one, the only... Heartbreak Hill.

I will never forget what one of our DSs told us that day, as we approached the completion of our *final* road march. To put it into a better perspective, it was December, yet we were hot, exhausted, sore, filthy, uncomfortable, dizzy, covered in blisters, sweat, sand, salt, and doused in plain ole misery as we neared mile twenty-three, or so. We had already conquered Misery and Agony that day, and they were long, steep mothers, too. Little did we know that in the next few moments we would learn how *Heartbreak* had etched its name into the history books. We would learn that it was written in the earned blood, sweat, and tears of the soldiers that conquered it before us.

The DS stated, *"ONLY A FEW MORE MILES, MEN."* We had only recently graduated from being referred to as men, versus ladies, which was a rare occasion indeed. Our lead DS was there marching in front of us, maybe five-to-ten meters, when he began telling us how close we were to completion. He said we were nearing the end, that we could do it, if only we could dig down deep into ourselves and *push our minds and bodies toward the goal.* He regaled us with the pride with which he felt at our accomplishments up to this point. He was telling us things that we'd not heard from our DSs, ever; granted, it was less than two weeks before graduation. He was actually praising us for one of the first times during our training. It was like a breath of fresh air on that cold, miserable day. It was a foreign tongue indeed, to hear of his pride in us. He was *finally* stroking our egos. It was what he said next that really confused me.

He said, *"MEN, THESE ARE THE BEST DAYS OF YOUR LIVES!"*

I'll never forget what I was thinking. *That sonofabitch is fucking crazy. He doesn't have a clue what he's talking about!* I was sure he had lost his mind, entirely. Granted, we were exhausted, filthy, sore and damn sure ready to be done with training, as the human body can only take so much, but still, this was unchartered territory for DS-to-soldier dialog. We had all but reached our limits this day. This road march was, by leaps and bounds, the toughest to date. It truly challenged a man and what he can do when he applies himself. With only a few months into being eighteen years old, I was performing the most difficult task to date. Regardless, *that sonofabitch was crazy* remained my lasting assessment of him that day as we marched along on blistered and calloused feet.

This all happened within moments of rounding the next wide, sweeping left-hand curve. The trees parted, the clouds in the sky seemed to unveil the sun, and there was a commotion in the ranks ahead as they rounded that curve. Then, like a panoramic picture of the Grand Canyon, the earth just dropped out from beneath us and rose back up again in the distance. *Heartbreak Hill* lay before us. It was, and still is, the most gravity-defying paved road I've ever seen in my life. Maybe it was the angle or the exhaustion, but this was one bad mother-fucker. It was a massive hunk of earth splayed out before us, and it had our asses in its sling. We had to march down the smaller side and up the larger, steeper one. Again, these DSs knew exactly what they were doing. Though I couldn't see anyone's face in front of me, I was quite certain it wore the same pained grimace as mine did. It was a monster of a hill.

The DSs reminded us, with genuine concern mind you, to have our chin straps buckled tight as we descended the hill. What the hell that meant made no sense to me, as they'd never spoken like that before. Going down, we just kind of leaned our backs into the hill behind us and kicked our toes out with each step that burned our calf muscles to no end. Each boot made a clumping sound as each heavy step fell into the paved earth. Once we found our balance, our body just numbed the pain away and found a pace. Our minds had learned the difficult lesson of how to drown out pain. Whatever mind-tricks were played against us, we'd better have mastered them when approaching Heartbreak Hill.

As I reached the bottom, to a small, paved flat, I did a brief turn-around to see what I had descended, before I truly grasped how far down it really was. I turned back around from the guttural depths of hell to look up the hill I now had to ascend. It was unreal. Words cannot describe this gargantuan of pain and suffering that lay before me. I knew not to stop, as my body would just shut down. I dug deep down into my psyche, into the *I can fucking do this* place. I mustered up a healthy appetite of *GET SOME, SOLDIER!*

I started my way up the hill, no problem. I knew I had to complete it. It wasn't easy, but I couldn't stop, for if I did, I was done for. I was dehydrated, exhausted, and simply out of *oomph*. I trudged on. We'd suffered shin splints before, but this was a level unbeknownst to any of us up to this point in our lives. It was like a Kung-Fu master beating your shins with fresh bamboo poles. I was about halfway up when I really started to dig down deep into who I was, and what kind of grit I was chiseled from. I literally had to hunch over to keep my balance. Had I not been holding my rifle with both hands, I could have, literally, reached out to the paved earth in front of me, touched it with my index finger, and still maintained my balance to continue up that God-forsaken hill. Some guys were falling out and falling over. Some were simply falling down, face first. With each step, it seemed like the toes of my boots were going to strike my splinting shins, given the sharp angle of incline. There's not an inclined treadmill the world over that could mimic this angle.

Given the angle and circumstances, it was a struggle to really look up and see what was happening in front of you. You just kind of held your head down and dug your boots securely into the ground, so as to make every forward progress count. With each step came a gain of mere single-digit inches. Grunts, groans, and panting ensued like a symphony of torture and pain.

Then one of those, *oh, shit* moments happened, like they always do. I was marching along taking quick peeks here and there to make sure I wasn't going to run over the guy in front of me, when that *moment* almost hit me square in the face. It assuredly would have been PVT Pinky's Coup de Grace, in terms of face rearranging's. At the very moment I did a visual spot-check, a thud hit the asphalt, and then I observed a Kevlar helmet inbound towards my face. I was ugly enough, I certainly didn't need any assistance. I knew the guy behind me was going to eat it as I just managed to duck and bob out of its way. Fortunately it just missed him and skipped its way down the hill without incident. Then came the owner of the helmet half-rolling down the hill, just to the right of my travel. That was close, I thought. *Aha!* The securing of the chin straps. I never looked back to see the melee, but I heard some choice adjectives and phrases bellowing from my brothers.

I trudged towards the top. I was out of breath, every inch of me in pain. Hell, the fucking hairs on my head were sore. My shin splints were nearing kelvin temperatures of the variety nearing the sun's surface. I hurt on the molecular level. After it was done, after I reached the pinnacle of *Heartbreak*, I pulled off to the side of the road and stopped for a brief moment to take it all in. With the exception of a couple of guys that fell out, I knew we'd accomplished something that day. Twenty-five grueling miles and conquering Misery, Agony, and Heartbreak; it was a rite of passage. I was proud of not only myself, but proud of the entire platoon at that moment. We had all come so very far in our time together at Knox.

That night and the next day, we felt exhausted, but alive. In *MISERY*, but confident. In *AGONY*, but very much aware of ourselves. The *HEARTBREAK* of trading childhood for manhood had entered our bodies, our being. The pain of challenging ourselves and the unknown limitations to our abilities were forever the victors. I felt like a man, no longer a boy. It was the first time I felt like a real soldier.

I guess it was about ten or twelve years later when I thought back to that long, awful day at Fort Knox. It was truly one of the toughest we'd had in our 4½ months of training. This was, obviously, long after I'd separated from the service and had time to reflect on my training and experiences. I thought about those hills, about the challenges I put my body and mind through. I thought about how I'd conquered any and all doubts in myself as I crested that final hill. I reflected on the struggles of not only HEARTBREAK, but the *struggles* within. Then I also remembered what our DS said to us. *"MEN, THESE ARE THE BEST DAYS OF YOUR LIFE!"*

For years, I had the constant belief, and justifiably so, that that guy was certifiably nuts and hadn't a clue what he was talking about; he had clearly lost touch with reality when he spoke those words to us that afternoon. I never wavered on my beliefs or thoughts about what he said that day, before we conquered Heartbreak, but as I sat there, drinking a few beers, all those years later, thinking about all the struggles, the pain, and the anguish, I realized…*THAT SONOFABITCH WAS RIGHT!*

21

THE M1A1 ABRAMS
BATTLE TANK

I went from riding motorcycles and driving my '74 Super Bug to driving a 70-ton beast designed for pure fucking murder. The contrast was not lost on me, or any of us for that matter. I was intimidated the first time I drove our tank, *Creeping Death,* so prominently painted on each side of its gun tube. You just don't get that kind of satisfaction with many firsts in life. That is the stuff of legends—a moniker so befitting a beast such as the M1A1.

Like most other things in the Army, there were weeks and weeks of training leading up to the day we were actually allowed to drive and shoot the tanks. We had to spend countless hours in the actual tanks, and several more inside the tank simulators.

The temperature was freezing the morning we left the motor pool. The twin-turbine engine whirred and spooled up to speed, forming a very unique sound when coupled with the tank's tracks as they crackled and clunked into place, propelling the tank forward. The driver has two positions from his station in the front slope of the tank. He can either sit upright with the seat raised, exposed to the elements, head sticking out of a small, funky, oval hatch; or, he (and she, nowadays) can lay back, hatch closed, and look out of three, devilishly small, rectangular periscopes. It offers a single, straight-forward view and a forward left and right oblique view, essentially, a large V-shaped forward view.

That morning, for the sake of safety, I was in the upright, open-hatch position. It was miserably cold, but the exhilaration numbed the pain of that brittle, Kentucky wind. It drove nothing like my classic Bug. There was no accelerator pedal or steering wheel, per se. It's more of a 'T' bar steering device with a motorcycle-style accelerator, though both handles twist simultaneously. It was very familiar, yet very foreign at the same time. In light of driving a real Army tank, my mind seemed to have blocked out the cold, entirely.

We stayed on the pavement for the beginning of the trek, then moved to the tank trail, what the civilian world calls a dirt road. It was a lot of vehicle to maneuver, and my mind's spatial capacity was extremely challenged and over-inundated with information. It soon became addictive and empowering. To be at the helm of the most advanced battle tank the world had ever seen, that America had ever produced...the thrill of it still courses through my veins over twenty-eight years later. You never forget that moment. It stays with you forever. Every single time I see a tank, either in film or sitting in front of a VFW post, I still hear the creaking sound of the tracks in my mind's eye. What was once so loud and intimidating, is now a symphony of sweet, chaotic noise.

At slow speed, the chatter of the tracks is almost comically and obnoxiously loud, but as soon as you start to turn, the chatter roars at you like an angry lion. It creaks and moans so loud, it sounds like a horrible construction accident where metal and steel are unwillingly being manipulated into a crumple of waste. As your speed increases, it becomes more of a steady, freight-train-like juggernaut of noise that would scare any Army before it. I can only imagine the pure terror those first men felt when faced with the English MARK V tank in 1916 during WWI.

The horrifying din is an integral part of the awe-inspiring power of tanks.

The ride itself is surprisingly smooth. Fuck a HMMWV (high mobility multipurpose wheeled vehicle, colloquially known as a *Humvee or Hummer)*. Tanks are the tits. You could run over a log, or a serious transition in the road, and feel nothing. You wouldn't even know you'd done it, had you not actually seen the road conditions. Driving a tracked beast soon became second-nature to us.

Eventually, we were allowed to operate the weapon's systems aboard the tank. We literally spent hours upon hours learning how to disassemble, clean, reassemble, name each component, describe its function, load, unload, and clear a jammed round, remove barrels, operate head-space and timing, or determine a *GO* or *NO-GO* for the weapon before we were ever allowed to fire them. When that day finally arrived, we could barely control our excitement. We were like an only child on Christmas morning with *shit and tons* of presents waiting under the tree. We were down-right giddy. The training paid off. It evoked the kind of confidence one definitely needed to go and effectively operate serious military firepower.

There are four weapons systems aboard the M1A1 Abrams: the main gun, gunner's coax MG (machine gun), loader's MG, and the TC's (tank commander's) MG. The main gun is a 120mm, smooth-bore, M256 cannon with bore evacuator, or the big dick. Next is the gunner's coax, the M240 MG, with a 7.62mm bore and mounted parallel to the main gun, thus it traverses and fires in-line with the main gun via the turret. Then, there is the loader's rail mounted M240 MG, and finally, the TC's rail mounted Browning M2 Heavy Barrel .50 Caliber MG. This weapon is affectionately known as the *Ma Deuce*.

We started with the loader's M240. It fires anywhere between 650–750 RPMs (rounds per minute), with an MER (maximum effective range) of up to 3,725 meters at 853 m/s (meters per second). It's fast and furious. It can lay down some serious firepower on troops and equipment. It's great for troop suppression, as well as plenty of battlefield melee. We basically went to the range and each man fired 150–200 rounds of ammunition. It was definitely cool, and was to near certainty the very first time any of us were allowed to fire a fully automatic weapon. Expended brass and linkage spewed all over the deck of the tank, and then rolled off to the surrounding earth. I think I got a little chubby during the first exercise. It was definitely the stuff I signed up for, as you can feel the power of this one in the palms of your hands.

Next was the gunner's coax. Also an M240 MG operated from the same controls as the main gun via the gunner's station. Due to it being securely mounted inside the turret, it has a far greater accuracy than does the loader's MG. It was a more personalized weapon to the gunner, as he could see exactly where the rounds struck and adjust the target on-the-fly through the magnified sights.

What was cool was the noise from this weapon was right next to your left ear and echoed immensely inside the turret as it spit expended brass and linkage all over the place, which greatly intensified the whole affair.

After the M240s, we graduated to the Browning .50 Caliber MG. Now this was some serious firepower. After my father explained to me each and every picture he had from Viet-Nam, I knew that the Ma Deuce was capable of blowing a man in half with only a few well-placed rounds. She is one serious bitch. The Ma Deuce shot out a slug about the size of your thumb end, at a rate of 450–600+ RPMs at a velocity of 890 m/s. She could easily reach out and touch you at over 2500 meters. You'll always see these amazing shots through walls at like, a mile out, in the movies…imagine that weapon on steroids and shooting a whole building or vehicle up with holes. Through flesh, it punches in a hole about a ½" in diameter and forms an exit wound large enough for a housecat to crawl through.

The cool thing about the Ma Deuce was that she would *talk to you* as the rate of fire would fluctuate as you cycled through ammunition in long bursts. It was like a hit-and-miss engine, or an old motorcycle with a slow rate of combustion where you could almost count the RPMs off. *DUT…DUT…DUT…DUT…DUT…DUTDUTDUTDUT… DUT…DUT…DUT.* It was like a symphony of death playing for both you and the enemy. It was beautiful. Like the sound of the tracks creaking and grinding, it's one of those sounds you never forget and love to hear whenever possible. It is distinctive, to say the least.

The Ma Deuce has been used since its inception immediately following WWI, and has yet to be surpassed in reliability or firepower. It is still the preferred mounted MG of choice for vehicles and positions of all types. The M16, the M240, the M60, and M249, or SAW (squad assault weapon), are definitely a lot of fun to fire, but nothing like the Ma Deuce. Should the opportunity to fire one ever become available, I highly recommend it, as they are, like hand-grenades, *so choice, so sweet.*

Ladies and gentlemen: last, but certainly not least, the M256, 120mm smooth bore main bore cannon, or main gun. Holy mother of God… the awesome power of this cannon is utterly mind-bending and bewildering. It recoils about sixteen inches into the tank with lightning speed. Should you be in its path, it will literally shatter your bones before it moves your extremity out of the way. This profound tool of merciless decimation fires a five-inch-diameter projectile at 1575–1750 m/s (yes, nearly a mile per second), with an MER of about 3500 meters, but was proven to be effective at up to 4000 meters during Operation Desert Storm in 1991. There were several tanks in our outfit, as we were mostly two-man crews, three with the TC, so I guess there were about fifteen tanks, give or take a couple. As our tank was not one of the first to tee up to the firing line, we were able to witness the first one from behind. *WOW*, just wow!

The best way to describe this unholy event is to search for videos, but it still would not do it the justice it rightly deserves. We watched and listened with open hatches from our tank when the first tank expended a round, maybe 50–60 meters in front of us. Even at that distance, it shook our 70-ton tank to its core. It is truly an awesome display of fire-power. When the main gun expends a round, it's as if Lucifer orgasmed from a 120mm, smooth-bored pecker. We watched as the fire ball from the muzzle end enveloped the airspace around the forward space of the tank, for what must have been as big as a short-bus, you know, like the ones they cart the infantry around in. Yes, that was a friendly dig. I couldn't help myself. We call infantryman *Crunchies*…it's the noise they make when we run them over with the tank.

I digress. Depending on your vantage point and location, you can see the round strike the target before you actually hear it. The really cool thing about our tank was, at the time, it was one of only a few in the world that could shoot a target while traveling at 40–45 MPH across the battlefield. That means we can eviscerate a target while on the move. The gun-tube stabilization system is an awesome feat of human engineering. The hull, or bottom of the tank, is going through ruts, ditches, and uneven ground, but the gun tube stays locked on its target and can fire on a stationary or mobile enemy target. It gives a Tanker a complex of sorts, a sense of invincibility.

Nerves were strung as we moved into position on the firing line. The TC's voice came through my CVC (Combat Vehicle Crewmen), or another fancy acronym for a helmet. *"GUNNER. SABOT. TANK,"* the TC says to me. That means, *Hey, gunner, we will be firing a Sabot round at a tank on the battlefield, and loader, we need you to load a Sabot round. Get ready, assholes.*

I reference the weapons system to fire a SABOT round. *"UP,"* Real Deal screams, after loading a round into the breech block and throwing the arming lever into the *up* position.

I scanned the battlefield and found my target, before screaming, *"IDENTIFIED,"* into my CVC. I quickly *lazed* the target to determine its distance from our position. *Yes, we have frickin' invisible laser beams onboard.*

"FIRE!" the TC yelled with conviction.

"ON THE WAY," I yelled, which, in the language of Tankers, means, I'm going to ejaculate a hell storm of thunder and fire!

"TARGET. CEASE FIRE!" said the TC.

The main gun recoiled into the tank and spat out an AFT-CAP, or what remained of the forty-plus lbs. of munitions I just sent into a target, center-mass. I had killed my first plywood target. I was so proud. My heart raced. It was deafening: a din of war, of hell, of beauty. My ears rang. My chest could still feel the shock wave just sent through the tank. My whole body was woozy at the sheer, raw power of the Hell that just happened. If I had a little chubby after firing the M240, I was in a full-blown hard-on after the main gun went off. It was a drug, and I was hooked.

The airborne infantry have their glory jumping out of airplanes, pilots have theirs in flying, and armor has theirs when the main gun goes off like the gods of war screaming for victory.

22

BRAINS?

Towards the end of training, as mentioned, we were given some liberties we had not yet enjoyed during our luxurious stay at Fort Knox. Chow was a very sordid affair up to this point, as we'd always ran to the mess hall, chow hall, dining facility, choke and puke, whatever you want to call it, screaming like turbo-assisted assholes with three to five minutes to eat our meal. There were, in the four-plus months of my tenure at Fort Knox, no memories of me enjoying a single meal there. Well, maybe the last one was enjoyable, but that doesn't mean it tasted good. However, there was certainly a *memorable* meal, as in, I will never forget it.

FTX was behind us, and we'd just entered Red Phase. We'd passed most of our exams and were all but done with our training. During this final phase, we were *finally* allowed to eat a dessert in the mess hall, but only at supper time. Now, we were allowed to walk and talk like normal human beings in route to the chow hall. It doesn't sound like much, but it was a huge deal. It was on this first night of this newfound liberty when my next story begins.

There were many choices for dessert that particular evening: cake, cookies, pie, cobbler, you name it. I opted for the gelatin. I had a beautiful, square blob of red gelatin stuck to a small plate on my tray. It shook and jiggled ever so gloriously as I walked to my table. It beckoned me to eat it first, but patience was with me this evening.

I sat with a few buddies and started talking about anything other than the Army. After four months, this really was a liberty. We enjoyed the moment as we had time to breathe between bites and actually chew our food. We tried not to taste it, though. Strange phenomenon, I know. The subject of movies came up—what we were going to watch when we were home and what good ones we'd missed during training. We were aware of the new movies in theatres through phone conversations and letters from home. Our family and friends kept us up-to-date, as anything non-military was always welcomed news. There was a horror movie coming out we all wanted to see, so naturally, we started talking about the best and worst in scary movies.

Like gentlemen, we patiently listened to one another's stories, and being polite, we kindly allowed the conversation to move in a circular fashion around the group. As the conversation moved around to me, naturally the attention of the group came my way. They could tell I had my mouth full, so to indicate that I, indeed, had something to contribute, I held my index finger up to imply a pause until I could politely respond. They looked at me a bit weird as my mouth was full and I was visibly busy with the contents, but anxious to speak. What they didn't know was as they were talking and looking at one another, I'd slipped a huge bite of my gelatin into my mouth and began to squish it between my teeth to stir it into a semi-soupy mixture. Once I felt I had attained the right texture, I dribbled the contents out of my mouth and onto my plate as I recited a movie quote, *"BRAINS!"* Laughter started to break up their long-awaited reply from yours truly, until… *"TURNER!"* echoed forcibly through the entire chow hall. I looked up to see ole Guts-N-Gravel, First PLT's DS, looking at me like an angry junkyard dog. This was the DS that gargled asphalt and concrete rubble with his coffee each morning, which amplified the terror even further. We all feared this guy since day two, especially after I thought he shot a guy that was just a few feet behind me moments earlier. He was an intimidating guy, no doubt.

My body froze, my eyes turned into billiard balls, following my break-neck reflex to meet his eyes and acknowledge his gruff existence. I knew I was stone-cold busted. I quickly tried to wipe the gelatin from my guilty face and recover into a military-*esque*-bearing, but I knew my ass was grass and he was the lawnmower. *"YOU GET THE FUCK OUT OF MY MESS HALL, TURNER. YOU BETTER BE STANDING TALL OUTSIDE OF MY OFFICE WHEN I GET THERE, FUCK STICK,"* his voice boomed out to me, instantly casting a demonic hex on my fearful soul. That was all he had to say to elicit an instant physical response from me.

He rose to take his tray to the clearing station. I soon realized that he just lit the fuse attached to my ass. I was now a man on a serious mission: to beat him, to not only the tray-clearing station, but back to the barracks, so he could rip me a new one. Luck is a double-edged sword, as is often the case in any situation I'm in. Luck had placed me closer to the clearing station than him, so I had that going for me. But Lady Luck, being a real bitch, had also placed me into my current state of Puckered Asshole Syndrome, A.K.A., Nervous Soldier in a World of Shit-*itous*. I was about to complete my happy meal with an entire shit sandwich for dessert.

Fortunately, I had downed all required nutrients before squishing brains back-and-forth through my teeth. I would need those precious vitamins, too, for I was about to expend them all in one fell swoop. I raced to the clearing station and tried to not make eye contact with him, as he had, fortunately, stopped to harass his own troops. Things were really looking up, I'd say. Nah, not a fucking chance. I was done for.

In a matter of minutes, I had screwed away my dessert and a walk, versus a run, back to the barracks that night. Like I mentioned before...*soldiering, I was killing it.* I ran back and waited at his office in a semi-attention position, as I knew he was not far behind. In the interim, I bellied a plethora of abuse and taunts from First PLT soldiers. They were all smiles and laughter until that big, steel door swung open and his intimidating form entered the bright light emitting from the mercury-filled tubes overhead. I snapped to attention faster than a bullet from a muzzle break. I puckered up and wished I'd wiped the sweat from my brow before I snapped to.

Without a glance, he walked into his office. I quickly and nervously wiped away the sweat resulting from my less than leisurely jog back to the barracks. I could hear him settle into his chair and rustle a few items around his desk. I then heard that brown and round hat hit the desk, striking with the efficiency of mashed potatoes slung from grandma's big spoon onto a flat dinner plate. I knew that meant pain was on its way.

He called his PLT guide into his office. Other than a few muttered words, I couldn't make out what they were discussing, before the DS issued a sharp *"DISMISSED"* to the PLT guide. He quickly entered the hallway and ran upstairs. Nervousness grew inside of me as the silence crept in.

Moments later, the DS emerged from his office with a smirk on his face. He had obviously been amused to the point that he asked me exactly what the fuck I was doing back in the mess hall. I explained the situation up to the point he'd understood the gist, then I thought I saw chunks of concrete spew from his mouth as he belted out, *"DROP, PRIVATE. KNOCK 'EM OUT, TURD BREATH."*

This being month four of our training, we were all pretty efficient at just about every form of disciplinary exercise they could dole out. It was to the point that when we started a disciplinary exercise, we didn't stop until told to do so, we just kept going and going. The days of ten or twenty PUs and resting in between were long gone like yesterday's farts. We were lean, mean, fighting machines. They say a 1,000 mile journey begins with the first step, and this was going to be no different. I started out with PU number *one* and a few short minutes later, I finally took my first pause at number *one hundred twenty-five*. Yes, one-hundred and twenty-five fucking push-ups. The whole while I was receiving an earful from Drill Sergeant Guts-N-Gravel himself, about how dumb I was.

After PUs, it was dying cockroaches, hello Dolly's, wall-ups, mountain climbers, more PUs, flutter kicks…you name it, and I did it. He smoked me for a good forty-five minutes. I was soaked in sweat when he finally released me. Then I ran upstairs to my floor to only be greeted by my own DS. No doubt, Guts-N-Gravel had his PLT guide inform him, as if he were not going to hear my screamed responses from one floor below. It would've been far too easy to sneak into my own room without a confrontation with DS Thomas. This wouldn't have fit into the master plan.

"TURNER," his voiced echoed through the hall, *"GET IN HERE."* My heart dropped back into my stomach. *Fuck me*, I thought.

"PRIVATE TURNER, REPORTING AS ORDERED, DRILL SERGEANT," I screamed out as I came to attention in front of his desk. A snappy and sharp exchange of Q&A time ensued.

"I HEARD YOU LIKE RED GELATIN, PRIVATE," he exclaimed.

"YES, DRILL SERGEANT," I said, as my stomach turned to shit.

He smiled and asked, *"DID YOU HAVE FUN PLAYING IN FIRST PLATOON?"*

"NO, DRILL SERGEANT," I said, still sweating.

"WHAT THE FUCK WERE YOU THINKING, TURNER?"

"I WASN'T THINKING, DRILL—" He cut me off mid-sentence.

"FRONT LEAN-ING REST PO-SI-TION…MOVE," spoken sharply to accentuate each vowel, with a brief pause in between for further effect. *"IN CA-DENCE…EX-ER-CISE. COUNT 'EM OUT, TURNER."*

"ONE, TWO, THREE, ONE. ONE, TWO, THREE, TWO. ONE, TWO, THREE, THREE…" I began. After about thirty or so PUs, *"RECOVER. STOP FUCKIN' AROUND, TURNER,"* he said with a wry smile across his pursed lips. *"DISMISSED, SOLDIER. MOVE OUT."* I quickly exited his office and made haste to my room, just down the hall. *"TURNER!"* His voice echoed again.

I quickly ran back to the door of his office. *Fu-u-u-u-c-k me!!*

"YES, DRILL SERGEANT," I responded whilst running through his door.

"NO DESSERT FOR A WEEK," he ordered.

Ready for it all to be over, I smartly screamed, *"YES, DRILL SERGEANT."* I quickly tried to retreat back into the hallway.

"TURNER," his voice yet again bellowing off the walls like a familiar yodel in the Alps.

"YES, DRILL SERGEANT," I said. My thoughts immediately went to, *Play time is over, and now he's going to smoke me, too.*

"JUST FUCKIN' WITH YOU. QUIT GETTING CAUGHT, TURNER." A more noticeable smirk on his face. At first, I was a bit dumbfounded at this remark, but it made perfect sense on graduation day.

"ROGER THAT, DRILL SERGEANT. THANK YOU, DRILL SERGEANT," I said.

"GET THE FUCK OUT OF MY DOORWAY, TURNER," quickly dismissing me again.

"YES, DRILL SERGEANT," I said as I bolted.

I ran to the latrine as fast as I could, so as to ensure I couldn't be called back to his office, at least for a couple of minutes. He didn't call me back. Being me, I'm willing to bet I ate that red gelatin every day after punishment until the end of training and it was the best damn gelatin I'd eaten in my life.

At the time, I wasn't that impressed with doing one hundred and twenty-five PUs without a pause, but now that I am in my mid-40s, it's damn impressive. For the record, I still love cherry flavored gelatin and think of that experience every time I eat it, too.

23

HEY, LOTTY DOTTY

We had all these inspiring (sometimes funny) cadences that we would *call,* or sing, while running or marching. The cadence caller would begin his cadence as his left heel would strike the ground, as would everyone's. Thus started *time* or tempo for the cadence. He would say a verse, pause, then the PLT or company would do the same as their left heel struck the ground. Singing or calling cadence would depend on whether you were marching or running in formation. It was a great way to take your mind off the blisters, shin splints, and misery a soldier generally felt while moving from one location to the next.

Here are a few examples to either reminisce over, or if you are new to this stuff, look them up on video. They will get you motivated, even sitting on your couch. Albeit, there are many, many lines I could add, I'm throwing the basics out there to remind my fellow brothers and sisters of the old days.

MAMA, MAMA

Mama, Mama can't you see, what the Army's done to me?

They put me in a barber's chair, spun me round, I had no hair.

They took away my faded jeans, now I'm wearing Army greens.

I used to date a beauty queen, now I love my M16.

NO SWEAT

One mile, no sweat. Two miles, better yet.

Three miles, gotta run. Four miles, just for fun.

How are you? We're OK.

Here we go. All the way.

How do we go? In the snow.

Where do we train? In the rain.

Where do we run? In the sun.

Hoonga. Gimme' some. PT.

Good for you, good for me.

MY GIRL'S A VEGETABLE

My girl's a vegetable, she lives in a hospital.

She has no arms or legs, just a set of wooden pegs.

I used to love to watch her strip, now she's on an IV drip.

My girl has long, blond hair, it's in patches here and there.

She has her own TV, it's called an EKG.

ALL THE LADIES

Oh, I wish that all the ladies were bricks in a pile,

And I was a mason, oh, I'd lay 'em all in style.

I wish that all the ladies were holes in a road,

And I was a dump truck, I'd fill 'em with my load.

I wish that all the ladies were rats in a steeple,

And I was the king rat, there'd be more rats than people.

A few more great examples are: Yellow Rose, Airborne Daddy, and Chain Gang.

The Chain Gang cadence is one of my favorites. DS Thomas, being a black dude, naturally had some *soul* to him, so he taught us how to do a march and cadence combination that was a lot fancier than the regular drill and ceremony we were accustomed to. We went well away from the other PLTs and practiced for days on end. When we finally got it down pat, we were so proud and we loved to show off our new marching skills. We did it when we entered the gymnasium for family day, too. I know we looked good, because we all worked so hard as a team. DS Thomas was a great teacher, DS and all-around good guy.

The cool thing was that no matter how fast or how slow a PLT or Company marched, there was a cadence for the occasion. It instilled pride in the unit. I enjoyed calling cadence when I had the chance. It was a little nerve-racking at first, but then you realized that we recruits were not DSs calling cadence every day, so we were excused to fuck it up until we got it right.

Before we could call cadence, we first had to learn to march in formation. You thought passing inspections were tough? Imagine getting thirty-plus men to march or run, all in-step. That means every one of us were marching face-forward, equally distanced from one another, feet and arms moving in unison as we advanced our position as a group. It's easier said than done.

Once you get it, you do it for the rest of your life. If I walked onto a training post right now and heard a passing PLT calling cadence, and without actually having to see them, I would immediately get in step with them. You could watch my left heel strike at the same time as theirs…and just like that guy on television selling suits, *I GUARANTEE IT!*

24

KENTUCKY OUTHOUSE BLUES

When I started training in September of 1992, it was still hotter than Hades in Kentucky. I wouldn't complete my training until the third week of December, when it would be as cold as an igloo in them there hills, complete with snow. As they say, *IF IT AIN'T RAININ', WE AIN'T TRAININ'. IF IT AIN'T SNOWIN', WE AIN'T GOIN'.* I swear, we marched for what seemed like every single inch of Fort Knox, twice, but this is another subject that will capture the hearts and minds of the soldiers that have served some of their time at Knox: field latrines, or outhouses.

Again, I debated on whether to include this chapter, but I know there are a few generations of soldiers that can share my less-than-fond memories on this matter. As you have figured out, we walked, ran, and marched *everywhere* we went. Going to the range, we walked. Going to eat, we ran. Going on bivouac (Army camping), we walked. Going to formation, we ran. Like Forrest, *we were running.* It came down to the task we were performing that dictated our actions.

Perhaps, it's best if I paint the scene before I delve right in. We were marching along the tank trails in the heavily wooded areas of Knox in full battle-rattle: the works. As we walked along, the trees parted to an open expanse, almost stripped or devoid of trees entirely. Even scenic, if you will. As it was around 25° F, we were bundled up to the nth degree. Strangely, it seemed better to keep moving, as a body in motion produces more heat than one sitting still, but we were ready for a break. We were exhausted and cold. It gave us time to rehydrate and rest our bones while we changed our socks. Besides, it was time for me to answer the call of nature.

As luck would have it, I couldn't just relieve myself in the bushes. Nature had other plans. Luck did smile on me, though. There was an outhouse about a hundred meters away. One would think that it's as simple as picking yourself up off the rucksack you'd carried *mile-after-mile* and walk over to the outhouse in the middle of the expanse, but oh, Hell no. One must load up all their shit: weapon, rucksack, pro mask, helmet, etc., and take all that shit with you. Then, you could drop your gear on the ground while you went inside to do your business. All but your weapon that is, as it was always to remain within arm's reach.

As I marched, the wind felt like it was laced with tiny razors that could, at any moment, slice open chapped skin with a healthy gust. It was truly miserable. As I neared the outhouse, the smell hit me: the lukewarm chemical reaction that emitted from that tiny building was simply horrible. I immediately stretched my undershirt over my nose to semi-filter the odor. It seemed to help, but ultimately it didn't. Microscopic pieces of shit were hanging in the air like rotting carcasses on a hook in the middle of summer, though no frozen cadavers here. It was truly an assault to the olfactory. I thought about calling in a chemical attack on myself, *Gas, Gas, Gas,* which meant I'd have to don my NBC mask, thereby filtering out said microbes, but handling my M16 was going to be challenging enough.

I swore, right then and there, that Davy Crockett himself had taken a dump in that very outhouse. It was the ricketiest, most dilapidated turd hole I had ever laid eyes on. It bore no door. It was a tin-roofed wooden structure that looked as if a good wind could blow her down. It consisted of a small partitioned knee wall, with 2x4 supports to the roof, and a quasi-mesh of torn, rusty screen, that wouldn't have filtered a full-sized buzzard, much less a gnat.

As I neared this structure of stench, I noticed a peculiar sound coming from inside. I haphazardly inched closer, eyes in a dead squint, no doubt with a dumbfounded look across my face. *What the fuck is that?* The smell had become this *living thing* in the air, or deadly thing, rather. It was awful, an overwhelming shock to the system. Seriously, there are not enough words in the English language to describe this horrendous odor.

Mouth and nose disguised in my undershirt, I noticed a rucksack sitting idly by the door space. With each step, the noise grew louder. The wind howling over my freezing ears muffled the noise until I was within a stone's throw of the shit shack. It sounded like someone was dying in the building, though the wind still toyed with my numbed ears. I pressed forward, with all of my curiosity running amok at this point. Fuck it. I wasn't standing around to find out, I was there on business of my own.

I threw my shit down on the ground as fast as I could, because after a hundred meters, I didn't have the time to ponder life's little mysteries. I was a man on a mission. I had my clock, and Mother Nature had hers, and the alarm was ring-a-dinging. My rucksack hit the ground with a reassuring thud that told me gravity was still working just fine. I temporarily rested my weapon on my rucksack, then struggled to get my helmet, LBE, and protective mask off, while fending off the stench from my ever suffering nose. My gear strewn on the ground, I recovered my rifle and headed in. Momentarily, I questioned my decision to leave my NBC mask outside. As I passed through the space that was devoid of any door, the *odd noise* aligned with the odorous punch to my face…My mind immediately connected the dots.

I thought I would find a fellow PLT member, but no, there sat some random-as-fuck guy from god only knows where. There wasn't one sighting of another platoon, squad, or any other life in those hills that day. It was Second PLT, trees, and this lone outhouse. There he sat occupying one of three holes in the devil's den. Location in today's terms: *#FuckingNowhere #LLMF #BumFuckEgypt*.

That is my first and last attempt to be modern in this book. You're welcome.

There he sat, still donned in his helmet, pants to his ankles with his weapon thrown to the ground and lying in old, stale piss. He sat over one hole and dry-heaved into the center one. It was an awful sight. In his less-than-stellar moment, he peered up at me with these blood-shot eyes, drool dribbling from his lower lip and this distinctive, *kill me now* look etched on his face.

In true soldierly fashion, I asked him was he okay? *"HEY, BUDDY, ARE YOU..."* I paused, before interrupting my own sentence with, *"ARUUUGGGHHHH,"* thus, began my own spell of the dry-heaves.

He didn't answer my question. The winds were whipping around in every direction that day, so there was no hiding from the soured bowels of hell's sewer. My nose had to eventually accept the fact that I'd entered a gruesomely fouled existence, right? I couldn't hold my breath forever, so my nose gave up on reaching for oxygen and fueled itself with methane and shit particles. I accepted the consequences of the severe *dain bramage* I sustained with each new breath. Consequences be damned, I was still on a mission.

Beyond the threshold, I found one remaining wooden oval. In my predicament, I couldn't afford to wait on my temporary battle buddy to finish. I began the unbuttoning process immediately after dropping my ruck, so my bowels were well aware of the situation and prepared to deliver. *TARGET IDENTIFIED. FIRE. ON THE WAY!*

The wood felt petrified to my bum. Cold, unforgiving, breezy. PVT Shit-N-Guts was still retching his innards out as I settled into my own heaving fits. There we sat on that cold afternoon in Kentucky, both in a Hell of our own. Funny how you forget that you'd signed on the dotted line, held your hand up and swore an oath, and this, however unfortunate, was part of that wonderful experience.

He eventually finished, leaving me to my own devices, but not before muttering out a stifled and guttural wish for my good luck as he exited. I swear, that place housed the asses from recruits as far back as the Civil War, perhaps, even the American Revolution. But hey, no one was shooting at me while trying to do it.

Yours Truly—1: Army—0.

TARGET…CEASE FIRE.

25

GENTLEMEN, YOU ARE GOING TO GERMANY!

One day, about a week or so before we were to graduate, the DSs called the entire platoon to an informal formation. We didn't have to stand at attention; we simply stood in a large gaggle. DS Thomas held a small stack of papers in his hand. The entirety of the group could feel that this was a pivotal moment, as there were few times, if any, that we were not standing at attention. Our TCs waited on the tanks.

He gave a small speech about our orders coming through and how the needs of the Army far outweighed the needs of the soldier. This was not, in any shape or form, a decision that the DSs were responsible for. Orders came directly from the DoD (Department of Defense). We had, of course, filled out the infamous *Dream Sheet*. It was to suggest that should the needs of the Army be met, which was about as likely as pigs conducting a state lottery, that you would get to choose *your* desired duty station.

First, he separated the Nasty Girls from Regular Army guys, because the NGs went home, versus we who were going to our permanent duty station. Then, the DS called out maybe six names and told them to gather to his left. He informed them that they had orders to report to South Korea. He said they would love it: it was cold, cheap to live, drink and chase women, and generally considered a great duty station; but also considered a hardship tour, as families couldn't accompany them. Some guys looked happy, while others looked miserable.

This, of course, spawned a lot of subtle chatter amongst the group. We all pretty much knew at that point, there were only a few options remaining for Tankers: America, Europe, and maybe Japan. America and Europe were the likely contenders.

The DS instructed us to listen up as he began the next round of names, and instructed us to gather to his right. My name was called. This group was considerably larger than the Korean one. It comprised a sizable bulk of the group, though not as large as the remaining men.

Pointing to my group, he spoke. *"GENTLEMEN, YOU ARE GOING TO GERMANY!"*

Then, redirecting his attention to the remaining men, he softly, almost saddened by the news he had to deliver, said, *"THE REST OF YOU ARE ORDERED TO REMAIN IN THE CONTINENTAL UNITED STATES WITH THE REST OF US."*

My Uncle Chris had been to both Korea and Germany during his time in service. He was both enlisted and an officer in the Army, which afforded me knowledge of some of his exciting exploits. It wasn't the first thing to cross my mind when the news hit me. I knew our family heritage was German, I spoke a little and had read and studied some German history, but none of that registered in my adolescent brain at that moment. Instead, terror ripped through me, because I had pretty much surmised what would happen if I was stationed so far away: my girlfriend and I were probably not going to make it. I was young and thought I was very much in love with this person, my high school sweetheart. At that age, you hope your love will last forever. Thankfully, and I do mean very thankfully, mine did not.

It took about two days for the news to really sink in. I spoke to several of my buddies within the PLT, and we realized how cool this was actually going to be. Europe was to be our playground. We were about to live in another country for what I hoped would be my three-year enlistment. I'd have the chance to see the battlegrounds I'd studied. Many of my uncles fought there in WWI and WWII. After that, I was floating on cloud nine.

Years later, I learned that my seventh great-grandmother, Ann Kalb, was born, lived, and died in the same state of Germany where I and Uncle Chris were stationed and great-great-uncle Maxi fought in WWII.

26

TRANSFORMATION

What so many people do not realize, is the transformation that happens to someone after such an intense regiment of physical and mental exercise with a healthy dose of reprogramming. Some people think you're brain-washed or implanted with chips that make you into robots. It's not like that at all. This is no normal 9–5 job, either. We volunteered for this shit. We raised our right hands and made an oath to defend the constitution against all enemies, foreign and domestic. We had, by all rights, signed an open-ended check for our very lives. We could be called for duty in a hostile combat zone and, perhaps, die. We knew this was always a possibility even before we signed on the dotted line. Hell, I prayed for war so I could earn and wear a combat patch affixed to my right shoulder, like so many others in my family had done.

This is no ordinary job where handicapped spaces are provided at the office or insurance subsidized weight loss clubs. There are no handicaps for flat-feet, poor eyesight, mental and health problems. You either make the cut, or you are escorted out as not fit-for-service. We are, especially in combat-arms MOSs, trained to win at war. We were not construction workers, bankers, salesmen, or clerks. We were soldiers, and expected to perform as such.

Most of us were eighteen years old and had no idea the profound impact or far reaches of where this adventure would take us. Our lives had been transformed forever. Nearly every peer we'd ever known was either (still) living at home, attending college, working for their family, starting careers of their own, getting addicted to drugs, or who knows what else? We were live-firing rifles, machine-guns, tanks, throwing grenades, and were about to move to another country, another continent. Our lives were never going to be the same.

I would like to prepare the reader for what is coming in Part(y) II, as it is nowhere near as innocent as training. I implore you to exercise a bit more leniency in your judgement towards me, towards all of us. We were all young, wild, and free.

Fuck it. I have made my peace with those I thought I'd wronged in the past and I sleep just fine at night, knowing I've made reparations. I make no excuses for who I was or who any of us were. What's important is who I became after the dust settled.

1992- With my parents, Paul & Brenda, after graduation at Ft. Knox, KY.

1992- Road march at Ft. Knox, KY.

1992- Training at Ft. Knox, KY.

1992- Infamous 3rd PLT fuck-up.

1993- Repelling off a WWII bunker in Lampertheim, Germany.

1993- Spud & I on our fuzzy night in Amsterdam, Netherlands.

1993- Eiffel Tower, Paris, France.

1993- Battle of Bulge bunker where Patton met the 101st Airborne.

1993- Caricature at Notre Dame in Paris, France.

1993- Jim Morrison's gravesite in Paris, France.

1993- Part of the Liberty Road in Belgium.

1994- Me driving a WWII half-track after winning the divisional boxing championship.

1994- Tom Dever and I drinking in San Sebastian, Spain.

1994- Dodging multiple bulls in Pamplona, Spain.

2015- 1ˢᵗ Reunion in Dothan, Alabama.
From Left to right: Fritz, Spud, Me, Tire Iron, Sgt. J, Wildman, and Byrdman.

2018- 3ʳᵈ Reunion outside of Dallas, Texas.
From Left to right: Top row: Weatherford, Sgt. J, Cheeseburger, Spive,
Fritz, Lake, Vegas, Wildman, Me. Bottom row: Duffster and Spud.

2020- Spud and I at Mount Rushmore, S. Dakota. Enroute to the 4th reunion.

2020- 4th Reunion in Stillwater, OK. Left to right, top row: Wildman and Vegas. Bottom row: Spive, Spud and Me.

PART(Y) TWO

A
SOLDIER
IN
EUROPE

27

PIZZA & BEER PARTY IN FRANKFURT

I flew in from Hotlanta. It was around 2300 hours on the 5th of January 1993, when I touched down in Frankfurt, Germany. The ground was covered in snow and ice, and it was bitterly cold. One of my first memories of Germany was seeing this extremely hot blond woman walking around the airport in a green and white leather jacket, sporting an Uzi sub-machine gun. She was an officer in the *Polizei* (German police). I was both intimidated and excited at the same time. It was very different from the airports in America.

This should be interesting, I thought. Of course, we didn't have search engines back then, but through reading, I *thought* I was very informed about Germany and Europe in general. My brother took some German in high school, and our family lineage was from Germany. I was ready, right? I drank beer all through high school, and now I was in the beer capital of the world. *What could possibly go wrong?*

Everyone knows the story about the ink blot on the linen cloth. Well, we were the epitome of that story, as we could be spotted a mile away with our fresh skin-close high-and-tight haircuts and wide-eyed faces.

With white-wall skulls, at least for us white boys, we more resembled someone sporting a Yiddish yarmulke.

There was a liaison waiting for us in the baggage area. He confirmed our orders, then led us to an awaiting bus that would drive us to *Rhein-Main* Air Force Base, where every soldier processes into Europe. My word, was it ever cold. We were checked into radiator-heated, near-freezing rooms close to the in-processing center. Breakfast was from 0600–0700, then began the task of completing our *in-country* paperwork. Already, this was an improvement over training, as we had an entire hour to eat!

On the way to breakfast, I ran into a couple guys I recognized from Knox, though from different PLTs. We all quickly buddied-up, as we were the only familiar faces in this very busy place. Vehicles were zipping to and fro; there were people running around everywhere. We had just spent over four months living the military life, yet this was completely foreign to us.

We sat down and ate breakfast, and thanks to the United States Air Force, we enjoyed the food here so much more than in Fort Knox. Unlike Army food, it was not devoid of any and all taste. It was actually good. As we walked outside, the snow began to apply another layer to the tree branches, ground, and parked vehicles. It was bitterly cold. We smoked a cigarette or two, then realized we hadn't a clue where we were to report to begin our processing. Officially, we were Lima Lima Mike Foxtrot. Land navigation wasn't helping us now.

We broke down and asked for directions and were a few moments late, but no one yelled, screamed, or made us assume the front leaning rest position. It was a whole different animal in the regular Army. I knew it was always different during training, but none of us had any idea it would be like this.

We had to do all sorts of stuff. I believe I updated *every single piece* of paper I had ever completed for the Army. It wasn't as bad as OSUT, though. It was still shit and tons, nonetheless. Then, the most amazing thing happened. They released us for lunch at around 1115, and told us to continue our paperwork at 1300 hours. This had to be some sort of mistake on the Army's part, though they never screwed up. We had almost two hours to ourselves. What the fuck were we going to do with that much time? Hell, we could eat in three minutes flat, which meant we had an extra hour and forty-two minutes. Did they not realize what mayhem we could get into with that much time on our hands? Apparently, not.

Fortunately for us and the Army, lunch went without a hiccup, as we visited the PX for some light shopping. It's the singular place where you could get most military necessities, as well as civilian ones, like groceries, housewares, and electronics. That afternoon, we finished our paperwork with regular breaks in between. Every hour or so, we would travel from one building to the next, with a 10–15 minute gap in between. It gave us time to bullshit and smoke cigarettes in the falling snow. We were shivering cold, but excited to be in Europe. The untold thousands of men and women that had processed through here…and now it was our turn, our time.

I guess it was about 1530 hours when we finally finished up. We were all starting to feel the effects of jet lag. We were 7–8 hours out of whack and two weeks out of OSUT, but, all of us being eighteen years old, it allowed us a great deal of leeway in terms of how much we could withstand. We were accustomed to such abuses on the mind and body. As a near full-day had passed, our motley crew of Echo 2-13 guys grew to four. We decided to forgo the complimentary Air Force meal, in lieu of the pizza parlor we'd seen earlier. The Army had well delivered on its *three-hots-and-a-cot*, so it was our turn to feed ourselves for a change.

We met up at the decided time, maybe around 1700 hours. We had beaten the end-of-day dinner rush. Had we not been on a military post, we'd have looked like a high school club meeting. We were all so young, and especially young-looking with our fresh haircuts and clean-shaven faces. We were soldiers, but ones that looked fresh out of the package. Looking back on it now, I think how naïve we really were. This was day one of our first *real* day in the Army. Oh, how we fancied ourselves. I guess every soldier, in every corner of the world, had to have a first day, so why should we be any different?

We took a booth in the back of the restaurant, facing the front door. It was on the outskirts of the room overlooking the bulk of the dining area. It certainly felt warmer inside, more than we'd felt all day. Hot pizza sounded so awesome. The waiter came over and gave us some menus and asked how we were. No doubt, he could spot us as *brand-spanking-new* servicemen. We ever so slyly asked about the specials posted on the chalkboard at the front door. He said, *"IT'S PERFECT FOR THE FOUR OF YOU. TONIGHT'S SPECIAL IS TWO LARGE PIZZAS, WITH TWO TOPPINGS, AND TWO PITCHERS OF BEER, FOR $XX.00!"*

Our eyes must have lit up like an airport landing a 747. Simultaneously, we had the same thought, *They are serving us beer.*

Now mind you, a few weeks earlier while at Fort Knox, our DSs informed us that the same laws of the United States, also applied to us here in Germany: namely the one concerning beer, wine, and liquor sales to those of us under the age of twenty-one. Undoubtedly, that was the first thought to enter our beer-hungry brains, thus the only law they discussed. We entered this vacant-like existence of disbelief. We all sheepishly looked at one another, eyes quickly darting back-and-forth beneath our bowed brows, in a *holy shit* astounded moment. Time stood near still, as a quiet came over our table. We could hear our own hearts beating inside our chests, as if in a *fight or flight* moment.

Was this some altered reality? Had he mistook this group of newbies as really being over twenty-one years of age? Was he that dense? No, he's like thirty years old, surely he knew better. Maybe, he was just *being cool*? This was, after all, a military base in Germany. Eventually we retrieved our jaws off the floor and decided on some toppings. He said, *"ONE PITCHER OF HEFE-WEIßBIER, COMIN' UP. UNLESS YOU WANT THEM BOTH NOW?"* In our race to complete the transaction, we opted for both…foolishly.

"SURE, HEAVY LIGHT (sic) BEER SOUNDS GOOD," I responded nervously. What the fuck was heavy-light beer? Who gave a shit? We were about to be served beer at the tender age of eighteen.

He retrieved our menus and said he would be right back. We giggled like school girls talking about their first, grade-school kiss. We leaned in, hunkering down to immediately break down the events, play-by-play. We confirmed with one another that we had all, in fact, received the same speech from our DSs. *Was it all bullshit?*

We soon decided that there was no mistake on the part of the waiter, as he soon showed up with two beautiful, wonderful, glorious pitchers of beer and four tall pilsner glasses, not plastic cups. Albeit, the beer was a cloudy looking concoction, of the likes we had never seen before. It was golden in color, frothy on top, and had this swirly looking sediment that had been imparted to its body. The pitcher found its place before us, suds resting and settling before our thirsty eyes.

He spoke. *"PIZZAS ARE IN THE OVEN, GENTLEMEN. THEY'LL BE UP SOON."*

"OK. THANK YOU," we responded in a semi-bewildered state.

But, being the soldiers we were, we wasted very little time in pouring this cloudy nectar into our glasses. It frothed up like a freshly shaken keg at a freshman frat party. We slightly tipped our glasses as we poured, but this cloud water superseded any of our beer-pouring abilities. The first and second attempts were equally as pitiful. It was as if they were our first beer pours ever! The glass was, maybe, a ¼ full, after each pour. This was next-level shit. Thankfully, for our egos, we were not spotted by the other patrons. Once the sudsy version of Mount Saint Helens had settled and it rendered a drinkable form in the bottom half of the glass, we opted for a friendly cheers.

Little did I realize the life-changing moment that was about to tran-spire upon my hairless lips. We lifted our glasses, clinked the rims excitedly while speaking the magic word in unison, *"CHEERS!"* Our guided hands quickly closed the gap between those beautiful glasses and our lips, allowing the golden flow of hops to displace the air in our throats and mouths. *HOUSTON, WE HAVE CONTACT.*

Through our sudsy glasses, we looked at one another with a wide-eyed wonder rarely found in the human experience. It was the most wonder-ful thing we had ever tasted. It was nothing, I mean absolutely nothing, like the swilled piss to which we were accustomed. In nothing less than leaps and bounds, this cloudy quencher surpassed the crap we had sto-len from the country gas station or from our fathers' cabinets. This was truly the nectar of the gods, and it was at that moment I understood that phrases do not simply make themselves up, they are born from moments like this, from beers like this. *Nectar of the Gods* made perfect sense to me now.

Again, we were like teenyboppers at a sleepover pajama party, playing truth or dare after a middle school dance. We were fucking giddy with excitement. To us, it was a phenomenon, as if we were now in a secret club. Not only were we members, we felt like we were the presidents of that club. It had to have been extremely comical for the flies on the wall. This beer was awesome! It went down sweeter than water; so smooth and full of flavor. It didn't suds up so much in your stomach like that American piss water did. I hate to beat-up on American beer, but sometimes, the truth hurts. It didn't seem to fill you up…ever.

We had sauntered through the first pitcher and were well into the second when we started feeling the effects of this glorious liquid, long before our pizzas arrived. I asked the waiter what *heavy-light* beer was.

He laughed and politely corrected me. *"HEFE-WEIßBIER. IT'S GERMAN WHEAT BEER."* (*Hefe-Weißbier* has many variations: *Hefe-Weizen, Hefe-Weisse, Hefe-Weiß*, etc.)

"OH, OKAY." My trepidation and nerves having worn thin about half a glass earlier. *"WHY IS IT CLOUDY?"* I probed.

He responded, *"IT'S UNFILTERED. THAT'S ALL THE WHEAT FLOATING AROUND. YOU GUYS LIKE IT?"*

"WE…hiccup…LOVE IT." I asked the guys if they wanted another one, and I believe a resounding, *"HELL YEAH,"* was the answer.

The waiter topped off our glasses and said, *"COMIN' RIGHT UP, GUYS,"* before disappearing with two emptied pitchers.

The pizzas were a welcomed addition to our stomachs, as it had been about seven hours since our last meal. At the time, it was a feast fit for gods. Hot pizza and semi-cold beer. It sounds strange, but German beer is not supposed to be ice-cold, like our American excuse for beer. Sorry, America, but the Germans have a lock on this one. We do freedom, like they do beer! (What do American beer and fucking in a canoe have in common? They're both close to water.) No one seemed to care since it tasted so wonderful.

We were in a frenzy, damn near inhaling both the food and the beer. It was as if we were in a dream and we didn't want to wake up. We absolutely stuffed ourselves with a half pizza each and nearly three pitchers of beer. The third pitcher sat a ¼ full in front of us. All of us sat googly-eyed, sizing up our beer appetites. The beer, though wonderful, could not be consumed. We were each, ten pounds of shit in five pound bags.

Belches, burps, and hiccups abounded like flies on a fresh turd. My eyes squinted, my brow furled, and my lips pursed in unison as a grumble came over my stomach. It was more like a gurgle from the intestines of Hell. I burped a couple times to release the building gases from my overstuffed gut. A bead of sweat slowly formed across my forehead, and my dominant hand found its way below to soothe the outside of my stomach: a worthless gesture of the body and mind, as if to support my stomach from falling to the floor.

Another gurgle formed and sent a ferocious, yet startling, uncontrollable belch to my previously pursed lips. It shot out of me with such a sharp release, which under normal circumstances would be blown into the faces of my buddies in a moment of comic relief. I was, I believe, more unprepared for this moment than they were, given the silly look that undoubtedly adorned my face. They didn't jump in fright as I had. It was like a hiccup and burp all at the same time, almost painful. It caught me at my most unawares.

Another gurgle overcame me. A few squinted grimaces came across the faces of my buddies as they asked, *"ARE YOU ALL RIGHT, TURNER?"*

This was where, again, luck was on my side, and yet totally against me. Yin and yang, and the whole good-versus-evil storyline. During the entire time that we'd consumed 2¾ pitchers of this glorious beer, did any of us bother to locate the latrine? No! This is where luck was against me. We had, however, parked our asses right next to the rear entrance of the building. This is where luck, albeit dumb, was on my side, like an old familiar friend.

Perhaps a quick lesson in beer math would help: 60 ounces multiplied by 2¾ pitchers = 165 ounces of German wheat beer, at roughly 7% alcohol (versus the 3–4% swill we were semi-accustomed to drinking), divided by four newly minted soldiers, meant we'd each consumed nearly eight American beers inside of an hour. Quick beer answer: we were all fucking wasted.

"I DON'T FEEL SO GOOD, GUYS," were the next, and obvious, words out of my gob-smacked mouth. I eyeballed the sign to the latrine and surmised that it was, in my current condition, nearer to the maximum-effective range of an M16; therefore, it was way too fucking far for me to stumble to. I opted for the piling snow outside the doors just behind us.

One of my buddies started with, *"YOU LOOK LIKE SHIT, TURNER. GO TO THE BATHROOM AND—"*

I didn't bother to stay and hear the rest of his fine speech.

I stood from the booth, performed an about-face, 180 degrees, then quickly rounded the booth towards the double-doors exit another 90 degrees. One would be inclined to think that these were a normal set of doors, but one would be wrong. It was of the German design; hence, logical in every sense. It was a set of double-doors with the bar across the width of it, like in grade school; sturdy, weather-resistant, and secure.

As the cold air began to hit my face and body, so did the upward journey of my mostly liquid dinner. Those logical Germans had constructed a small area in which to knock the snow from one's boots, or to retract an umbrella. As logical as it was, it was doing me no favors that evening. I needed every inch between me and the snow-covered ground to be as minimal as possible. The cold hit me like a polar bear challenge and was an instant shock to my already beer-weakened body.

I made it to the first set of doors, before scrambling to the next, with an even greater sense of urgency, especially upon realizing that the goalpost was farther away than anticipated. My body, however, had different plans altogether. It slowed down in its state of shock. In a semi-daze, I stammered to the second set of doors. Whether I liked it or not, it was time to exorcise the demons that were performing a satanic séance in my belly. Devils be gone!

I shot that left door open with a fury, the night air slamming into my discombobulated form. It was also the moment my stomach imploded and let loose a fiery stream of tomato sauce, pizza dough, and that wonderful liquid concoction that had put me in this befuddled state. It was the most wonderful feeling of relief I had ever felt, at least up to that moment in my life. It felt awesome to let loose the dogs of war that were gnarling against my innards. I came to, after the bile-like tears of Satan were ripped from my soul.

Spent, but with wonderful relief, I slowly opened my watery eyes. I found myself on both knees, one hand still clasped to the door in a white-knuckle death grip, and the other splayed flat on the icy, cold sidewalk. My body was contorted and doubled-over, half in the doorway and half outside. As my sight returned and I gathered my wherewithal, I noticed the hot, heaping pile of that night's chalkboard special, steaming in front of me. But, my creation was not alone. No, no, ladies and gentlemen, my monstrosity was held high into the night air by an airborne jump boot—the right boot, to be exact. Between the chunks of pizza and the film of *now* red-colored beer, I could see the reflection of a very drunk PVT in the U.S. Army. In my horror and shame, I looked up and found a very disappointed 1SG, giving me a whole new meaning to the name, Top. My life flashed before my eyes. He was a very large and in-charge black dude, that looked about as happy to see me, as I was him.

I wasted no time in my apologies. *"OH GOD, TOP. I AM SO... HICCUP...SORRY. I-I-I..."* stammering and stuttering. I know he could see that I was (a) a newbie; (b) drunk off my ass; and (c) in no condition to clean his boots. His face looked pained. I knew I was toast. I thought, *I am in trouble and I haven't even been in country for 24 hours.* I know I had to have looked terrified, because, quite frankly, I was.

"ARE YOU HERE ALONE, SOLDIER?" he asked.

"NO, TOP. I'M SO SORRY, I SWEAR TO GOD I DIDN'T MEAN TO—" I began to mutter before he interrupted. He was surprisingly calm, considering the situation.

In a firm, but controlled manner, he abruptly said, *"FIND YOUR BUDDIES. PAY FOR YOUR MEAL. SEE TO IT THEY GET YOU BACK TO YOUR RACK. UNDERSTOOD, PRIVATE?"*

"YES, FIRST SGT. I'M SO SORRY," trying to reassert my remorse.

"DO NOT, UNDER ANY CIRCUMSTANCES, LET ME SEE YOU AGAIN TONIGHT. DO YOU UNDERSTAND ME, SOLDIER?" he said with a voice that came with the kind of assurance that (a) he could kick my ass; (b) he could seriously kick my ass and was considering it; and (c) he could have my ass arrested, because he seriously outranked me, but he was not going to as long as I heeded his orders. Yes, that kind of assurance.

I quickly composed myself into a staggering gaggle fuck of, *I gotta get the fuck out of Dodge before he reconsiders his handling of the situation.* I rounded that booth, threw an *Action Jackson* ($20.00 bill) down on the table, and said, *"GENTLEMEN, I HAVE TO LEAVE…NOW!"* They were witness to the mercy that was adjudicated me, and they too, felt it best to pop smoke, or immediately get the fuck out of the area.

I started stumbling out when they grabbed me and assisted my exit at the front door. After that, I remember getting to my room and passing out for the night. I think it was 1930, maybe 1945 hours—not late at all. In fact, it was relatively early, but the jet lag assisted in my early retirement for the evening. I woke up the next morning before my alarm.

To this day, I do not know why he took such pity on me. He could have indulged in the pick of the litter, in terms of the disciplinary actions at his disposal to throw upon me. But, mercy was on his mind that cold, snowy, January night. He looked down on me in that moment and saw the sheer terror in my eyes, perhaps thinking, he, too, was once a young PVT that relied on someone's pity. That was so many years ago, yet I remember it like it was yesterday; only the hangover from that evening has dissipated.

Top, I don't know if you're reading this, but thank you. I mean, thank you. You saved me from a lot of trouble and probably saved yourself a ruined supper from all the fuss and paperwork associated with busting me. Either way, I am forever in your debt for taking pity on this young and dumb soldier on his first night in Germany.

I have gathered from the several young soldiers I have spoken to in recent years, that these days, superiors are ever-itching to bust guys for any and every infraction, including minor ones. I cannot attest to that firsthand, but I know we had some of the same issues with certain individuals when I was in. It truly was a simpler time, though. I am thankful for all the times I should have been in trouble, but avoided it through some devious plan of my own or from the kindness of others.

I have no doubt, that 1SG Steaming Boots has told that story a few times since then, too. I have a feeling his version may be slightly different, as the perspective was reversed, but I am sure he can laugh about it now, about that one time in Frankfurt, Germany, when this white boy from Detroit Ralphed all over his right boot. Thanks again, Top.

28

REMEMBER, WE WERE YOUNG

I felt it important to preface the remainder of the story before you, the reader, continue. I am not sure how to explain *me*, twenty-five some-odd years later. Once that spark of youth is gone, it's gone. I will never be that young man again. I have aged and wised-up over the years. I will never have the zeal and lust for danger like I once had. It's the natural course of life, of time. Throughout the writing of this novel, I have had twinges of feelings and memories of my former self, but it's never quite the same. I am now stuck in the conundrum of describing the conceited asshole I once was, from the viewpoint of the person I now see in the mirror each morning. It's difficult to piece together the character, irresponsible behavior, and lack of fear that once lived, breathed, and dominated every breath of my being. I feared no man, no consequences; I feared nothing, really. My philosophy was that if you weren't living on the edge, you were taking up too much space.

As an author, one hopes many will read his or her work. There are many that will read this, and will hopefully see the young man I was then, and have some understanding—empathy, if you will—for the wild, fearless soldier I personified. There will also be others who may think, what a self-serving, drunken, conceited prick…and both accounts would be correct. I guess I am trying to preface, or evoke some form of mercy from my readers, some *generosity of spirit* in regard to what you read about that time of my life. I was young and have grown from these experiences.

Although it does not paint the entire picture of my life while in service, or the lives of my buddies, it does paint what, I hope, is a great snapshot of a special moment in time in the prime of our youth—a glimpse into the way the world was, for us, twenty-eight years ago. I, like so many of my brothers, were dedicated, professional, and patriotic soldiers. We just lived a little closer to the edge than most would have considered normal.

Herein lies the *booze-hounded* debauchery of life in an American Armored Unit in Germany, circa 1993–94. I hope you enjoy reading about these exploits, as much as we enjoyed living and drinking them.

29

WELCOME TO THE SPANISH ARMY?

After another day of paperwork, processing, and nursing a slight hangover, I boarded the bus to be delivered to my unit. I was going to a little town named *Käfertal-Wald* (or *Käfertal*-Forest), just outside Mannheim, in the state of *Baden Württemberg*. It was near the location where General George S. Patton was injured and ultimately led to his dying in nearby Heidelberg. *Käfertal* was home to Sullivan Barracks, located inside the [American] Benjamin Franklin Village. It's a tiny town just off Autobahn 6, between Frankfurt, Stuttgart, and Heidelberg. The autobahn is Germany's famous high-speed highways. America's Interstate system is based on it, but at much slower speeds.

My great-great uncle Maxie Butler was an anti-tank gunner during WWII, and coincidently travelled through Mannheim during the war. The funny thing about his time in Seventh Army, was that he was the best marksman on his anti-tank weapon, yet he drove a truck for the duration of the war.

After the Allies liberated Europe and stopped the Nazis, my Uncle Maxie was chosen for Color Guard duty in Frankfurt, for what would be General Patton's final parade before his untimely death. Color Guard is the large, good-looking guys in the white gloves, boot covers, and helmets, sporting the white rifles. It is a coveted job and an honor to be chosen.

As the truck pulled into Frankfurt, excitement got the better of him and he hopped out of the back of the truck without removing the canvas troop strap above the tailgate. His foot got entangled, and he fell to the concrete. Due to a hand injury, he was unable to perform his Color Guard duties. He was still to participate in the parade, though. When asked about his experience, he simply told them that he'd driven a truck with an anti-tank weapon in tow. Naturally, they put him in the parade driving a truck, with none other than an anti-tank gun in tow.

The cool part of the story is that on the 50th anniversary of the parade, it was re-aired in his small town in Cullman, Alabama. He just happened to be clicking through the channels when he saw the driver of the third truck of the column, his younger self. He said he about jumped out of his chair as he started hollering for his wife, my great-great aunt Charlotte, to come see him on television. I loved hearing him tell that story. Maxie was bigger than life in character and laughter.

Mannheim was most famous for its water tower. During WWII, the Allies kept the water tower intact as a reference for over one-hundred and fifty bombing raids, meant to cripple its industrial efforts for the war. We used it as a drunken reference to find our way back to the barracks. It would serve as the backdrop to many of our adventures.

It was late that night as I got to my unit, the 3rd Battalion of the 77th Regiment of the First Armored Division. I checked in at the CQ desk (or Charge of Quarters, the person(s) guarding the front door of a barrack). In layman terms, he answers the phones and signs-in people like me on cold, snowy nights. Most everyone was asleep. He called the

Supply SGT to meet us at the CQ desk, so he could issue me some sheets and a blanket for the night. I was to sleep in Headquarters building until they could decide where I was to go.

It was absolutely freezing that night as we moved out to the cargo boxes to get my stuff. As Mannheim was in the lowest elevation of Germany, there wasn't as much snow on the ground as in Frankfurt, but cold nonetheless. As we got to talking, I noticed he had a touch of a Spanish accent. He told me that supply was operated by all the Spanish guys: Mexicans, Hondurans, Guatemalans, etc. I asked him where he was from. He told me he was originally from Mexico. I turned to him and asked, *"DO YOU KNOW WHY MEXICANS ALWAYS HAVE THOSE LITTLE SMALL CHROME STEERING WHEELS ON THEIR LOW RIDERS?"*

He looked at me for a second and shook his head, no. I said, *"SO THEY CAN STILL DRIVE WITH HANDCUFFS ON."* Now he was looking at me like I'd sprouted bolts from my neck and horns from my skull. Here was this white boy cracking Mexican jokes with him not fifteen minutes after our meeting.

He wanted to crack a smile, but he didn't. The jury was still out on this one. I looked over and said, *"IN ALL SERIOUSNESS, SGT, I KNOW QUITE A BIT ABOUT MEXICO. ACTUALLY, I KNOW MEXICAN JUDO."*

"REALLY?" he said, clearly with no prior knowledge of *Mexican Judo*.

Then in my best Mexican accent, I said, *"YEAH, JUDON'T KNOW IF I GOTTA KNIFE, JUDON'T KNOW IF I GOTTA GUN. JUDO KNOW NOTHIN, HOMES."*

He lost it after that. He started cracking up laughing. He said, *"YOU GOT BALLS, TURNER. YOU'RE CRAZY, MAN. THAT'S SOME*

FUNNY SHIT. NOW, TELL ME MORE. I GOTTA TELL THESE TO THE OTHER GUYS."

I proceeded to tell him every Mexican joke I could think of. He told me that no one would tell them these jokes, because they were of Spanish descent. He even had some good white guy jokes. I now had a buddy in supply. I got my sleep wares, and he showed me my room upstairs at HQ. As we parted, he smiled, shook my hand, and said, *"WELCOME TO THE SPANISH ARMY."*

Much later, as my time wore on in the unit, because of my joke telling abilities, I was the only *non-Spanish* speaking guy that could walk into supply and get whatever I wanted. They liked me, for some strange reason, jokes and all. I can still hear my superiors saying, *"TURNER, GO TO SUPPLY AND SEE IF YOU CAN WRANGLE SO-AND-SO OUT OF THOSE GUYS."* I would always return with said items in tow.

My brother gave me some of the best advice that I will now impart to anyone that's reading this and considering joining the armed forces. He said when I got to my unit, that I should try and make a friend in every department: the mess hall, supply, the mechanics, etc. He told me that it would improve my quality of life in so many ways, and boy, oh, boy, was he ever right. It was some of the best advice I'd ever received about reporting to my permanent duty station.

30

UNCLE SAM'S

It didn't take long for me to get out and about into the German countryside. I was soon drinking with the guys, on the economy, or any establishment off post and not operated by the Army. We would have to exchange our tax payer-paid wages into *Deutsch Marks*, otherwise the Germans would offer horrible exchange rates to accept the US Dollar. Roughly, $33.00 would get you DM50, which was more than enough to get drunk, buy a girl a beer or two, and fund a round trip on the *Straßenbahn*, the highly effective, state-operated train system. There were several bars the Americans frequented: Uncle Sam's, The Irish Pub, The Whitehouse, and The Skyline, or as we called it, The Skydive, as it was a rough place.

Uncle Sam's was quite a bit farther away from post than the other bars, but it was a nice mixture of Americans and Germans. I am still friends with the door bouncer, Claus Much, a big German guy that served in the *Bundeswehr* (German Army), as a paratrooper. It was my first *real* night on the town in Mannheim. I recall there being a lot of German girls there, which was a plus for a young G.I. like myself.

It was very different in Europe. The women there looked and dressed different, and even socialized differently than American women. It didn't take long for one of those young ladies to come over and say hello to me. I was taken aback, at first; the thought of a girl just walking over and saying hello in a bar was so foreign to me. In fact, everything was foreign at this point. Five months earlier I was in high school, popping pimples and making time with my high school sweetheart. All of my buddies were getting settled into college but still two to three years away from the legal drinking age of twenty-one. Whereas I was legally in a bar in Central Europe and a cute girl just walked over to ask if I would like to drink my *beers* (yes, plural), with her and her friends. Naturally, I said yes, and the blood from one brain starting flowing south to the other. I was barely into one of my two beers, and I was surrounded by a group of beautiful girls. Before continuing, perhaps it is best if I explained why I was holding two beers and not one.

As I mentioned early in the book, I looked young; very young, in fact. This was my first night out onto the economy, so I was, for all intents and purposes, *green*, or wet behind the ears. Provided by the Army, I had been through Head Start, a week-long course on the basics of German language, customs, and how-to's; how to count, their thirty letter alphabet, how to ask for directions, beer, food, etc. Head Start could not have failed me more than on that night. The only German I had a strong command on was, *"EIN BIER, BITTE,"* or, one beer, please.

After breeching the entrance to the club, I was so cool, so suave, as I strutted over and bellied up to the bar. I eased an elbow up onto the hard, smooth wooden top, as I took a pull from my cigarette. Fucking James Dean moment, I tell you. I looked the bartender in the eye, smiled, held up my left index finger and poured out the manliest voice I could muster. *"EIN BIER, BITTE!"*

I said it like a pro, nodding my head as I spoke, laying on the coolness of yours truly. I was so proud of myself. I had this whole *speaking German thing*. I was hip, cool, with it. Fucking cake-walk, man.

She smiled, spoke something in German, and quickly darted off to retrieve my beer. I was so pleased with myself. I waited, real cool like at the bar. My friends back home were stealing beer from the little country store, or asking their older friends to buy it for them. I was ordering a beer in Germany. I was about to once again enjoy that wonderful taste from Frankfurt. I could hardly wait to hold that glorious glass in my hand. It was going to be a ½ liter pilsner glass of pure, beautiful genius. Damn I'm good at ordering beer.

I thought to myself, *Well played, sir...well played, indeed.*

A couple of minutes later, she returned and sat *two*, yes, *two* full one-liter steins in front of me—both frothing slightly over the rim. My face contorted into an abysmal grimace. They were not the little half-liter glasses I had so briefly accustomed myself to in Frankfurt. No, my friends, she delivered two full-on ½ inch thick, glass handled, one-liter steins with an oak tree emblem on them.

My mouth started pouring out in protest that I had only ordered one beer. *God, this sounds horrible. Whining about too much beer.* In my protest, I was waving my index finger vehemently into the air in the same manner in which I had ordered. I repeated myself, *"FRÄULEIN, EIN BIER. EIN BIER."*

She leaned in with a smile on her face, wishing to speak to me up-close and personal. After leaning in, she asked me if I was new to Germany. I nodded yes, as I held up two fingers and told her I'd been here for nearly two weeks. She asked if I had yet ordered a beer during that time. I nodded no, dismissing the American pizza parlor in Frankfurt. Her smile grew, and palm to me, she held up her index finger, then explained that in Germany, a single index finger implies the number *two*. She then lowered her index finger, held up her thumb, and while twisting her hand around, palm facing her, continued to explain that that meant *one* in Germany.

I had just learned a valuable lesson. I was bitter, but knew that she had me by the balls, as Claus Much (not yet my buddy) was guarding the door. I took my licks like a man. I paid for my beers and took one into each hand and walked away, pride *somewhat* intact.

So, back to being surrounded by beautiful women. I knew a little German, but it didn't prepare me for this. I was surrounded by young, beautiful, confident European women that were asking me questions in broken English and talking amongst themselves in German. My German elicited a few laughs, but not in a bad way, as I was politely corrected. Taking note of my current situation, I knew I wanted to learn as much of the German language as humanly possible.

Silka was the one who invited me to join her and her friends. She was cute, fun, and bubbly, but I couldn't help but take notice of her friend, Claudia. I spent the evening with Silka, being polite and kissing her goodnight, but it was obvious that Claudia and I were attracted to one another. Soon thereafter, Claudia and I were dating.

Through this relationship, I learned much of the local slang, times to ride the *Straßenbahn* without a ticket and not get caught, the coolest bars to frequent, and a lot of the local history of Mannheim and nearby *Ludwigshafen-Oppau*. Twenty years later, I nearly married Claudia, but that is another story.

The girls introduced me to another bar, perhaps, the coolest one in town: the Broker's Inn. It was an eclectic collection of attorneys (one of which I dated), lay-folk, G.I.s, and all walks of life in and around Mannheim. It worked much like the stock market. The local beer was called, after translation, Oak Tree, and yes, I'm withholding the name for copyright reasons. It was also known as *Corpse Bier*, or *Graveyard Bier*, as the brewery is located right next door to a graveyard. Yes, the waters used to brew this beer were pulled from the earth below the graveyard. They started brewing this wonderful beer in 1679. It was, and still is, my all-time favorite beer in the world.

Back to Broker's Inn. Two or three electronic boards listed the most popular drinks and their constantly changing prices. Market forces determined how much you paid for it. As demand rose, so did the price of the drink, until it was priced beyond affordability (demand plummeting) and the market would crash. Then began the stampede to order more drinks as the price, inadvertently, plummeted with the crash. Then it cycled again, and again. It gave everyone something to smile and interact about as we eagerly watched the price board.

I still have a hardback menu from Broker's, and after calculating the exchange rate, it equated to around $1.00–$1.20 for a ½ liter of the finest beer this side of the Danube River. Damn, I miss those days. We all had a lot of wonderful nights at Broker's.

31

SUPPORT PLATOON AND HERMANN, THE FUCKING GERMAN

I was stationed in HQ Company, SPT PLT (or Support Platoon), 5-Ton Squad. I know, *what the fuck?* I just spent 4½ months training at Fort Knox, Kentucky, the Home of Armor, learning how to load, drive, and shoot the greatest fucking battle tank on the face of the planet, and I ask myself, *What the fuck is SPT PLT and what the fuck is 5-Ton Squad?*

However, it would prove to be one of the most awesome experiences during my time in service. We had this crusty, old PLT Daddy that was never seen without a cigarette in one hand and a cup of coffee in the other. The question of how he saluted officers was often pondered, until we actually saw him do it with the proficiency of a fish to water.

I was to learn how to drive a 5-ton truck and, wow, did I ever learn. I wound up being the second-most licensed soldier in our unit, next to the CW-4, or Battalion Maintenance Chief. I sometimes volunteered, but, more often, was *voluntold* to get licensed and certified on nearly every vehicle in the unit's fleet.

We had 5-Tons, Deuce-and-a-Half's, bob tails (military versions of semis/trailer haulers), with 25 and 56 foot trailers, and of course, the 10-ton M977 & M978 HEMTTs (Heavy Expandable Mobility Tactical Trucks). You name it, I had a license for it.

I was sent to all kinds of schools, too. How to drive in the snow, on ice, high-speed driving on the Autobahn—it was awesome. It came at a price, though, as my friends and family hated riding with me after I returned home armed with so much driving prowess. I may, or may not, have been notorious for correcting the habits of horrible drivers for a decade, or two, but who's counting? Now, I simply avoid them—corrections and horrible drivers.

The PLT was a hodge-podge of soldiers. There were 19Deltas (Mechanized Cavalry Scouts, or the cavalry, less the horses), 88Mikes (Truck Drivers), and a couple of other MOSs, but mostly it was 19Kilos, like me. The unit was over-inundated with tankers, so we were pushed into SPT PLT. It all goes back to the needs of the Army, not yours. In the beginning, it was so foreign to me, as everyone was so busy and comfortable being a soldier, and I simply felt out of place.

By February I was like the others, comfortable being a soldier, complete with an eat-shit attitude. I was comfortable in the unit, in my PLT, and in my squad. The next month we left for the field (or Specialized High Intensity Training, also known as S.H.I.T.). We left for the German state of *Bayern* (Bavaria in English), near the Czechoslovakian border, to train at the world-class facility known as *Grafenwöhr* Training Area.

It was formed in 1907 to train the Bavarian Army, until the Nazis procured it and used it to practice their famous blitzkrieg tactics. After the war, the Americans commandeered it. It's the largest NATO (North Atlantic Treaty Organization) training area in Europe. Americans, French, Germans, Dutch; if it's NATO, they use it as proving grounds for their armies. It's our heavy-metal playground for tanks, howitzers, mortars, infantry and air-to-ground combat flight missions. It's a lot of work, but a lot of fun to play with military-grade hardware.

Going to the field was commonly referred to as a *field problem*. It meant long hours, often times with very little sleep. It also meant a lot of training on weaponry, vehicles, combat formations, and sadly, very little beer drinking. It wasn't completely out of the question, but it wasn't near the amount we consumed in garrison (barracks, or in the rear with the gear). So, as was customary, the night before a field problem, we got wasted.

I know this is hard for some of you newer soldiers to believe, but in those days, the SGM actually brought beer to the field with us. After mealtime hours or returning from the range, we could go to the mess hall and purchase beer. The SGM had strict rules about this beer, too. There was to be a *two-beer* maximum, per soldier. I quickly reverted back to the *four-count* math I learned at Fort Knox. My perspective told me to follow the SGMs rules by consuming the first and last beer and to not count the ones in between. This would come back to bite me in the ass…almost.

Graf, as we referred to *Grafenwöhr*, was a huge facility. It housed and trained thousands of NATO troops at the same time. During my first field problem, it was my responsibility to ensure I was trained and licensed on the 5-ton and HEMTT. Before I could even drive one, I had to ride shotgun with someone until I got my studies completed and tests passed. I eventually received my interim license, until we could get back to garrison for my hard copy.

So, there I was driving these huge vehicles over the tank trails of Graf. As far as civilians go, they see a bunch of cool guys on cool vehicles doing cool Army shit. I used to also see it like that, but all of that changed after we had to go to the wash rack, or military carwash. All that cool dirt, dust, clay, piss, shit, and German muck found on every tank trail in Graf was now on our vehicle, and before it could be returned to the motor pool, it had to be cleaned.

I guess we'd been in the field for a few weeks when we pulled into the wash rack to clean our HEMTT. I believe we had delivered munitions to a group of assholes firing off cool military toys. Yeah, a little jealousy shined through there. Mostly we delivered mortars, small and large caliber munitions, and shit and tons of tank rounds. We pulled into the wash rack, and little did I know that those German lessons with Claudia and Silka were about to pay off.

We parked our HEMTT near a German howitzer. A howitzer is a single-bodied, tracked-vehicle with a huge 150mm+ gun tube sticking out of the front, yet it lacked a turret in which to traverse around, and so it was very much a *behind-the-lines* combat vehicle. This young German guy in a drab green uniform and black beret was washing his howitzer, as we were washing off our truck. I stepped over, said hello, and offered him a cigarette, making conversation with him in what German I knew.

Fortunately, his English was better than my German, but he appreciated that I first spoke German with him. He knew where in Germany I was from, too. As I had not really learned my German in a proper school, I picked up the dialect from the area, known as soft, or relaxed German. It wasn't so strict and blunt like *Hochdeutsch* (high, or standard German). *Hochdeutsch* is what is taught in school or printed in publications.

He was as young as I was, though he looked younger than I did, stretching the limits of possibility. He was the first German soldier I had ever met after all my studies on both world wars. The end of WWII was less than half a century removed at this time. I didn't know what to expect, so I just spoke to him like two soldiers sitting in a bar, with respect, admiration, and genuine interest. For him, I was the first American soldier that he'd met.

We shared a couple of my American cigarettes, and I began to admire his uniform, and he mine. His had cloth ribbons on the shoulders, a leather and semi-canvassed set of boots, though the beret really caught my eye. It was a sharp-looking, black beret. It had a large tank surrounded by a swath of wreaths and a small German flag in the bottom of its symbol. My soft cap body and bill were rolled into my head like my Airborne-Ranger brother had taught me. It looked sharp. My uniform was filthy, but serviceable. Its only accoutrements were three patches: (a) my nam-etag; (b) the U.S. ARMY tag; (c) and my unit patch located on my upper left sleeve. Coincidentally, we were about the same size and build.

He removed his beret for me to inspect, and I my soft cap for him. We were both in awe at what the other country wore as a uniform. I thought his was way cooler than mine, and I guess he thought mine was cooler than his. Sometimes the grass *is* greener.

Hopeful, I offered to trade him my head gear for his, but he didn't have a spare one with him. Shit. We smoked one of his cigarettes and spoke some more about this soldierly exchange. Soon, we realized that we were both near one another in the barracks area. He offered to meet near the American mess hall and exchange entire uniforms. I more than happily agreed.

My uniforms were about seven months old by March of 1993, but they were my originals from OSUT, so they were very broken-in. I picked up the rattiest one I had, a pair of my basic boots, and an extra soft cap and went to the mess hall to wait. He was late, as I stood there like an asshole, uniform in hand. I waited and smoked a few cigarettes until, thankfully, I saw him approaching. We shook hands and began to over-look our exchange. We swapped entire uniforms—hats, boots, belts, trousers, and jackets. He was so happy, and hell, I was equally ecstatic.

His uniform looked so good compared to mine. Whereas I took one of my rattiest uniforms, he brought one of his best, as his were newer than mine, by only a few months. He one-upped me, too. He brought a patch for the shoulder and breast, as well as extra ribbons, shoulder epaulettes, and a last of the *rocketeer* unit's qualification badge, patch and pin. That dude hooked me up with a kick-ass German uniform. I was so stoked. Quite frankly, I wished I would have taken him a nicer uniform, but he was happy, so it worked out.

I returned to the barracks and my Section Sergeant, SSG Lomio, looked over and said, *"NO SHIT, TURNER. YOU HAVE A GERMAN UNIFORM. LOOKS LIKE THE WHOLE DAMNED THING, TOO."*

"ROGER THAT, SERGEANT," I said, with a shit-eating grin across my face.

"LET'S SEE IT. WHAT'S THE FRONT LOOK LIKE? WHAT'S HIS NAME?" he asked.

My smile grew as I turned it around for most of the platoon to see. In unison, they all muttered, *"HERMANN, THE FUCKIN' GERMAN."* SSG Lomio was impressed that I had not only done some horse trading, but I had the best of the traded goodies at the end of my *first* field problem in the Army. Fate had surely shined on me that day. A few of us had traded various items, but none like the one I had secured. I still have that uniform hanging in my closet.

Hermann, the fuckin' German, was an expression we often used to describe an unknown male German. Hermann the German was also a real, historical figure known as Arminius, a tribal leader that decimated three Roman legions in the forests of Germany, at a time when the world thought the Romans could not be defeated.

Towards the end of the field problem, I was well into my own element and very comfortable as a soldier. So, on the last day of the field problem, as we loaded the trucks, I simply followed my character and earned my first AAM (or Army Achievement Medal). I saw a problem in the loading of a very large box. Standing there looking on were two Specialists, a CPL and a SGT, watching a group of guys try and load an awkward box into the back of a 5-ton. The task was not getting done, so I simply started barking out orders as to how I thought it should be loaded. Nobody batted an eye as to why a PVT was barking out orders to get shit done. SSG Lomio saw this and remarked how kick-ass it was that a PVT was taking charge of a SNAFU, also known as *Situation Normal, All Fucked-Up*. I was promoted and awarded my first of three AAMs. It was a very successful field problem for me.

Earlier in the field problem, while training on the HEMTT with SSG Lomio, he turned and asked, *"TURNER, HAVE YOU EVER HUNG AROUND?"*

"YEAH, SURE," I said. *"HUNG AROUND WHAT, THOUGH, SERGEANT?"*

He laughed and said, *"DO YOU WANT TO GO HANG A ROUND WITH THE MORTARS?"*

Still not understanding the full depth of what he was asking, I said, *"SURE. I KNOW A COUPLE OF THOSE GUYS. YEAH, LET'S GO HANG OUT WITH THEM FOR A FEW AND WATCH 'EM."*

He looked at me trying to determine whether I was serious or not, then spoke. *"NO, YOU IDIOT. HANG A MORTAR ROUND, NOT HANG AROUND. DO YOU WANT TO FIRE A MORTAR ROUND?"*

"OH, HANG-A-ROUND." The light illuminated for me. *"FUCK YEAH, SERGEANT. YOU MEAN, ACTUALLY HOLD THE ROUND OVER THE TUBE AND FIRE IT?"*

As he instructed me to turn into the range, he said, *"YES, TURNER, HANG A ROUND!"*

I received some quick training on each mortar position. I relocated rounds to the area where charges were being loaded onto them. I then helped attach *cheese charges,* or nitroglycerin squares, which are used as extra propellants for ranging the round. Then the guy breaks off a little piece of it and says, *"PUT THIS UNDER YOUR TONGUE."* Bad idea, especially seeing as I needed my wherewithal to do a mortar fire-for-effect. But that is another story.

Then I handed off the rounds to the guy actually hanging the rounds over the tube. Then came the big show. I was the guy holding the rounds over the tube for, what must have been, a ten-round fire-for-effect. A fire-for-effect is like making it rain ten, 81mm mortars throughout an area that would be eaten-up with the enemy. I didn't realize the concussion from these things was as big as it was for the M252 81mm Mortar. It was no tank, but it was impressive.

All-in-all, Graf proved to be a great field problem.

32

FIRSTS IN LIFE: THE AUTOBAHN & MY FRENCH EXPOSÉ

After successfully taking charge of loading the 5-ton, I was, shockingly, slated to drive a HEMTT from Graf to Mannheim, a 200-mile journey. It was about a six-hour road march. We all formed a long column of vehicles and slowly moved out towards the Autobahn, towards my new home in *Käfertal*. It was a beautiful day that April, still chilly outside, but the sun was shining bright. If you are not sure what a fuel HEMTT is, then this is a good time to perform a search; it's a 10-ton, 8-wheel-drive tactical vehicle, with 2,500 gallons of jet fuel strapped to the back. It is a *helluva* lot of truck at 8-feet wide, 34-feet long, and a turning radius of 100-feet.

Just to put this into perspective…inside of five months, I'd upgraded from driving motorcycles and Bugs, to driving tanks and 10-ton trucks on the Autobahns of Germany. The Army had entrusted me with quite a bit in such a short period of time. Life was interesting as an eighteen-year-old soldier in 1993.

I was nervous, but confident that I could do it. I had driven this beast around Graf. *What could possibly go wrong?* Besides, I had one of the most senior lower-enlisted guys with me.

Fuel: check. Pogey bait: check. Pogey bait is a term to reference sweets or food. In use since WWI, as guys in the field rarely get treats. Water: check. Cigarettes: check.

It's 315 km to Mannheim. We have 2500 gallons of fuel, a half-a-pack of smokes, it's sunny out, and we're wearing shades…hit it!

We left Graf and hit the Autobahn. No problem, I had this. The plan was to drive the six-plus hours and be home in time to unload and get drunk before 2000 hours. The German countryside outside of my window, the sun shining through, things were awesome. The first hour goes by without a hitch.

Suffice it to say, HEMTTs are not exactly built on a chassis that is famous for comfort, but okay, I'm on the world-famous Autobahn, cruising at a top speed of 88 km, or 55 mph. Yeah, this story could be in a supercar with a hot German blonde sitting beside me, but let's keep it real, folks. My shotgun was an ugly SPC4 seated across the cab of a HEMTT. He was, however, kind enough to allow me to smoke in the vehicle, so long as I rolled the window down, as smoking in a military vehicle is a big no-no. We seamlessly drift into hour number two. Life is still good.

I did mention that HEMTTs are not exactly built for comfort, right? Fate stepped in and told me that I had to piss in the worst way, which meant life was no longer good. My bladder and kidneys were getting *beat-the-fuck-up*. HEMTTs ride like a train on square wheels. I was soon handed an empty, wide-mouthed, plastic bottle in which to relieve myself. I had this blank stare on my face. That was very trusting of my shotgun. I thought, I can piss into a bottle, no problem. But, can I piss into a bottle while driving a HEMTT down the Autobahn at 88kmh? I was in quite the conundrum. I opted to wait.

Another half-hour goes by, and it's not going away. It's only getting worse. I really had to piss now, akin to an Arabian racehorse.

I thought for a couple minutes about my decision. If I were to wreck the truck and survive, I could potentially be left pissing into a colostomy bag for the rest of my life. I formed a plan. Eyeballing the bottle on the doghouse, or large transmission cover between myself and the shotgun, I knew how it had to happen. My eyeballs were yellow and floating at this point. The doghouse only allowed a view of the tops of each other's torsos, as if I gave a shit, anyway. I had no shame.

I took the wheel firmly in my left hand, then started taking off my BDU top, swinging each arm out. Done. I undid my belt buckle and all four buttons to my trousers, flipping, to each side, my camouflaged fly. Done. I inched my trousers down to expose my boxers. Done. So far, so good. *I had this, right?*

Life is funny sometimes, as it likes to throw you curveballs when your back is turned and your head is the target. I was about to be in a real conundrum, as the Autobahn gods were making me pay for that German driver's license I'd received for only $12.00 (DM20), the same license the Germans paid thousands of DMs for. This was my penance, and I was about to pay big league.

I whipped my pecker out and splayed it out on top of my boxers, soon realizing that that was not going to work. I had to pull my boxers down as well. Done. I was pretty wide open at this point, but traffic couldn't see me from my bird's-nest height inside the confines of the ten-foot-tall HEMTT. There was no chance of *exposing* myself like a creep, to half of the Bavarian population on the Autobahn.

Enter curveball. The federally operated *Bundesautobahn* (proper name of the Autobahn) had decided long before my arrival, that repairs were needed, and through, you guessed it, the very section I was traveling that day. This shit was not part of the plan, dammit. I was sitting in a seat that could, more appropriately, be likened to riding on a dirt bike on the whoop-dee-do section of a motocross course. All the while, a plastic bottle awaited an intimate interlude with my frank and beans. A construction zone…For fuck's sake, why a construction zone? Why now? Why on my first trip on the Autobahn? Clearly, I had angered the gods to a great degree.

Needless to say, I was fairly committed to my plan at this point. I was maneuvering through heavy traffic, curves to the left and curves back to the right in this landscape of cones, flags, lights, and expensive German automobiles, whilst maneuvering a 10-ton truck I had absolute minimal experience driving.

To paint the picture a little more vividly, it had been about a month since I'd seen a woman, so the prevailing winds, as it were, were fucking perfect that day as the bumps relentlessly continued to abuse my bladder. I guess between the nervousness of maneuvering the construction, and the incessant bouncing, my dick developed a *self-induced* boner. Not a chubby, but a full-blown stiffy that was so hard, that you could have had a boat sail hung from it. My pecker, George, was now the fifth appendage to my body. Yeah, yeah, I was a kid when I thought my pecker needed a name. George seemed regal. I was maybe seven or eight years old—it stuck! I knew damn-well that I wasn't going to piss into that bottle given the current circumstances. I was more than likely going to wildly spray the inside of the windshield. What does one do in this situation, you might ask?

Naturally, I did what any red-blooded American would do in that situation. I rolled the window down and smoked a cigarette, in the hopes of the cool air knocking the wind out of George's sails, as it were. I was still navigating a fucking HEMTT through a construction zone, mind you.

George was bouncing in the wind, and the Germans below had no idea. No clue at all. They popped-up, no pun intended, almost like ants in my mirror. I grinned to myself and thought who would believe that my first time driving on the Autobahn, I'd be doing it naked and with a raging hard-on? After a month in the field, I was just a few, albeit long, strokes away from ejaculation. I owned it, though.

I was trucking along, when I noticed something odd in my peripheral. A strange something that soon began to *fill* the reflection in my door mirror. It was large and slowly gaining ground on my HEMTT. I leaned into the mirror a bit, crouching my head in order to gain a full view of this double-decker bus overtaking my truck in the left lane. Of all the times for a bus to pass! It wasn't just the one bus, either. It was a convoy of about twelve French tour buses passing our entire column.

As they neared my position, I noticed two distinct things in my mirror. I first noticed what looked like faces, pressed into the windows of the bus. Second, I noticed that the windows of the bus were about a foot or so higher than mine. Translation: George was no longer going to enjoy the privacy he'd once commanded from the *cockpit*, pun intended, of the HEMTT. So, upon notifying my shotgun of this revelation, he promptly grabbed my BDU top as hostage, thus keeping me from covering my exposed appendage. I would've been angry, but I'd have done the same to him were the roles reversed, so who was I to complain. Good one, buddy!

I will explain a little further. Have you ever driven down the expressway and someone passes you so slow that even at 80mph, you have time to look over and see if he or she is black or white, fat or skinny, what kind of clothes they're wearing? The kind of slow where you almost make an informal introduction to him or her and their entire family? You know, the kind where you think, *They look like a nice family,* or *Holy shit they look like a carload of assholes.* Yeah, that is the kind of, dare I say, speed, in which they were overtaking me.

It wasn't so bad until I noticed that it *wasn't* a tour bus of old decrepit pensioners, or a university football team with accompanying entourage. No, it was bus after bus of young French girls, maybe between the ages of sixteen and eighteen. Had this occurred in today's modern world, these girls would've been transfixed onto their phones, thus occupying their near full attention. Or, quite possibly, I'd have been captured on video and gone viral as a perverted internet sensation by the end of the day, but this was 1993 and there were no mobile phones. The parade of G.I.s and Army vehicles had enraptured the attention of these young impressionable French girls. Americans, especially soldiers, still had a mystique to the rest of the world back then.

In 1993, to be an American soldier in Europe, actually meant something to Europeans. We were still *Jolly Green Giants* walking the land in the name of freedom. We were still very welcomed across the European landscape. We were the sons and grandsons of the liberators and heroes of WWII. America, and American soldiers, were very much still respected and admired back then.

So, naturally, these young women were doing the admirable thing. They were all pressed into the right-hand windows of their buses and delivering friendly waves and smiles to America's finest. And, speaking of America's finest, George and I were sitting there, open to the failing winds that, coincidentally, had not delivered the calming effects I'd hoped for. George was bouncing up-and-down like a drumstick at a rock concert, still responding to every bump in the road that the Autobahn could dole out.

So, being a young ambassador to the United States, I also did the honorable thing and waved back…twice. Yes, shy me did nothing to preserve my dignity or hide my pride. I kept smoking my cigarette while steering with my right hand, as my left exuberantly returned friendly waves in observance of friendly international relations. It didn't take long to notice that the newest patrons of my French Fan Club were exiting the side windows in favor of the overly large, single window in the back of the bus, to further their zeal in waving to me. There were several blown kisses, as well.

No doubt, my shotgun and I laughed at the irony of the situation. The chances were astronomical to that ever happening again. As fate would have it, the buses all passed and a few short kilometers later, construction was completed. Go figure? The bumps subsided, as did George, and I was able to finally relieve myself, much to the pleasure of my bladder.

Once in garrison, with the road march complete, I remember being approached by the guy that was driving the vehicle behind me, and him saying, *"MAN, TURNER, THOSE GIRLS ON THE BUSES SURE LIKED YOU!"* I then had to explain the situation to everyone. That afternoon, we promptly started cleaning our equipment and drinking our normal copious amounts of beer.

So, you drove on the Autobahn, eh? That's cute. My first time was in an 8-wheel-drive, 10-ton HEMTT, half-naked, with a raging hard pecker hanging out, and with a very pleased and smiling international audience of ladies. A monster was born!

33

SWASTIKAS AND BIER MACHINES

Our home at Sullivan Barracks were leftovers from WWII. The staircases still bore swastikas emblazoned into the cast-iron newel posts, or top and bottom spindles. The ceilings were 10-foot high on each floor, giving the impression of a much larger state room. Behind our barracks, in the *Lampertheim* Training Area, lay other remnants of the war; an intact Nazi bunker that would be the site of my first rope-repelling experience. There was also a combination trench-berm meant to disrupt a tank assault. The idea was that when the tank crested the berm, and landed atop this large concrete double-X structure, it would hold one-half of the tank up off the ground, thereby rendering the tank immobile and incapable of firing horizontally.

The Army really did care about our well-being, to the point of installing beer into the vending machines in lieu of sodas. That beautiful machine was a mere five meters from my door. It was DM2 for a semi-cold beer. I'm willing to bet those are no longer an option in today's Army. Like the old Army slogan, "Be All That You Can Be… In the Army," even if that included being drunk. Unless you count that one time that we (whose name I will not mention) figured out that inserting water into the coin slot would give you all the free beer you wanted.

The unfortunate part of this story is that those barracks are all gone now. They were torn down just a couple of years ago. The overwhelming opinion is that they should've been torn down sooner because the Nazis built them, but that simply isn't the case. Those barracks housed so many soldiers in their seventy-plus years of existence. We didn't care there were swastikas in the handrails—to us, we were living inside of history, instead of reading about it. In the basement of our barracks were tunnels the Nazis constructed to transport troops, small arms, and supplies around Mannheim without above-ground exposure. Those doors were heavily alarmed and very off-limits. There has to be a balance of what history is to be preserved, and what of it is to be destroyed. Obviously, these old buildings were the developmental battlegrounds of my first two years of adulthood, so they will always be special to me.

Upon our return, SPT PLT had strengthened its ranks with a batch of new guys, which meant I was no longer the FNG, or Fucking New Guy. Amongst that group were the guys that are still my best life-long friends and brothers: Joe *Spud* Powell, Don *Wildman* Ward, CPL *Shithouse Lawyer* Fritz, *Tire Iron*, Ray Weatherford, Glenn *Hamburger* Martony. They were as destined to be a part of this rat pack as I was. Some of the guys that were already in SPT PLT were, SGT J, Spive, Tricky Dick, Brad *Vegas* Gold, John *Duffster* Duff, J. *Halterhomo* Halterman, Tim *Byrdman* Byrd, and so many others that made the experience for me, how shall I say, enlightening and fucking nuts.

The partying only intensified as summer soon rolled around. This is when the real madness and mayhem started, when we really got to see who was who. Our quad parties were near infamy. They lured in the crazies from all over the soldier and civilian worlds in and around Mannheim.

On the weekends, par for the course was that we partied in the quad until dark, and then got ready to go into town. As our budgets were constrained once economy prices were in play, we first had to get liquored-up at the barracks. Cue our savior, the Class VI. It was always there to properly aid in the destruction of our livers. The Class VI was/ is a military operated liquor, beer, and wine store. A 1.75L of the finest Kentucky bourbon then, without all of those pesky U.S. taxes, came out to a whopping twelve glorious dollars and seventy-five measly cents. A carton, yes, ten packs of top-name cigarettes, were four dollars. With a two-dollar-off coupon, my American and Turkish blended coffin nails were a cool two-dollars per carton. It was terribly beautiful.

Where once I was a novice in all things *Hefe-Weißen*, by summer's end I was hopelessly devoted to her imbibing. The natural procession of things was that it eventually took more and more of her to feel the same spark from which that love was born. By the time I left Germany, I could easily put away *ten* glorious liters of *Hefe-Weißen* and still want more. I was what one might call a *professional* beer drinker. In the land of beer and beer boots, *my sole was going to heel.*

LET'S GET THE FUCK OUT OF HERE

One night, while out with my roommate, Vegas Brad, we decided to hit up the fanciest of clubs, Windows. It was located downtown on the thirteenth (yes, the thirteenth) floor of this circular, glass-encased building. We were dressed to the hilt, because to even enter the elevator up to the bar, one had to pass a dress code inspection. It was a rare treat to gain access. We partied-hard and decided to go back to the barracks. We wanted to get to the *Straßenbahn* at the water tower before the train stopped running. It would damn-near deliver us to the front gate of our barracks.

As we were walking through downtown, Brad got hungry, so we stopped into the *arched* cheeseburger place. Hint-hint, wink-wink. It was busy, as it was the weekend. Brad ordered a burger and fries. I started picking some of the fries from his tray before he barked out, *"FUCK, TURNER. GO GET YOUR OWN, DUDE."* So I sauntered up to find a bunch of Turks, or folks of Turkish descent, operating the joint. I knew they spoke German, so I ordered in German. By summer, my German had exponentially improved.

The food was delivered cold, but, in the spirit of being an ambassador, I kept my cool and spoke in German. I told the manager that the food was cold, and that I would like it hot. We argued back-and-forth for a spell before he told me take it or leave it. I lost it then, saying, *"LOOK, MOTHER FUCKER. THIS IS AN AMERICAN RESTAURANT AND I'M AN AMERICAN. I WANT MY FUCKING FOOD HOT, ASSHOLE!"* This immediately caused a scene, which he didn't want.

Palms down, he started giving the international symbol for calm down and said, *"OKAY, I MAKE HOT."*

A couple of minutes passed before he offered my food at the side door, closest to where I was standing. As I turned to grab the tray, the door quickly swung open and a pair of large hands stretched out to pull me into the kitchen area. The door was promptly slammed behind me. There stood the manager, tray in hand, along with three other employees, two of whom were monstrously large. I knew my goose was cooked.

The manager sat the tray down and said, *"OH, YOU BIG AMERICAN, YES?"* As he spoke, he pulled at my tie and forced me into the wall while eyeing my well-heeled clothes up-and-down. *"YOU BIG MAN NOW?"* he continued angrily.

I spoke. *"ALLES KLAR. ALLES IN ORDNUNG. ENTSCHULDIGUNG,"* which means, *all is okay, everything is in order, I apologize.* I threw my hands into a palms out, hands-up pose, or international surrender.

I calmly said, *"ICH GEHEN,"* meaning I would leave. They seemed happy with my response. They eased up and motioned for me to leave through the door I'd entered. I turned to open the door, and in doing so, blocked off access to one of the gorillas, so it somewhat evened the odds. Oh, boy.

Brad is sitting down, unaware and still enjoying his meal. I turned to leave and decided, *Fuck this, I paid for a meal and I'm getting my money's worth.* So I hauled off and delivered a beautiful right hook to the manager's chin. I saw his eyes roll into the back of his head and knew gravity would do the rest. He was out cold and falling into the path of the one remaining gorilla. I slammed the door behind me and started hauling ass towards the door. I was a fast runner, had always been. I could run the Army two-mile PT (physical training) test in just under twelve minutes. My buddies hated me, sometimes. I would snuff out a cigarette before the run, then be waiting at the end of the run smoking another one as they rolled in. I was an asshole, albeit a fast one.

I was dressed to kill that night, but not dressed to kill a two-mile run. I'd worn those slick-ass loafers that looked great on the dance floor, but terrible in a *fight-or-flight* situation. I struggled to gain speed across the greasy floor, as Turkish curse words slowly began to get louder, and louder at my back. I remember screaming, *"BRAD, LET'S GET THE FUCK OUTTA HERE,"* precisely the moment I was tackled by three french-fry cooks in the middle of the lobby. I'll tell you, it was a whole-new low in customer service.

I squirmed for a moment before getting onto my backside where I began to deliver a hail of kicks, punches, and my own treasure trove of American curse words. The restaurant stopped dead in its tracks. Yet, I distinctly remember looking over and seeing Vegas calmly chewing on his burger, barely watching the freak show unfolding in the middle of the restaurant. He didn't get excited, or even anxious. He was kind of like, *Meh…it's just Turner fighting again. No big deal.* He knew I could handle myself in a fight, but damn, this was ridiculous. I looked over and with a sarcastic, but serious tone, I asked, *"A LITTLE FUCKING HELP, DUDE?"*

Perturbed, and visibly pissed, Vegas calmly weighed his options. He actually watched the situation for a moment, deciding whether to intervene or not. I'm sitting there wrestling three of these fuckers and he's deciding whether he wants to interrupt his meal. Reluctantly, he opted to come to the rescue of *yours truly*, but not before taking a final bite of his burger and grabbing a couple of fries for the road.

We hit the sidewalk and headed towards the *Straßenbahn*. The first words from Brad's lips were, *"THANKS A LOT, TURNER. I WAS FUCKING HUNGRY, DUDE."* My buddy wasn't pissed at those assholes, no. He was pissed that he didn't get to finish his food. As we walked, he remarked about how we couldn't go anywhere without me getting into a fight. I said something about there being a lot of assholes in the world and it was my job to sort them out. He, of course, forgave me, and we laughed it off.

DATE WITH A DENTIST

I will never forget the night that Brad, Duffster, and I went to The Skyline, or Skydive bar. If you didn't get lucky in town and you really needed to get laid, or wanted to continue drinking until 0400 hours, this was the place. We had to stumble under the Autobahn down this long brick tunnel to get there. We walked in, grabbed some beers, and started scoping the place out for women. We hadn't even finished our first beer when this cute girl walked up to Brad and asked, *"DO YOU WANT TO MAKE A PARTY?"* In Germany, wanting to make a party was translation for, *You're attractive. Would you like to hang out, have some drinks, and get to know one another?*

Duffster and I couldn't help but notice that she had two friends with her. There were three of them and three of us…the night was shaping up nicely. Did I mention that she was cute? Well, in the dark and before speaking, she was attractive. As soon as she parted her lips to speak, the first thing we noticed was that she was missing one of her teeth. No, not one of her lower premolars or upper molars, where it could be hidden with a shy smile. No, it was one of her *upper incisors*… like the Christmas song about two front teeth. No smile at all would have hidden that damaged truck grill. She had a horse smile to boot, which meant you could drive a Deuce-and-a-Half through that gaping hole. The problem is, Germany is a somewhat well-to-do society, which translates to options for its citizens, namely dental care.

Vegas reared back and held up his dukes with his wrists and knuckles curled inward, as if about to enter a bare-knuckle boxing match. He exclaimed, *"GODDAMN, BABY. YOU NEED TO MAKE A PARTY WITH THE DENTIST."*

Duffster and I couldn't help but laugh. She didn't understand his words, but she wasn't dense to the message behind our laughter and his body language. She did an about-face and retreated back to her girlfriends. Of course, Duffster and I didn't waste any time in asking him why he didn't take one for the team. In one fell swoop, he negated any chance Duffster or I may have had with her cute girlfriends. We, of course, forgave him, and we laughed it off.

I WILL KICK YOUR ASS, MOTHER FUCKER

The Skydive was always full of German women looking for the *great green card in the sky*, or an American visa. It was also full of liquored-up G.I.s, looking for women and often looking to prove their manhood in a bar brawl with other G.I.s. I happen to fall into the latter category. This one particular evening was no different.

While I was crossing the dance floor, I found myself vying for the same empty hole in the crowd as this Lurch-looking mother fucker. Had we been the same height, we'd have bumped shoulders. As we both tried to fill the same real-estate, my shoulder struck his elbow. He towered over me and everyone else in the bar. We gave one another a stern, menacing look to imply that neither were backing down. The crowd noticed, and immediately gave us a wide swath of floor space. He said something about my attitude for such a *little man*. Evil-eyed and with a knife-hand, I told him in no uncertain terms, *"I WILL KICK YOUR ASS, MOTHER FUCKER. LOOK HERE, STRETCH, I WILL END YOU!"*

The crowd was itching to see this rumble go down. He looked me over and realized I was not backing down one-single-inch. After a short pause, his demeanor changed to a non-defensive posture. He then held out his hand and said, *"YOU KNOW WHAT, DUDE? I FUCKING BELIEVE YOU."*

We shook hands and introduced ourselves. We had a couple beers to-gether that night, shooting the shit about everything under the sun. He told me he wanted to get into a fight for so long after he'd joined the Army. After enlisting, he was in better physical shape and felt confident about himself; due to his size, he'd always wanted to fight someone, but could never get anyone to take him up on his offer. He confessed after he saw the lack of fear in my eyes, he knew I was dead-fucking-serious about whipping his ass. He said, *"I'VE NEVER HAD MY ASS KICKED, BUT FOR THE FIRST TIME IN MY LIFE, I BELIEVED IT WHEN **YOU** SAID IT."*

We only saw each other a few more times in and around Mannheim, but it was always fun when we did run into one another. It became a fun game for us in whatever bar we happened to meet. With curse words, knife-hands, and name calling, we acted as if we were caged animals closing the gap in a fight for our lives. The crowds would rear-back in anticipation of our brawl, though it looked more akin to David and Goliath. Then, as we approached one another, the smiles and laughter would break out between us, and he would give me this huge bear hug. He was like a gentle giant, and I was like his side-kick whenever we saw each other out and about. Although we were in different units, I wished I'd maintained contact with him, as he was a cool guy.

THE SULLIVAN SLASHER

I can tell you a story about a seriously dude in our battalion: Midge, or the *Sullivan Slasher*. One night, he and some girls were hanging outside the gymnasium, located directly behind the entrance to HQ. Midge was not a big guy in those days. In fact, he was closer in stature to a flagpole, not unlike the ones you see in front of government buildings. No, it was more akin to one of those small ones that children hold up during a parade. Sorry, Midge…the truth is the truth. In his defense, he has now filled-out and sports a proper beer-belly like the rest of us. Welcome to the club, brother.

Anyhow, these four guys came over and start fucking with him and the girls. As there were four of them, he tried to pop-smoke and get the fuck out of Dodge. One of the largest guys in the group grabs Midge by his coat and starts to wrestle him to the ground. So, he arms himself with his multi-tool, then flips out the knife portion, and slashes the guy right in the gut.

Midge was arrested and trialed. He was relinquished of all charges after the group came clean and confessed, amounting to, *They got what they deserved*. A few months later, the JAG officer, or Judge Advocate General (a fancy name for military attorney) called Midge and told him the guy died from surgical complications.

COWBOYS & INDIANS AT THE WHITE HOUSE

Another interesting night was when we were getting shitty at The White House. It was a night like any other when my buddy sat down and asked if I would *inspire* someone to stop fucking with him. I obliged, as he was a bit of a pacifist. The guy in question was from our sister unit, 5-77 Armor (the Steel Tigers), and also the on-break bartender of The White House.

I sat down next to the guy whom we shall call SPC Cook, because he was, in fact, a cook. My buddy took the seat across from him. I calmly looked over to Cook and asked him to leave my buddy alone. I told him that I wouldn't ask a second time. He smarted-off with something that didn't agree with my peacekeeping mission. I told him that if he opened his mouth with anything other than an affirmative to my request, I was going to end his night. I am not the biggest, nor am I the toughest son-of-a-bitch alive, but you might say, I'm one densely packed, mean mother-fucker when I need to be.

SPC Cook proceeded to open his cock holster with another smart-assed remark aimed at yours truly. So I did exactly what I said I was going to do and *ended his night*. I gave him a quick right elbow to the face, then reached up and over his head with my right arm and did my best to grab that little tuft of hair atop his crown. I reared his head back as far as the mounted chair would allow, and then, leaning my own body forward, followed through to the table, head in tow. He wasn't completely knocked out, but he wasn't serving anymore drinks that night. He was slumped onto the table, bleeding and dazed as if he'd run headfirst into a brick Kremlin. I calmly stood up and continued drinking.

The next thing I know, this 11Charlie, or mortar man, from my unit came over with a huge smile on his face and said, *"THAT'S THE MOST BAD-ASS SHIT I'VE EVER SEEN. WHAT'S YOUR NAME, MOTHER FUCKER?"*

I was now friends with Jim M. He bought me a beer, and we were soon talking about everything from his time in the Gulf War, to home life. But our happy story ended when we were rudely interrupted by an angry mob from 5-77 Armor. One of them was a gargantuan American Indian. In our group was Big Steve, Lake, Flaze, Jim M., and your drunken-hero author, *moi*. We decided to take it outside into the middle of the street. It was early into the evening yet, so the after-work traffic rush was still in play.

Once in the street, the brawl exploded into all directions. I was repeatedly kneeing this guy in a red flannel, until that gargantuan Indian got ahold of me. He was fucking huge, and I started screaming, like a bitch, for backup. Big Steve came and saved my ass, just in the nick of time. We continued kicking their asses, while traffic, at least twenty cars deep in both directions, was at a complete standstill. Wild is an understatement.

Once they'd had enough, we parted ways and reckoned that the *Polizei* and MPs (Military Police) were well on their way. We decided to pop-smoke and haul ass down the tracks of the Straßenbahn. The MPs caught up with us at the next RxR crossing. We did manage to sweet-talk our way out of it, though. Just remember, you cannot spell wimp, without MP. That was the joke we could never tell them, so I'm sharing it with you, my wonderful readers.

Apparently, one of the miscreants of 5-77 was left laying across the train tracks, but we never heard anything about it afterwards, otherwise, we would have all been in military prison, or a German one. I learned of this years later.

FUNSHINE OLYMPICS

One of my all-time favorite weekends was when I volunteered for the Special Olympics in Heidelberg. It was as if fate had stepped in and saw that I wasn't *all* bad. During a normal, end-of-day formation, Top stepped out and asked for two volunteers for the coming weekend. I thought, I'm overdue for some kind of shit duty, whether in the mess hall scrubbing pots and pans, or helping the company armorer clean weapons. It's always better to volunteer versus being *voluntold*.

After volunteering, Top said we were getting not *one*, but *two*, four-day weekends as a reward. I didn't realize that the assignment itself was my reward. We were going to be volunteers at the *Funshine* Special Olympics, hosted by the American Armed Forces in Heidelberg. I had an Aunt Carolyn with Down syndrome, so I knew it was going to be loads of fun.

It started with erecting tents and tables, but after being released from my duties, and having access to the entire event, I soon found myself on the track making friends and cheering on the contestants—probably louder than anyone else. I never even asked about my *reward* weekends, as I'd already been rewarded. Eventually, Top told me to take my weekends before he gave them to someone else, so I took a trip to Belgium with Spud.

Fate had stepped in and allowed me to do something that *wasn't* on par with my (then) normal selfishness. It was the most fun I'd had in Germany whilst completely sober.

34

SOGGY BISCUIT

As time went on, things only got worse in terms of our debauchery. I am, by nature, a trickster, a prankster, and at times (*was* being the operative word here) a real shit, as this chapter will testify. I had grown into a very cocky soldier as the weeks and months passed. I certainly lived up to every inch of that truth and stretched it as taut as humanly possible. I can only be all too thankful for the friends I have today—as they say, you are only young once.

Given the circumstances of this next story, it's safe to say that in to-day's Army, I would have been charged with traumatic sexual, physical, biological, and emotional harassment, found guilty before a military tribunal, and assuredly court-martialed out of the Army. There would have been a slew of other charges such as bullying, fighting, and hazing, facilitated in every known degree. No doubt, it would have included charges like lewd and crude behavior, public drunkenness, and a list of other offences. I am not sure where this chapter falls betwixt all of those charges, but, somehow it does. I will take this opportunity to re-mind the reader, I was young. I am no longer that asshole. I have a wife and family, and I am a mostly changed man. I am a much kinder and gentler soul, that, somewhat, regrets his past. That said, I'm still prob-ably going to hell for this one. I hope God has a great sense of humor.

Our group was, how shall I say, *the cool guys*. When we received newbies, naturally, they all wanted to party with us. Because of our craziness, we had to be selective about who was *in-the-know* and who wasn't. We had a plethora of deep, dark, sinister secrets to protect. We heavily screened who we allowed into our inner circle. When they wanted to drink and hang out with us, we had to give them a trial run, or two. This normally consisted of some light and heavy barracks drinking, served with a side of psychological torture. We also watched them carefully at work to see if they were going to tattle-tale at any or every misstep. They were on double-top-secret probation.

We had this one kid from California…he was new to the PLT and assigned to the HEMTT fuel section. He wanted to party with us in the worst way, though he was very suspect to *not* be one of the cool guys. There was something amiss from his character. I instructed the PLT to direct him to me whenever he would inquire about drinking or hanging out with us. No matter what, I was to be the guardian of all things debauchery.

We shall call this new guy, PVT Gullible. He pestered me for several days to come and hang out with us. I promised him that he was not ready to party at our level, despite his protests and promises that he was. I assured him he was nowhere near the veteran level of liver-destroying sin upon which we operated on a near daily basis. PVT Gullible kept after me, and the PLT kept after him to deal with me. He kept chomping at the bit, day-after-day. I kept stringing him along.

Payday was nearing, and PVT Gullible asked me what was going down that weekend. I looked him in the eye and asked if he wanted his chance to party with the big boys. He assured me he was ready. I told him to be sure of what he wished for, as he just may get it. He swore up-and-down he was crazy enough, he was ready for us to bring him into the fold. I told him that if he *pussied* out, he would be the laughing stock of the PLT. Oh, no, he was ready. I instructed him to bring a six-pack of beer and $30.00 cash to my room about 1730 hours, for some pre-party drinking. Thirty bucks to a new PVT was a decent amount of money back then. He promised he would be there.

1730 hours rolled around, and sure as shit, he *actually* showed up. We sat down, cracked a beer, and it didn't take long for him to ask what was on the agenda. I told him that there was still time to back out, if he wanted. He assured me that he was ready. I told him, this is next level shit, we were crazy out there, and that he could save himself the ridicule by simply walking away. He was hooked. I asked to see the money, ensuring he'd done as instructed. He looked confused. We cracked another beer, and I began to explain the situation.

I told him that the money was to get him into the room upstairs. That every payday we placed a little wager on something we called, *Soggy Biscuit*. Still confused, he asked what it was. I told him that about twelve-to-fourteen guys would go upstairs, pool the monies, sometimes upwards of $300 to $400 and bet to see who won the pot. His eyes glistened. Naturally, he asked what we were betting on. I told him that we gathered into a room with blacked-out windows, turned off the lights…his face contorted and I asked him once more if he was sure he was up to the task. He assured me he was, though perhaps now regretting his bravery.

I informed him that we didn't exactly advertise this kind of shit to everybody in the unit. He could hardly stand the anxiety of it. I said, *"OKAY, AFTER THE LIGHTS GO OFF, WE ALL START JERK-ING-OFF IN THE ROOM."*

"OH, BULLSHIT, TURNER," he said.

Quickly, I responded, *"BULLSHIT NOTHING, MOTHER-FUCKER. I KNEW YOU WEREN'T COOL, I KNEW IT. I KNEW THIS WAS TOO MUCH FOR YOU. IF YOU SAY A FUCKING WORD ABOUT THIS TO ANYBODY, I SWEAR—"*

He listened intently before interrupting me. *"YOU'RE SERIOUS, DUDE?"*

I said, *"YEAH, I'M FUCKING SERIOUS. I PLAN ON WINNING THIS MONTH. I HAVE STAVED OFF PUSSY AND JERKING-OFF FOR TWO SOLID WEEKS IN ANTICIPATION OF BANKING THE POT."*

He was completely and utterly dumbfounded as to what to do next. I could hear sheered cogs falling to the floor of his brain. The look of, *What have I gotten myself into,* grimaced his face. He didn't want to be a pussy, but this really was next level shit; a level that he was clearly not comfortable with.

The wait was over. I butted into his inner-dialog. *"FUCK IT, DUDE, YOU'RE NOT READY. I KNEW I SHOULDN'T HAVE LET YOU JOIN. YOU'RE A PUSSY, DUDE. I JUST DON'T KNOW HOW EVERYBODY IN THE PLATOON IS GOING TO FIND OUT ABOUT THIS…?"*

Against all rational thought and behavior, he forcibly blurted, *"I'LL DO IT."*

SUCKER, shrieked through my mind.

"OKAY, GRAB YOUR BEER, GULLIBLE. LET'S GO. I HAVE A HOT DATE LATER."

We went upstairs to my buddy's room and performed the classic, *pop-goes-the-weasel* knock. That should have been the sign for him to run, but he stayed, like a crayon-eating fuck stick. I handed the money to this cool black dude from New York. As fire-for-effect was well in play, he immediately started talking shit to me. *"YOU'RE GOING DOWN, TURNER. I GOT THIS SHIT THIS MONTH. FOR THREE WEEKS I HAVEN'T CLEARED THE PIPES, DUDE."*

You could see the horror strike PVT Gullible's face as the reality of *This isn't bullshit, after all,* set in. You could see the lightbulb flicker, then illuminate as he realized he was in a whole new world of *psycho* that he never thought possible. Nothing in his life had prepared him for the room he just paid to enter. Disbelief quickly whisked away, as fear set in.

I made my rounds through the room, bullshitting with everyone while introducing our newest member. The plan went over like a beer in a barroom. This was working more beautifully than I ever thought it would. Finally, after about half a beer and some small talk, someone broke the ice by saying they had plans and the party needed starting. The stage was set with the spotlight aimed. The windows were closed and nearly $400 was collected and placed into the pot. We made our way to a *personal* area in the room and set our beers down. The word was passed, *"LIGHTS OUT, MOTHER-FUCKERS."* PVT Gullible was in way above his head, but to his credit, he dug down deep and went all-in after the bell rang.

With the lights off, silence quickly set in, then the sporadic rustling of belts and buttons momentarily drowned the silence. Then absolute silence struck again.

Minute One: The soft clap of skin could be heard from every nook and cranny of the room. The squishy workings of men rubbing themselves could be faintly heard. The occasional spittle of saliva could be heard exiting someone's mouth and clapping onto their hands, with a quick return to the pitter-patter of self-gratification.

Minute Two: Heavy breathing began to mix with the clip-claps of wet skin on wet skin.

Minute Three: Breathing and slapping intensified. The room was drunk on itself. The darkest side of the moon was coming into view...

Minute Four: In a busy fervor, PVT Gullible spoke, *"I'M GONNA CUM. I'M GONNA CUM. I'M GONNA FUCKING WIN."* That's when the lights were flicked-on, and PVT Gullible found himself in the middle of the room stroking his pecker at full-speed. The only problem was, he was the only guy in the room, pants at his ankles, servicing himself. We had been simply sitting there clapping our licked palms together, giving the *audible* appearance of masturbating. I was a horrible person, I know.

PVT Gullible's world quickly crumbled; hopes of winning the pot were swept away and dreams of glory were dashed beyond his grasp, no pun intended. I have seen a lot of people grow angry in my life, but never at the breakneck speed in which he did. He was *abso-fuck-ing-lutely* livid. If ever a person could describe the definition of rage, it was at that moment, him. I thought he was going to come unglued, again, no pun intended. He couldn't get his pecker tucked into his pants quickly enough. He was multi-tasking like a mother-fucker. He struggled to stow his deflating glory while bolting for the door, all the while screaming at the top of his lungs, *"I'M GONNA TELL THE FUCKIN' SERGEANT. I'M GONNA TELL THE FUCKIN' SERGEANT."*

It took four or five guys to hold him back before he made the door. He squirmed and fought like his life depended on it, but it was futile. They were not to be overpowered. He was not going to get away, because, quite frankly, our lives did depend on it. That could have been a catastrophe, had he actually told the CQ SGT. That would have meant our hides, an investigation, punishment: *the works!*

Still struggling, I asked him, *"WHAT, EXACTLY, ARE YOU GOING TO TELL THE FUCKING SERGEANT, PVT GULLIBLE? REALLY, WHAT THE FUCK ARE YOU GOING TO TELL HIM? THAT YOU WERE JERKING-OFF IN THE MIDDLE OF A ROOM FULL OF GUYS?"* I explained to him that that may not go over very well for anyone if he marched up to the CQ desk making such outrageous claims, and that he'd likely be labeled a pervert, or psychopath.

I continued. *"BESIDES, IT'S YOUR WORD, AGAINST OURS. WHAT'S IT GOING TO BE, GULLIBLE? THE EASY WAY, OR THE HARD WAY?"* Still calming himself, and recognizing the situation, he considered his actions very carefully.

He eventually calmed all the way down and realized that we had gotten him pretty damn good. We returned everyone's money and told him we were taking him out for an all-expenses-paid night on the town. We bought him plenty of shots and beers, showing him our drinking haunts. He was ripe drunk and happy as a clam as we walked back to the barracks later that evening. I don't remember who said it to Gullible, or the exact phrase, but it was something along the lines of *not jerking-off in formation the next morning,* or something to that effect. That was obviously not the right choice of words, as the earlier lividity from *room erotica* entered a full-blown relapse. He struggled to form his drunken face into focus on, you guessed it, kicking my ass, or so he thought.

He broke into a full-on stammering trot towards my position. I swung my body around and gave him a little left-hook to remind him that I was still well in control of my faculties. I told him to calm down as we all broke into laughter. Again, he calmed down and came to his senses. I threw my arm around his shoulder and said, *"WELCOME TO THE CLUB, BROTHER."*

He didn't care much for me after that night, and I still don't understand why. Go figure? I was such a nice guy, once you got to know me. If, by some strange chance, PVT Gullible were to read this, don't get any weird ideas, I'm still a bad mother-fucker when I need to be.

35

BOX, TYPE, ONE EACH, GOES TO HAUS II

I debated on whether to include this story, but after speaking with his mother night-after-night when her baby boy, my brother, Box, was dying in a hospital in California, I decided to include it. I wanted our brother to be remembered in some capacity, beyond the memories of only his family and friends. She always told me to remember her baby, for us all to remember her son.

Box, Type, One Each (an ode to military naming), Fuck *Duuude* (sic), Butt-Head, or Tricky Dick—whatever you called him—undeniably, he was one of the funniest guys you would ever want to meet. As most of my brothers know, he is no longer with us. Two of my brothers, Spud and O.C., were able to make the trek down to see him right before he passed. It was a great loss to our small band of brothers. He was one of the few guys that I consistently kept up with over the many years that passed since we served together.

Tricky and I went on quite a few adventures together, like running with the bulls in Pamplona, Spain, and getting drunk in Paris, France, and going hiking around Mount Rainier, Washington. He was always there to deliver a smile and a laugh. His sense of humor, although dry and sarcastic, was always on point to the situation; you couldn't help but love him. In honor of our fallen comrade, I dedicate this chapter to you, brother Box. I hope I honor your memory well, my dear friend.

I will try and describe Box to those of you that didn't know him. He was about 5'8", skinny, brown hair and brown eyes, with a light physical build. He wore glasses that were so thick, I claimed he could see into the future or through walls with them. I can hear him now, *"FUCK OFF, TURNER,"* with a big smile across his face and extending one of his middle fingers. The thing is, a soldier will talk mad shit to your face, and honor you to the ends of the earth behind your back, so I mean no disrespect by fucking with him even after he's passed. He would want and expect it of me.

Now, Tricky was not like the rest of us, but it never stood in the path of anything he ever did. He had this humor and wit that could break down the strongest of wills and walls. The difference was that his hair didn't grow like ours. It was literally like someone had taken a set of close-skinned sheers and just did a quick arched *drive-by* over each of his ears, only it was permanent. They were like white-wall tires. It simply just didn't grow for about an inch-and-a-half above his ears, from his temple back to the base of his neck. One day while walking to the PX, when asked about his fucked-up haircut, he told the brigade SGM that he was struck by lightning. The spot-inspection was quickly dismissed.

Once night, Tricky, SGT J, Duffster, Spud, Tire Iron (surprisingly, Tire Iron was with us, as he was the sham master, being the colonel's driver, so he couldn't get into as much trouble as we did, but he was always there for the good stuff) and Gumby—maybe two car loads of us—drove up to Frankfurt's *Sachsenhausen* district. No, not the famed political prisoner concentration camp. It was a section of Frankfurt known to have lots of bars and a large red light district, or whore house, also known as the *Poof Haus* (haus is German for house). Whoring is a regulated and government-sanctioned business in Germany, and many places in the world. It's just like going to work at a restaurant or gas station. You're still giving a service, just a filthy one. I never frequented one as a customer, never had a reason to.

When we showed up to the bar and found a big table, we immediately broke out a chemical light stick, or break-n-shake light, and set it down on the table. These were very hard to come by back in those days and were, on the German economy, deemed very expensive luxury items. Of course, yours truly went to supply, told a joke, and got a couple of boxes. We could trade them to the Germans for drinks. We settled in and ordered some beers.

Tricky decided he wanted to go to the red light district and get laid. A couple of us said that we would escort him to the *Poof Haus* and check out the wares, as it was only a block or so from the bar.

We arrived, walked through the double-doors, and immediately put Tricky out front, as he was the *John*. As we were standing there gathering our bearings, I noticed another building out the back door, towards the interior of our building. I suggested we check it out. It had a sign that read, *HAUS II*, or house number two. We walked in and started up the hallway, perusing the women. The way it worked was, if you passed a doorway with an open door, she was open for business; if the door was closed, she was conducting business. Now, I will say this, there are some fine-looking whores over there. Beautiful blue-eyed blondies that would fuck or suck you off for DM50, or thirty-some dollars. A real bargain, right?

As we walked down the hall of *Haus II*, looking into each doorway, we noticed that these women were not exactly what one would call, *top-notch*. They were definitely eclectic: Asians, Africans, Hispanics, and most every walk of life other than European were represented. Every variety of each, too. Short ones, fat ones, skinny ones, ugly ones, old ones, young ones, freaky ones. It was an interesting walk, to say the least. We decided to try the upstairs hallway and see if Tricky's prospects improved. They did.

We were walking along the narrow, dimly lit hallway, when all of a sudden this huge, Amazonian chick steps out of her room. She was one of, if not, *the* tallest woman I have ever seen in my life. She was probably seven-feet tall, no bullshit. She was as black as night, and sporting a cheetah outfit and giving off the air of having actually skinned a cheetah to acquire her clothing. She had a huge afro, and appendages that were lanky, and proportioned longer than they should have been, given her size. She was skinny with a nice figure, but mind you, *Big and Tall* stores would be strained to clothe her. She literally looked straight out of the pages of an exotic book.

She stepped out, leaned her torso against the doorway, and extended her right arm across the width of the hall. Nothing weird here, until she placed her hand flat, I mean, fingers extended, palm out, hand lying flat against the opposite wall. It freaked us out just a little. A few years ago, I worked in Africa for a couple of months and have yet to see any shit like that. As we inched closer, she repositioned herself akimbo, hands on hips into the middle of the hallway, right in front of Tricky. His face didn't even reach her breasts. He had to cock his head back just to look up and see past her tits to glance at her face.

Tricky stood in awe, as did we all. Don't get me wrong—she wasn't ugly in the least, just simply a ginormous woman. We stood, waiting for a dialog that never came. Smiling, she eyed Tricky up-and-down, and then, without warning, she grabbed his shirt and drug him into her room. He just did manage to get in a small wave goodbye to us silent onlookers. We were dumbfounded at what had unfolded before our eyes. We didn't know whether to head back to the bar or go in and rescue him. We opted to continue drinking at the bar, since she could have probably kicked all of our asses.

About an hour later, Tricky swaggered into the bar wearing a huge shit-eating grin on his face. In the interim, we'd filled in the guys with the unbelievable details. We asked him how it went, and excitedly he said, *"SHE SUCKED ME, FUCKED ME, AND DIDN'T CHARGE ME ONE RED CENT!"*

I had heard a lot of crazy red light stories, but never one like that. We called bullshit, so he pulled his single DM50 bill from his pocket and said she never asked him for payment. It was always suggested to take with you only what you intended to spend. Only Box could have pulled that off. He never had a lying bone in his body, unless you were the BGD SGM questioning him on haircuts, so it stood as undeniable truth. Cheers to you, Tricky!

36

UN-ORGANIZATION
DRINKING DAY

What was supposed to happen each year, but didn't in 1994, due to the European drawdown, was Organization Day. It was a big three-day weekend event where the unit came together to celebrate ourselves. Just kidding, it was when we got to showcase our unit, our vehicles, and boost unit morale, with the wife, kids, and girlfriends in tow. Again, I jest, it was really a sanctioned day to get drunk with everyone in the unit, wives and girlfriends included.

What made ours so cool was that we had formed a relationship with a German military museum; one of the last *semi-operational* units of what remained of the NVA (or, *Nationale Volks Armee*, the National People's Army), of former East Germany. It was operated by an old German vet and his wife, a sweet older couple. Being licensed on nearly every vehicle in our unit, I was tasked with picking up and delivering the antique vehicles we were going to showcase on our Organization Day.

We borrowed a WWII M3 half-track, a vehicle that was half-truck and half-tank (seen in a lot of movies), a Willy's MB jeep, and a Korean-era,

M8, a 6x6 wheeled, Light Armored Car, complete with a small-arms turret, much like a tank. As I was to load and unload them onto my flatbed trailer, the old man gave me a crash course on how to drive each of the vehicles. Even though he would be present, it was better for me to have *some* knowledge of them, as I was transporting them to and fro.

Two boxing bouts were set for the light and middle-weight teams of both 3-77 and 5-77 Armor, vying for the division title, so there were a lot of guys from both units in attendance. I was set to fight around 1000 hours. They had a full, regulation-size ring set up for the matches. My opponent was taller and heavier than me; however, I was trained by a three-time Golden Gloves champion. Plus, I had always been a natural brawler since kindergarten. My first fight involved three boys that wouldn't allow me access to the pencil sharpener. Two black-eyes and a bloody nose later, they learned their lesson about this Turner!

Round one: He had the upper-hand, as he was a very good boxer. His jab was quick and effective. His counterpunches had a pause to them, so they were, seemingly, slow and predictable. He out-boxed me in round one, no question about it. My confidence waned a bit after that. Doubt began to creep in. It didn't help that there were a few hundred people watching our match. It was a bit more intimidating than fighting in front of a few dozen people, as in my first two bouts. Unit pride was on the line here, and I wanted 3-77 to look damn good.

Round two: He started out with some good jabs, and my confidence started taking a nosedive, as he was definitely out-boxing me. Then he struck me with a good right-cross. I felt the sting on my nose and the water swell in my eyes. It was the first time I'd been properly popped in the nose. My face felt like a balloon. I began to evade him and form a strategy, which if you've ever been in a boxing match, it's tougher than it sounds, especially with someone trying to knock your lights out. He had round one in the bag, and round two was not looking much better for me. He was about to have two, of the six scheduled rounds, in the bag.

I am not sure how to explain it, but whenever I get into a fight, I kind of lose memory of the actual events and literally see red in the heat of the moment. I rarely had the flight instinct, as much as I had the fight. I remember everything about that fight until he bloodied my nose. Then, I lost it.

This fucker had to go down, now! I had never had my nose bloodied, as I was always faster and smarter. I evaded his jabs and his combinations on my way into the inside, where I like to fight. I jabbed my way in, and then delivered a huge right upper-cut. He flopped back like a fish out of water. The match ended with a knockout. My right upper-cut proved to be the signature punch that took me all the way to winning the finals for the U.S. Army in Germany.

My buddy, Fritz, recorded it and said, *"TURNER, YOU FUCKING BROUGHT HIM OFF THE MAT WITH THAT PUNCH, DUDE."*

Several guys verified that I had indeed lifted his feet off the mat with that punch…otherwise, I'd have never believed it. I remember hitting him, but the details were fuzzy. My buddies wasted no time in recounting the victory I'd brought to 3-77 Armor that day. I was definitely the man of the hour. Okay, more like ten minutes, then we started drinking beer. After that, I had plenty of beers coming my way by officers and enlisted alike. I knew I'd made the unit proud.

I wasted no time in getting some beers in me before talking to the old man about driving that half-track for a victory lap. *"KEINE PROBLEM,"* he said, meaning, no problem. I couldn't believe he was going to let me drive around in a WWII half-track whilst drunk off my ass and unsupervised. My buddies didn't waste any time in getting their asses into vehicles of their own, to accompany me. We had a WWII half-track, a modern HMMWV, and a Korean-era jeep, all loaded down with drunken soldiers cruising around a military post. Per usual, *What could possibly go wrong?*

I was driving around in the half-track with a few guys, Halterman was in the HMMWV with a load, and God only knows who was in the jeep. It all started so innocently, then the alcohol took hold. First, we were speeding around a little, then racing, and then it was who could do the best power slide around a corner. Reckless driving with drunken soldiers hanging off the sides of the vehicles, an accident was bound to happen, and it almost did.

You'd think that would have slowed us down, but you'd be wrong. It only intensified the belligerent disregard for all things responsible. Tires were screeching, the tracks from the half-track were roaring down the roads like a Blitzkrieg, all hell had broken loose. Then Halterman came screaming around the corner, waving us down, telling us that the MPs had just rounded the corner at the front gate. I didn't think I could turn that half-track around so fast, especially without power-steering, but I knew we had to high-tail it back to the parade grounds. Fortunately, none of us were caught, but can you imagine the shit storm it would have caused having so many drunken soldiers in both U.S and German government-owned vehicles on the roadways? It would be a story that would be told much differently had we been caught. We returned our vehicles safe-and-sound. Tragedy averted.

I was so glad I made friends with the old man at the museum, because some months after that, a few of us were invited to qualify for our *Schützenschnur*, (German Armed Forces Badge of Marksmanship). We qualified with the nearest-to-current weapons at the time, as well as a few antique weapons around the museum. It is an award that is issued from the *Bundeswehr*. All German soldiers are authorized to earn the award, but only German enlisted soldiers are authorized to wear it. However, when issued to Americans, both officers and enlisted soldiers are authorized to wear it as a foreign award.

My only regret is that I didn't turn the paperwork into my commander before two of my duffle bags were stolen, as they contained all of my extra shit. I could of murdered a thief that day, as I had all sorts of extra goodies: gas mask, body armor, Kevlar helmet, my tank CVC, my *Schützenschnur* and accompanying paperwork, one of my hard-copy AAMs, a shit ton of other stuff I'd collected during my time in Germany. It was heartbreaking and still is. I loathe a fucking thief.

37

HAIRY NIPPLES & HELICOPTERS

I guess it's time to tell an embarrassing story on yours truly, thus concluding any attempt at being modest. Oh, the webs we weave. I was hanging out in the barracks one night without a date and without any plans. I was just drinking and listening to music. It was the weekend, so I must have been broke. Sometimes I was so broke I couldn't afford to pay attention. German bier (bought on the economy and brought home), and lots of it, were expensive for us lowly, enlisted soldiers. I usually sat around in my boxer shorts, as there were nothing but guys around and nobody gave a shit anyway. My roommate, Vegas, and our buddy, Duffster, were out on a double-date that night.

All of a sudden I get a light knock on my door, so I knew it wasn't a soldier. I open it to find a semi-cute girl standing there asking about Vegas Brad and Duffster. I knew this girl, as she'd been around their girlfriends, but I'd never had an inkling to pursue her. The guys, though, had given me an operations order in the event that this very thing were to happen. She was not to be given any details of their whereabouts, activities, etc. For whatever reason, they were avoiding her like the plague and wanted me to do the same.

"WELL, COME ON IN," I offered. After a bit of small talk, I made a move on her and she accepted. So we climb up on the top bunk, where my bed was located, and got a little more comfortable with one another. Don't laugh, it gave us more space, as it was both tight budgeting and tight quarters for us enlisted guys.

She asked that the lights be turned out, so I obliged. My humongous stereo system was of concert proportions and emitted enough light to hand-signal in a jet landing, so I could see what I was doing, nonetheless. Things were rolling along nicely; I played some sexier music and was laying down my mojo. It was as ideal as it gets. I didn't have to take her on a date, buy her a drink, nothing. It was like winning the sexual lottery.

I got her shirt off to reveal a fantastic, petite upper-torso. I inched her bra off and began the natural, next step. That's when it got weird, really fucking weird. We are all familiar with how, under natural and normal circumstances, a man or a woman might wind up with a hair in his or her mouth. But, I wasn't even rounding third-base yet. It made no sense to have a hair in my mouth. A definite, *What the fuck, moment?* I pulled this thin two-incher out and thought, *Okay, self, I'm hairy like an animal.* It was a fleeting thought, so I got back to business. She didn't sense my hairy dilemma, so she was still unaware.

So, I'm cruising along when I move to the other breast and viola, *pith, pith, psst...* I spat out another hair. I could sense that she noticed my dilemma. I did, however, snatch the lamp-pull to the *on* position before she could react. I found that she had these man-style hairy nipples. She was as equally shocked as much as I was frightened and bewildered. Her arms quickly crisscrossed to hide her yeti-style milk maids. In my drunken stupor, I couldn't help but be curious. I tried to coax her into letting me see them in the light, but she wasn't biting. If you didn't think I was an asshole up until this part of the book, be prepared to change your mind. I was young, dammit.

Reluctantly, she agreed to let me see her in the light. At her behest, I promised her that I wouldn't have a bad reaction to whatever I would see. What a *stupid and ridiculous* agreement for someone to make with my younger self. She slowly lowered her arms to reveal a set of nipples that looked like *Bigfoot would take pictures of her*. I'm not talking a few odd hairs, oh, hell no, this was thirty or so, two-inch-long nipple hairs…on each nipple. I thought, a razor or shave-less cream, something. They were almost transparent they were so thin, but not so thin as to be imperceptible. Beautifully shaped breasts, just hairy.

Again, I was young and drunk, so I started snickering to myself, trying to stifle my laughter. Then snickering turned into chuckling. I couldn't help myself, I'm fucking sorry. She promptly lowered herself from my bunkbed and got dressed. She then turned on me like a rabid dog. I should have seen it coming.

She became very angry, *oddly enough*, even after I tried to calm her down and apologize. But, in my defense she shouldn't have bedded me down, knowing damn-well she had Sasquatch DNA coursing through her veins. It all became very clear as to why she was single and on the hunt for a stud like me. I was polite and tried my hardest to remain respectful of her situation. Although I imagined that *downstairs*, it probably looked like she had a *Wookie* in a leg scissor-lock. Don't get me wrong, I love shagged carpeting, just not shagged drapes. During my time in Europe, I was even willing to accept that a lot of European women didn't shave their underarms in winter time, sometimes even their legs, but at hairy nipples I drew the proverbial line in the sand.

It was when she refused to leave my room that I became angry and stopped being polite. She insisted that she was going to sit in my room to wait for her friends that were out with my buddies on a double-date incognito. It escalated, and I thought, this is how soldiers get into trouble, as she could have said anything had happened behind closed doors. It became my life mission to get her out of the room, by any means necessary. It also became a life's chore, too.

I took her purse and tossed it over to the backside of our wall lockers, which was directly at the door. When she went to retrieve her purse, I cornered her, opened the door, and swooshed her out. She turned and starting dog cussing me in German and English. I lost any and all compassion at this point. I was now under the control of beer. I started yelling back to her with my own mixture of German and English adjectives. I, of course, had a much louder voice so it carried throughout the entire building.

At the top of my lungs, I told her, *"RAUS, RAUS!"* (German for [get] *out*). I said, *"OUT…GET THE FUCK OUT OF OUR BARRACKS."* This, of course, gained the attention of most *everyone* that was in the barracks that night, so doors started popping open up-and-down the hallway to see what I was yelling about. Had she any sense, whatsoever, she'd have taken the nearest exit, right across the hall, passed the swastika-laden staircase and bier machine, but, no, she took the scenic route.

During my rant and her walk of shame, and for extra measure, I threw in, *"GET THE FUCK OUT. YOU HAVE HAIRY NIPPLES, AND YOU SMELL LIKE FEET AND ASS."* She didn't smell, but the moniker was soon adopted by many of my brethren as a funny punch line. She made her way down the hall and disappeared through the back door.

I know, those were the good ole days, when you could ditch an angry foreign woman anywhere you wanted in the barracks. We didn't even have to sign them into the front gate. Then, years later, those sorry mother fuckers had to fly jumbo jets into the World Trade Center and fuck-up everything for everyone.

I bet you're thinking that that's the end of the story, but you'd be dead wrong.

So, after hearing the commotion, my then buddy, Devo, came downstairs to see what was going on. The beer flowed whilst I regaled the tale of hairy nipples. He took a piss break, and upon his return, he noticed her sitting on the steps outside of the doorway, near the bier machine. She wasn't alone, though. She was sitting there with my squad leader, CPL Dangerous Dave the Planet. I crept out for a closer look.

I told Devo, *"I HAVE A PLAN!"* He asked what I was going to do, but I told him to quietly wait in the hallway until I returned. I jumped out of my window and made my way around the building, spying on them, as she sat complaining about, you guessed it, yours truly.

I eyeballed them from the corner. I slipped off my beer-label-adorned boxer shorts and crept up on them in the shadows of the building. I was naked as a jaybird, less the crumpled boxers in my hand. I must have been about 3–4 meters from them when I threw my hands up in the air and started screaming and running at them like a possessed hyena. She reared back in nightmarish shock. Dangerous Dave just threw his head in his palm and started cracking up laughing. I ran past them and into the barracks, where, upon sight of me, Devo doubled-over in uncontrollable laughter as well.

I ran into my room, donned my boxers and grabbed a fresh beer. Devo and I were sitting there when Vegas and Duffster popped up in the window asking about hairy nipples out on the steps. Obviously, they were still avoiding her. I promised them that they were safe. I explained that she wasn't coming back to our room under any circumstances. Confusion adorned their faces as they realized I implied that she'd been in the room. They entered through the window and started drinking with us. We filled them in with all the *shaggy* details of the evening.

A little while later we heard a party going on in SGT J's room. They were in party-hardy mode, so Devo and I walked down to scan the scene. Brad and Duffster soon followed. Their dates and my semi-date had by chance met one another at the Straßenbahn station, and two of the three girls returned to barracks for god only knows why. At the time of their return, I was recycling beer in the latrine, and they entered SGT J's room without a fuss. Then I reentered the room, only to be greeted by their angry faces.

Furry Fun-Bags was sitting on the bed next to SGT J and Duffster's date, extolling her horrific evening to them. Everyone had yet to hear all the evening's excitement, so needless to say, they were all ears. I think Gumby (SGT J's roommate) was bench pressing some weights and told me that it was my turn. I pumped-out some reps and jumped up to my awaiting beer. She, the consoling friend, started in on me, complete with German accent. *"OH, YOU THINK YOU ARE BIG MAN, HUH? YOU MAKE FRIEND FEEL BAD. YOU ARE A BAD MAN, PICK ON GIRLS."*

I said, *"SHE STARTED BEING RUDE AND REFUSED TO LEAVE MY ROOM. SHE BROUGHT THIS ON HERSELF."* This was not going to help matters as she again started getting uppity and giving me shit.

I thought, this is not going to get better by arguing. It was a rare moment for me, especially at that age. I calmed her down and asked, *"DO YOU WANT ME TO APOLOGIZE TO HER? YOU WANT ME TO TELL HER HOW SORRY I AM? YOU WANT ME TO SAY I'M SORRY TO YOU BOTH?"*

She reluctantly agreed as she, pouting lips and all, nodded her head up-and-down. *"YES, TELL US BOTH THAT YOU APOLOGIZE. IT WILL MAKE US FEEL BETTER,"* she pleaded.

I hunched over them at the bedside and began apologizing. I said that I was sorry for laughing at her hairy nipples, I was sorry for kicking her out of my room, and I was terribly sorry that I made them upset. I asked if they would accept my apology, and they both agreed. All seemed right as rain in the world again. The girls relaxed and took sips of their drinks and smiled in satisfaction.

SGT J looked at me, like, *Who the fuck are you, and what have you done with Turner?* I slowly turned around, my back to the girls, and sat my beer down on the nightstand. I put my cigarette to my lips as a legend was about to be born. I moved my hands down to my beer label boxers and turned my head over my shoulder and spoke to Duffster's date, *"HEY! ONE MORE THING, SWEETY."*

She looked up and said, *"JA"* (yes in German).

"THIS," I said, as I turned around with my hand down the waistband of my boxers. Her eyes met mine, then followed my arm down to where my dick was hanging out of the slot of my boxers, hand busily swinging around what resembled a vertical helicopter. Thus, Turner's helicopter legend was born.

The room just fell about in laughter. All the guys were rolling on the floor and chairs. The girls huffed and puffed and abruptly exited the room. No one was in any condition to chase them down, either. SGT J laughingly said, *"THIS MOTHER-FUCKER IS CRAZY. YOU AIN'T RIGHT, TURNER, BUT THAT WAS SOME FUNNY SHIT, MAN!"*

For months after that, whether in formation or party mode, SGT J would just take his hand and swing it around like I did that night. A constant reminder of my crazy ways. Now, fast-forward twenty-seven years to the third, of what I hope to be many reunions, and guess who waved their hand around in a helicopter fashion to yours truly? Fuckin' trusty, ole SGT J! I guess that is one of those things that I will never live down. As you read this, SGT J, just remember *hamburgers and bat wings*, mother-fucker! That shit will come out after you retire, and be written into the second book, *THIRTY-FIVE YEARS LATER…STILL COMBATING HANGOVERS.*

38

WHAT IN THE HELL
ARE YOU DOING?

After rotations to *Hohenfels* and *Wildflicken*, another *Grafenwöhr* field problem rolled around, so again, another night of excessive drinking ensued. I guess it wasn't that we couldn't drink in the field, as much as it was that we couldn't drink with *women* in the field at our favorite bars. So, we drank to mourn the departure from our regular watering holes. Plus, the food was nowhere near what it was in garrison, unless it was Thursday. At our unit, it was famously known as *Soul Food Thursday*.

In garrison, each and every Thursday we did this really awful thing called Sergeant's Time. It involved direct NCO to enlisted soldier training from 0700–1200 hours. It was five straight hours of torture that I would compare to waterboarding. The only good thing about Thursdays was that our Mess Sergeant (or the head NCO responsible for chow) put on a meal that was to die for. Soul Food Thursday drew in the crowds from all around Sullivan Barracks.

Just in case anyone was wondering, yes, our Mess Sergeant was black and from the South. Back then, before the world was so easily offended by its own shadow, we could do this kind of shit without hurting any-one's feelings. It didn't matter whether you were white, black, purple, green, or red, so long as you did your job and the next man could count on your having his six, or his back when the proverbial shit hit the fan. We had ribs, fried and barbequed chicken, grilled sausages, ham-burgers, French fries, coleslaw, baked beans, and just about every other Southern staple known to man; being so far away from home and our families, it was comfort food. The shitty part was that if we were late being released from Sergeant's Time, we had to wait in a monstrously long line at our own damn chow hall.

I digress. Ah, yes, field problem, where we didn't do SGT's Time. I was chosen to drive the PLT Daddy, SFC Cigarettes & Coffee, to the field with me in the 5-ton truck. Everything was already loaded when we left out for a six-hour road march. I was still very much drunk from the night before. To spatula on the icing nice and thick-like, I was towing a 250-gallon pod of jet fuel behind my truck. Happy, happy, joy, joy. The nice part of it was, he was willing to forgo the rules, and thus, he allowed smoking in the truck. There was no fucking way he was going more than five minutes without a cigarette. I thought I was bad, but he was a steam-powered locomotive with a carton of cigarettes. I think he smoked three entire packs during our six-hour trip.

We were driving along, smoking and trying to eke out some semblance of small talk to one another. That proved very difficult, so silence crept in and stayed a little while. I was, of course, *drunk-over*, or still drunk and suffering a hangover at the same time. In silence, I got sleepy, so I (almost) smoked cigarette-for-cigarette with the PLT Daddy, to help stay awake. It didn't last long, though. I was *fucking* tired.

I remember it vividly. It was a lush green stretch of Autobahn with a slight, but long curve to the left. My eyelids felt like dumbbells were strung to them, and I was on my last possible repetition. In my mind, I knew there were vehicles and people on the Autobahn with me, plus shit and tons of jet fuel behind me. It wouldn't have been a normal crash. It would have been a carnage of scorched earth, an oil drip can full of extinguished cigarette butts and bones in the laid waste that would have been our remnants. It would've been bad. I had no business on the Autobahn that day, other than being in the shotgun's position sleeping off my stupor. Youth and stupidity and all that jazz.

I was driving, eyes feeling better and better in the closed position. I remember the green, tree-lined Autobahn and approaching that long curve when my eyes last closed. I'm guessing I didn't make the curve as I kept driving straight. It didn't last long though, as I was jolted awake with SFC Cigarettes & Coffee screaming, *"WHAT IN THE HELL ARE YOU DOING?"*

Luckily, I had the wherewithal to not instinctively snatch the wheel as I came to. I saw the trees that were once to my right, now staring me in the face. I was just at the shoulder's edge when I eased back onto the roadway.

It certainly woke me up, as well as the PLT Daddy. We started having some real break-through conversations after that. He had, shall I say, a whole new interest in *yours truly*. He wanted to know where I was from, about my folks, my love life, you name it, and he was willing to talk about it all. It was during that conversation that I learned he used to haul nuclear waste for the Army, as he was one of the few real truck drivers in our PLT. It certainly explained a lot about him. He was looking forward to retiring when he got back to the states.

This field problem would be our last rotation to Graf. It would prove one of our most difficult, too. We were being tested on all fronts, as things in the international political world were heating up. I was even able to trade some uniforms with some Dutch soldiers. The Dutch have a different Army than we do. It was comprised of both volunteer and mandatory one-year enlistees. Professionals, or the volunteers, wore camouflaged uniforms and the long-haired, marijuana-smoking (no bullshit), earring-wearing draftees wore olive-drab uniforms. I have one of each.

We did have some fun when we could fit it in. One of the guys had a birthday while in the field, so we helped him celebrate by taping him up inside of his sleeping bag, then hanging him from the crane of a HEMTT. Good times.

REAL DRUNK DRIVING, ARMY STYLE

Devo and I had earned an evening off, so we decided to go and join a few of the boys at the mess hall for some well-deserved beers. Besides, we needed to practice our arithmetic with some enlisted man's math, or counting the first and last beer, and not the ones in between. About the time our math started getting really fuzzy, was when SSG Lomio marched in and informed us that he had a mission for us. We had to go out to range 301, out in the middle of *Bum-Fuck-Egypt*, the farthest range from our camp. It was a horrible trip there and back, no matter how you looked at it. It could be upwards of a 4–5 hour mission if things went south.

He *voluntold* me and Devo to sign-out our weapons and our NVDs (night vision devices). Dread befell us. We tried to tell him that we were drunk and in no condition to go on a mission. He insisted and said, *"THEN DON'T GET PULLED OVER."* Herein lies proof that driving a military vehicle whilst drunk was not always *my choice* of approved activities, like driving the half-track on Organization Day. Sometimes, it was thrust upon me like a football-bat. I knew this was going to be *FUBAR*, or *fucked up beyond all recognition*.

We signed for our weapons and two sets of NVDs, but the armorer had no batteries. Fucking great! We were supposed to drive a 5-ton truck loaded down with live ammunition, in black-out drive without functioning NVDs, whilst drunk as a skunk. Black-out drive is operating a vehicle in a tactical state, or only with the assistance of tiny, AAA-battery-sized lights. They worked great with NVDs, not so much without. Uncle Sam always had a plan, right?

Devo and I drive out to range 301 and pick up the ammo. Two-plus hours had passed, so sobriety was inching its way in. We were still deep in the proverbial creek of shit, though. We knew we could almost make it back to camp and still salvage our buzz if we could finish the mission in time. Mind you, there is a speed limit in Graf, a very strict one. I believe it was 15 mph at night and 25 during the day. The MPs were assholes in Graf back then, and they would give you a ticket for farting too fast. Getting a ticket in a military vehicle spells huge trouble for any soldier, especially in our condition.

Naturally, in my semi-drunken stupor, I decided to speed things up a little, as we didn't see shit for MPs on the way out. The moon did offer enough light to see the tank trails, especially since our eyes were well-adjusted to the darkness. I turned off my blackout lights and sped it up to about 30 mph. The truck was loud as fuck, so we were not sneaking up on anything. I then inched it up to 40 mph. In my mind, I had worked it all out…*No, officer, I didn't see the speed limit signs, the batteries died in my NVDs.* I didn't realize I was doing 25 mph above the speed limit. It sounds as stupid now, as it did then.

Finally, I thought, if I'm going to get a ticket and get arrested for drunk driving, I'm doing it properly. I wouldn't say I eased it up after this, I'd say, I put the pedal-to-the-metal, or the heel-to-the-steel. I had that 5-ton cruising along at a comfortable 55 mph, sloshing through the loose sand and gravel of Graf's finest tank trails. Devo was like, *"I WILL TELL THEM THAT I ADVISED YOU AGAINST THIS, TURNER."*

"I KNOW, FUCKER," was my reply.

I was pretty much going to wind up in Coleman Confinement at the rate I was going (Coleman Confinement is one of four level-one, U.S. Army prisons around the world). Still, I trucked on. I was making killer time, and we could hear the beer calling our names, more so, my own. Then my little world spiraled towards the abyss as I could see black-out drive lights quickly approaching our six.

I said, *"OH, FUCK, DEVO. I'M FUCKING BUSTED, DUDE. I HAVE A SET OF BLACKOUT LIGHTS THAT ARE ALL OVER MY ASS. I BETTER GO AHEAD AND PULL OVER, BEFORE THEY HIT THE SIREN."*

Devo wasted no time in taking on a fatherly tone. *"I FUCKING TOLD YOU, TURNER. IT'S YOUR ASS, NOT MINE."*

I extinguished my cigarette into the oil drip can on the floor, which normally sat beneath the front axle when the vehicle was parked. I backed off the throttle and mentally prepared my defense. I was nearly stopped when I finally got an earful of what was on my ass. I heard him clutch in, give it a quick-shot of throttle, and then drop a gear.

"FUCK ME. IT'S A DEUCE-AND-A-HALF, NOT A HMMWV. I'M GOING TO BULLSHIT MY WAY OUT OF THIS," I said confidently to my shotgun.

"HEY, TURNER, JUST SO YOU KNOW, THE MILITARY POLICE DRIVE DEUCES, TOO," Devo quickly retorted.

I stopped for a second and said to myself, *Nah, no they don't.* My asshole did pucker up a little after he said that, but oh, well, I was committed now. *"BULLSHIT THEY DO, DEVO."*

I range walked back as the driver of the Deuce popped off his NVDs, jumped out, and asked, *"IS EVERYTHING OK?"*

I said, *"YEAH, IS EVERYTHING OKAY WITH YOU? WHY'D YOU STOP?"* I played it real cool.

He asked, *"YOU'RE NOT BROKE DOWN?"*

I said, *"NO. I THOUGHT YOU WERE THE MPs."*

We then shot the shit for a minute or two, when I told him I was cruising at 55 mph, asking him how fast he had been travelling. He told me that he was doing better than 65. I called bullshit, and he said his Deuce *may* be modified just a teensy-weensy bit. I asked if he'd thought about overtaking my truck before I pulled to the shoulder.

"I HAD CONSIDERED IT," he said, half-serious, half-joking. I believe to this day, given a good straightaway, he would have taken me. As he said, his NVDs were functioning perfectly. He was a little shocked when I told him I didn't have NVDs. He climbed into his Deuce and said, *"AND I THOUGHT I WAS CRAZY. KEEP UP IF YOU CAN."* I ran back up to my truck, threw it in gear, and floored it. That Deuce left me in his dust. I kept up for the first five or so curves, and then he was long gone.

We made it back to the barracks area, and Lomio looked at his watch and said, *"FUCK ME, YOU GUYS WENT TO THE WRONG RANGE."* A strange look fell across his face, as he looked again at his watch and, haphazardly, asked, *"RANGE 301? ALREADY?"*

We nodded yes.

"I DON'T EVEN WANT TO FUCKING KNOW, DO I?"

We shook our heads, no. He bought our first beer, as the count was reset back to another enlisted-inspired mathematical equation. God, how I loved enlisted man's math.

39

FROM BLOOD AND GUTS TO BASTOGNE

Another wonderful aspect of being stationed in Europe was the U.S.O. (United Services Organization; a non-profit program to aid soldiers and their families and a place to relax when off-duty). They sponsored these wonderful day and weekend bus tours to various places around Europe. Back then they were mostly historical and military-related tours. In my research for this book, I recently read they have discontinued a lot of their shorter tours around Europe. Granted, our presence there now is not as robust as it was then. It was an inexpensive way to see some of the rich military and civilian history of Europe and of the many wars fought there, especially World Wars I & II. The guided tours of the battle sights were tremendously informative.

Spud and I took one of these tours to Bastogne, Belgium, to see the site of the Battle of the Bulge. The really cool part was that we stopped in these little towns along the way to see monumentalized WWII tanks, anti-aircraft guns, and statues, stopping for coffee and lunch in the local cafes. I wished I had plotted our route better, noting these smaller towns and places.

I do remember us stopping in Hamm, Luxembourg City, Luxembourg, to visit the Luxembourg American Cemetery and Memorial. There rests, whom many consider the father of United States Armor, Old Blood and Guts, Bandito, The Old Man, Georgie, or as we know him, General George S. Patton. The cemetery is a time-standing testament to the sacrifices the common American soldier made to liberate Europeans from the last Nazi stranglehold. In that cemetery alone, there are twenty-two examples of brothers buried, side-by-side, in the confines of its fifty-plus acres of white marble headstones. They stand in stark contrast to the dark headstones of the German soldiers from that battle, buried less than three kilometers away.

We continued into Belgium, stopping just outside of Bastogne to walk a length of the famous *La voie de la Liberté*, or Liberty Road. It is a string of *borne* (French for markers), commemorating the *footsteps of freedom* of Patton's Third Army. There are 1,146 markers placed at every kilometer along the path of the Allied invasion, beginning at Saint Marie du Mont, France (D-Day), continuing through Luxembourg, and ending in Bastogne. The markers were suggested by Guy de la Vasselais, a French liaison officer attached to General Patton. The paint was thick, rugged, and aged on many of the markers, but the torch of liberty was clearly visible in the cast monuments. Some were a simple white, while others were beautifully painted in vibrant red, white, and blue.

We came to a large Fourth Armored Division plaque outside of a simple two-story home. I believe I remember it being yellow and brown, very non-descript. Across the street was a large, scenic, open field. The bus driver parked in front of the house and sent us backtracking to the memorial, perhaps 25 meters, which seemed odd at the time. After we looked the plaque over, we returned to the bus to find that the driver had spoken to the resident of the home. He informed us that she was returning in a few moments to give us something. We were intrigued.

This little *Oma* (German for grandmother) stepped out of her door with a large tray of glasses, one for each of us. Inside each glass was a shot of *Apfelkorn* (schnapps-like German liqueur). Oma's was not like the German stuff we were used to, as hers was a *damn* potent recipe. The guide explained that she made this herself. I wanted her family recipe, but no such luck.

She then explained to us that she had been a young girl living in the home with her family during the siege of Bastogne, telling us how they hid in the basement while tanks and soldiers waged war outside. She explained there was some damage to the home, but relatively minimal when compared to the battlefield. The bullet holes had long since been repaired by her father.

One thing that really stood out to me, was her recounting their hiding in the basement, and the dust falling from between the basement rafters as the tanks and grenades exploded near their home. She said it was a terrifying ordeal. Joe and I felt honored to have shared her history and Apfelkorn with her that day. Often, humanity needs to be reminded of what the world has been through, in order to starkly realize how fortunate we are in today's world.

After this, we drove to the pillbox, or bunker, where the 101st Airborne were rescued by the Fourth Armored Division, thus breaking the encirclement of Bastogne. It is a tiny thing that stands to this day and where General McAuliffe famously said, *"NUTS,"* when the Germans asked him to surrender.

Then we drove to the Mardasson Memorial located near the Bastogne War Museum. It's a humongous structure shaped like an American star. Engraved in it are each of the, then, forty-eight states and the names of the soldiers that were either wounded or gave their life in the pursuit of a Nazi-free Europe. It was a moving monument, as there is an unfathomable *76,890* names of American heroes that sacrificed so much for freedom.

40

BIRTHDAY IN BAD KREUZNACH

It was August of my first summer in Deutschland. The weather was beautiful, and I was loving life. Who'd have imagined I would be spending my nineteenth birthday living in another country? I certainly did not. I cannot remember a more fun time in my life. While my civilian buddies back home were doing the American thing, I was doing the European thing—living and breathing in the cultures of France, Poland, Belgium, and so many other places around Germany. Life couldn't get much better than this.

Several of us from First Armored Division were chosen for a detail (or mission), at First Armored Division Headquarters. We were to be makeshift casualties and secondary evaluators for medics trying to earn their EFMB (Expert Field Medical Badge). Next to actual combat experience, it was the test of their medical abilities. Upon successful completion, it meant they could prescribe ibuprofen faster than wet shit sliding off of a warm shovel.

The Army is notoriously famous for prescribing ibuprofen for a plethora of diagnoses such as: sore muscles, headaches, contusions, severe fractures, bleeding out of your eyeballs, multiple amputations, poisonous spiders breeding in your skull, sprains, neurosurgeries, crushed limbs, fatally infected blisters, cardiovascular explosions, diabetes, excessive flatulence, heartburn, gonorrhea, Tourette's, and last, but not least, a shaving profile. What is a shaving profile, my civilian readers might ask? A soldier had to be clean-shaven when reporting for duty, less a regulation moustache, but some troops would get these bumps on their necks, or breakouts from irritated hairs. Essentially, they were allowed to keep a five-o'clock shadow in order to mitigate these bumps, thus, a shaving profile.

There were, maybe, twenty of us from 3-77, twenty from our sister unit, 5-77, a few from 4-68 Maintenance, etc., etc. Each unit was set up near their respective lanes, and each lane was designated a different scenario upon which to test the EFMB candidates. I played a combination casualty, suffering from a sucking chest wound and a compound fracture to my fibula. It was rather boring seeing medic-after-medic come through your lane, either failing miserably or passing with flying colors. All-in-all, it was evaluating the basics of their aptitude, should we be deployed into a combat zone.

It was a proper training facility, set up in the beautiful, wooded, rolling hills on the outskirts of Bad Kreuznach. It is a very beautiful part of Germany. The detail consisted of lower-enlisted guys, like myself, with one NCO in charge of us, SGT Travis. He was single and lived right across the hall from me back in Mannheim. He was definitely one of the cool NCOs, as he could be found drinking it up with the boys, even though upper-management would frown on such behavior. He was soon due to ETS (Expiration of Term of Service), or *Getting the Fuck Out of the Army*, so his *give-a-fuck-o-meter* was pegged out in a vacuum at less than zero.

We had two GP medium (General Purpose) tents configured end-to-end, in a long rectangle, hitched together as a single unit. About 25-meters from our tent, 5-77 had theirs configured much the same way. Approximately 50 meters from us and 25-meters from 5-77 sat a single GP large tent. It housed the head honcho, a Staff Sergeant. She was in charge of the entire detail comprised from First Armored Division. By strange coincidence, she was also the wife of our own medic, PLT Daddy. We were, by proxy, her golden children of the detail. She was an E-6, and the only female in the lot of sixty or so guys comprising the detail. This was our first real experience working with, or for, a woman in the military.

It appeared that she was no ball-breaker either, as she was timid, soft-spoken, and very sweet-natured. She was a nice looking black woman with a very pretty smile, and an attitude that was confident and relaxed in a large group of young male soldiers. Our NCO, SGT Travis, was a tall, well-spoken guy, who seemingly knew his way around a woman. It appeared that she was smitten with Travis, thus she is aptly named SSG Smitten.

I wouldn't go so far as to say anything happened between the two, but he did exactly as I'd have done in that situation and took full-advantage of it. She favored us. It was a beautiful arrangement for us, and it would look pretty bad on her, to have thrown us *under the bus* for any minor, or major, infraction. Did we take some advantage of this situation? You better fucking believe it, brothers and sisters. It was prime-time for crime-time for yours truly, and his band of merry pranksters.

Our daily life was pretty drone and bore, watching the medics act out their spiel. It wasn't like we were waking up at the ass-crack of dawn to go running or pound our faces with push-ups, but it had its challenges. We woke up, got dressed, ate chow, and then moseyed to our lane, to then sit on our asses and evaluate medics. They had a gauntlet of core-tasks to perform, maybe ten, or eleven, in total. I was but *one* lane, with three-to-five guys to each lane.

I remember this captain—in fact, we all remember this particular captain—as she was a bombshell. We had never seen anything like her in an Army uniform. We were like giddy schoolboys, even though we were the evaluators. We were definitely hot for teacher. Blond hair, big blue eyes, and making a BDU uniform look sexy as fuck. We were not used to seeing soldiers like this, so we were all-eyes on her.

Given that I was suffering a sucking chest wound, I had to be maneuvered from a position of lying flat on my back, to an upright position, to facilitate aid to my chest wound. Boy, did I ever deserve an award for playing a wounded soldier. I was helpless in her beautiful arms. I was putty. Hey, before you judge, remember that I was eighteen and horny, so cheap thrills were hard to come by. Hard to come by…okay, no pun intended, but I should have inserted one. Dammit, inserted one…another pun to the wayside. I was, to some degree, a professional soldier, I promise. I was just a horny one. Back then, I was always bad company around a beautiful woman.

We were all in the same boat, as none of us had seen anything as lovely as her in camouflage. All told, we knew we never had a chance with her, but it didn't mean we were devoid of having some impure thoughts about a fellow sister-in-arms. So, sue me.

This detail was not like others in terms of training, gunnery, etc. It was like field time, but we were only four or five clicks (or kilometers) from Bad Kreuznach proper, meaning we could, without permission, go to town after evaluations were completed for the day. We were living in tents, without electricity and the normal creature comforts of the barracks, but it didn't mean that we were not in possession of civilian clothes (or civvies). One never knew when a just-in-case situation would present itself. Like the old adage, a good soldier is always prepared. We were good soldiers, just good soldiers with a hard hankering for pussy, beer, and nightlife.

I think the whole affair was about two weeks long, so it must've taken us only a few days (likely hours) to realize that we could get away with murder under SSG Smitten's command. We were not going to let some rule, like everyone had to stay in the detail area throughout the entire two weeks, hold us back. We were free Americans, dammit. Who were they to tell us that we couldn't walk a few miles through the woods of Germany to grab a beer, or ten, or twelve, or who the fuck even counts such ridiculous things? No SGM field problem math on this one! We viewed those rules as more of a challenge, really. As evaluators on an important mission, we were forming the irreplaceable bonds of esprit de corps, which far outranked any rules and regulations that leadership may have laid down. Did we push the envelope to the absolute brink? You can bet the fucking rent check on it. Besides, what kind of trouble could a small detail, away from the prying eyes of our direct chain-of-command get into, really? Hold my beer!

As one entered our tent, my mug was the first to greet them. The first time SSG Smitten entered the tent unannounced, I was, naturally, the first to see her and set the tone for all future visits. As she entered, she found me standing in my boxers and flip-flops, center-aisle, hand down my boxers scratching away at my sweaty balls, cigarette hanging from my lips. She looked a bit surprised, especially when I didn't break stride and kept scratching away. Lips pursed, I smiled through the rising smoke and said hello as she inched past me. We all flirted with her in a fun way, because we were, vicariously through her husband, her boys, too. After that, she was prone to giving us a courtesy shout before entering. It made no difference, as she enjoyed the attention, as much as we enjoyed laying it on thicker and thicker with each passing day.

The first test of how much we could really get away with came on the evening of my nineteenth birthday. We were going into town, damned be the powers that would stand in the way. Like a true leader, SGT Travis took one for the team. He decided he would stave off any and all interference from SSG Smitten that evening, by hanging out with her until after she made her final round through all the individual unit tents. We showered and got dressed into our civvies. The mission started at my cot and continued through the length of the tent towards the exit into the woods. There was an *impossibly catchy mission* tune being hummed along the way, so everyone was privy to the black-operations at-hand. *Dunt…dun, dun, dun. Dunt.* Cue flute: *doot-doot-doot…do-do-doooo.* I know, now that jingle is stuck in your head. You're welcome. It does help set the tone, for the mission was nearly impossible.

As it was still daylight when we departed, it translated to our making the trek in a very cloak-and-dagger manner. We were in quite a pickle as we left, as (a) we were not supposed to be running around in civvies; (b) we were not supposed to be running around in civvies while leaving the camp, to go and get drunk for my birthday; and (c) we had to play cat-and-mouse through the entire training area to pull this mission off. There were five of us, so our modus operandi of the evening was, don't get caught in or out.

We foraged through the woods for the perfect path to freedom. Ducking, bobbing, and weaving our way through abandoned trenches and tree lines to keep our civvies clean and not get captured. The first part of our plan was a success, so we relaxed our highly trained, animal-like senses. Five senses, *pffff*, we had closer to six, maybe even seven. We were trained killers, but mostly killers of livers, brain-cells, and the hearts of beautiful, young *fräuleins* (a now outdated German word for unwed women).

We were well out of enemy range when we came upon this large field. It was several acres of wide-open, semi-flat land. But, we were not alone. We stumbled upon a huge automobile meeting of the British *miniature-type*, all from the 1960s, nearly three hundred of them. Some were driven there in daily-driver condition, and others were in pristine, showroom quality. It was quite a spectacle. I'd have loved to stay with those guys and ogle over their cars, beer-in-hand, but town was calling and light was fading. We continued through the woods and hills towards our goal.

We reached town and decided to grab a beer at the first place we found. It was a little hole in the wall imbiss (street food stand). They are small, usually family-operated, street stands offering several würste (sausages) and sauerkraut options, among other German fare. This happened to be a Turkish imbiss, offering Döner Kebabs (A.K.A. gyro; not gyro as in gyroscope, but gir- rō).

No story about being stationed in Germany would be complete without at least an honorable mention to the ever-famed Döner kebab. The difference in the ones you find in America, versus Europe, are the fresher ingredients of those from the latter, as well as the meat. In Europe, the dürüm (bread) is generally prepared in old-world fashion, or handmade, and not in a factory. The meat is predominantly lamb, not beef, which changes the taste entirely, and for the better, I might add. It's juicier, more flavorful, and traditionally, more appropriate to what it would've tasted like a hundred years ago.

"EIN BIER UND EIN DÖNER, BITTE. OHNE ZWIEBEL." (One beer and Döner, without onions, please.) One did not simply walk up and order a kebab, like at a fast food joint. No, no. One had to wait as the attendant prepared your order, which took time. He would start up the vertical rotisserie and sear the lamb to a crisp brown, while the bread baked in the oven. After a pocket was cut into the bread, they would slice off, in near transparent morsels, little slivers of lamb that fell into the fresh bread. He would then squirt a tzatziki-style cucumber sauce onto the meat, and then top it all off with some lettuce and tomato. It was a taste of beauty, truly the perfect drinking food.

Whoa, got a little lost down Memory Lane there for a moment. If you were ever stationed there, I know your mouth is watering and you're dreaming about a Döner right now, aren't you? A warm Döner, wrapped in a little piece of aluminum foil in one hand, a local Hefe-Weißen in the other. Perhaps you are walking down the street, or sitting on the Straßenbahn with your girlfriend beside you. Maybe she's holding your bier for you. I know you can now see that Döner in your hand. Maybe the sauce is dripping out a little. You can almost smell it, right?

Don't hate me because I'm beautiful, hate me because I'm an asshole. If that were true, from here on out I'd throw the word Döner randomly into the text of the manuscript in some obscure place just to serve as a reminder of one of the wonderful things we all miss about Germany, but I'm not that kind of asshole. You're welcome.

We wound up venturing into a club or two, but they didn't really suit us that night. I do, however, still have a coin from one of the clubs for a free drink. It was a holographic coin with the club name on one side, and on the other, a naked animated girl controlling a string tied to a guy's pecker. Yes, there was/is some weird shit over there. We then ventured nearer to division HQs and found this up-scale bar that, literally, had not a single soul in it. We almost continued walking, but instead opted to have a drink in the comforts of air-conditioning for a change.

No sooner than we entered, the bartender informed us that he was about to close-up for the night. We begged him to let us in for one drink, explaining that it was my birthday and we wanted to celebrate with *one* proper drink in a nice place, not a club. He self-debated, before taking pity on us. He would allow us in for *one* drink. I know, I know, famous last words.

The place was a bit more upscale than the haunts to which we were accustomed. The bartender was a cool, slightly older, German guy. He said, he rarely had soldiers in, but would actually enjoy some company while he closed up. We asked him if he would suggest a birthday drink for us…what his favorite drink was. *"EINE MOMENT"* (one moment), he exclaimed. We waited.

He returned with a bottle of local white wine for us to share. I still have that bottle to this day. We poured that down our maws and waited while he clanged and clamored behind the bar. He then returned with a tray full of mind-erasers. It's a wicked good concoction made with vodka, coffee liqueur, and a club-style, clear soda, all layered and designed to be consumed with a straw. First the taste of coffee to thicken the pallet, then vodka to get you wasted, then soda to wash it all down. They were like liquid candy. I had never heard of these things, but they were doing the trick and quickly earned its name.

After a few of these, we started getting a little boisterous, which was, normally, cause for alarm in a swank place like this, but the bartender was so cool about it all. Even after a couple of other patrons entered the bar, he allowed us to carry on in a loud, drunken, soldierly fashion. It was awesome. The other patrons departed, and the bartender wrapped up his bar-closing duties. We invited him to join us for a celebratory drink, to which he accepted and obliged, but not before locking the front door. The party was on as he poured another round for us all.

He quickly downed his drink before turning up the volume on the jukebox that blared out classic American rock and roll. Then, we all proceeded to get absolutely stupid drunk. When I say stupid drunk, I mean sloppy, stumbling about like a plastic chair in a hurricane kind of drunk. We must have been ridiculously entertaining to the flies on the wall. I would love to see the security footage from that night. We were drinking shots of every variety—beer, wine, and booze. It was disgustingly beautiful. I think the bar tab was about DM25 each, which was preposterously cheap, given the amount of booze we downed. I think he appreciated the lively company and the party atmosphere that followed us through the door. It was one *helluva* nineteenth birthday bash in Bad Kreuznach.

I vaguely remember the bartender calling us a taxi. The driver needed an address to deliver us to, but we didn't have one. He was very suspect about delivering a large, drunken group of soldiers to an undisclosed location in the wooded hillsides outside of town. We knew there was a paved road leading to the miniature car show, so we knew we could get relatively close to our destination. That was a wonderful part about being a soldier; even in our drunken states, we knew exactly where we were and how to get back to where we belonged, as we'd been trained to always keep mental tabs on our whereabouts.

Much to the chagrin of our comrades, our return home that night was with a much louder and drunker impossible mission tune being hummed, moaned, and grunted as we entered the tent. Boos and hisses, along with other fine adjectives, were being tossed around like a baseball at spring training. We didn't sneak in, near as well as we'd snuck out. I passed out in my civvies, for our lovely SSG Smitten to see the following morning.

Our military-mom, Mrs. SSG Smitten, gave us a bit of an ass chewing that next morning, but no harm, no foul, as we made formation, albeit, *drunk-over*. We smelled like the gutters of a town that housed a brewery, distillery, and vineyard, all while suffering the throes of a Prohibition-era raid. No doubt, we were rancid with the stench of booze. I'm sure the candidates we evaluated that next day received a contact-buzz from our breathing on them.

It blew over like a single cloud on a sunny day. SSG Smitten was happy after our schmoozing leader, SGT Travis, eased her concerns around lunchtime. She couldn't stay mad at us, but she could certainly be re-angered by our other shenanigans!

BIRD IS THE WORD!

It didn't take long for us to wriggle out of the birthday bash before we cooked up another scheme to test the waters of our *fearful* leader. Playing nice for a day or two led to boredom, which, as all soldiers know, is the hunting ground of old Lucifer himself. So we decided to cook up some old-fashioned fun for everyone.

I have no clue who commandeered it, but somehow, somewhere, someone came up with a shiny silver War Eagle (or full-bird colonel rank). It is one of the most recognizable ranks in the Army. It's also one of the highest, as it's right beneath a general. It is a left-facing eagle, clutching arrows; thus it is known as a War Eagle. Wings in hand, our devious minds cooked-up a plan, much to the dismay of someone else's dissatisfaction. Who could pull off such a feat? Certainly not yours truly. I looked like a seventh grader, less the pimples. It certainly wasn't going to be SGT Travis, as he was as obvious as a man with a set of double-D tits.

Fortunately, we found a willing participant to impersonate a full-bird colonel. Now this may not sound like a big deal to my civilian readers, but trust me when I say, it's a huge fucking deal. It could get us into a lot of trouble, but namely, it could get the guy actually performing this ludicrous idea into much bigger trouble. It is punishable under the *Uniformed Code of Military Justice; Article 134: Impersonating a Commissioned, Warrant or Non-Commissioned, or Petty Officer or an Agent or Official.* I have no clue what the punishment would entail, but I'm pretty sure it amounts to nothing less than a loss of rank and pay, as well as a possible court-martial depending on the severity and extent of the impersonation. Ours was for fun, not spy-level shit.

Now, who would be the likeliest of recipients for such a marauding masquerade of comic-relief? Yes, you guessed it—our sister unit and our lovely military mother, Mrs. SSG Smitten. We decided to pounce on 5-77 first. We formed a plan that would be perfect during the hours of dusk, that mixture of bright light and dark shadows. See, we were tactical beasts. The guys would be relaxing in their tent, thus never expecting a colonel to waltz right in.

We eased over. I walked into their tent, amidst many weird looks. I then came to the position of attention and called out in a firm voice,

"GROUP, ATTENTION." They looked at me like I was bat-shit crazy, as they knew my face at this point. They thought it was a joke. There were guys lounging around in their skivvies or a towel in preparation of a shower, reading fuck-books (for my young readers that translates to pornographic magazines), while others were getting ready for the next day or wrestling around with their buddies. It was the poster-child for unpreparedness if ever there were one. They never saw it coming. Granted, who would have?

I continued to get these weird looks until Craig walked in with his brim pulled low over his eyes and that big, shiny, War Eagle standing out on his soft cap. Those guys jumped up and out of their skin, as though God himself had walked through the flaps of their tent. It smelled like dip, cigarettes, feet, and ass, and only lacked beer cans and bongs on the floor to look like the aftermath of a frat party. It did not take long for word to reach the other side of the tent, that some serious rank had entered their AO.

"CARRY ON, GENTLEMEN," Craig said in his best baritone, all the while stifling laughter. Our small entourage simply walked behind the colonel as he inspected their quarters.

We had our fun with 5-77, and they were none the wiser as we completed our quick walk-thru. Bad news travels fast, though, as it didn't take a Hong Kong minute to reach SSG Smitten's tent. We were in route, as she barreled out of her tent, still buttoning her BDU blouse. She was so flustered and in such a hurry, the alignment of her buttons to eyelets was offset, making her technically out-of-uniform to greet the colonel—a big no-go in the Army. Her headgear was crooked atop her head, giving notice to her nervous eyes as she exited.

She looked at Craig for a moment and then it hit her like hammer striking an anvil. She knew she'd been had, by none other than her beloved, Silver Knights. She smiled for a second, and then was on the warpath for SGT Travis. It didn't look good for us, but, per usual, it was soon smoothed over and she laughed it off.

Silver Knights—2: SSG Smitten—0.

OPERATION SCATTER...ASSHOLES!

The colonel incident should have told us that we were skating on thin ice, but who in the hell learns when they're miles ahead? It certainly wasn't our gaggle of drunks. Our heads were as thick as tank armor those last couple of days on the detail.

Boredom, the devil's playground, was again running a course through our devious, one-tracked minds, so we cooked up crazier ideas. We were trying to come up with something to fuck with our, you guessed it, sister unit...poor bastards. It was another beautiful afternoon in the woods near Bad Kreuznach, as we sat outside our tent preparing dinner. We had MREs for breakfast, MREs for lunch, and MREs for dinner, which translates to not shitting for a full month during and after the detail was completed.

The only difference during this field problem was we had unlimited access to FRHs (Flameless Ration Heaters), used to heat up our MREs. Essentially, it was a plastic bag with a perforated wafer inside, and when mixed with water, would form a chemical reaction to heat up the main course. It was a small, but relatively significant luxury, as we were unaccustomed to having them. However, when time permitted, it was nice (I never thought I would use the adjective *nice* to describe an Army meal) to have a hot meal in the field. I think I had the Chicken-Ala-King that night, my favorite of the shit options. You would have to knead the contents, drop it in the bag, add water, wait for ten-minutes, and then dig in.

As we sat waiting on our meals, we were inspired with a stroke of brilliance. One of the more experienced guys, James "Shadow" Yura, remarked about something they often did in the first Gulf War when our barracks/unit was 8th Infantry Division (their unit crest was an upward arrow going through the number 8, so naturally, we as soldiers, using the polite term for fucked-up, used *eight-up*, or *ate-up* [as in, ate-up with the dumbass] in its stead), thus our ears perked up and our eyes widened in anticipation of this wonderful concoction to combat boredom warfare. We listened with the kind of intent rarely found in human beings, as if we were learning the secrets of producing fire or conjuring beer at the snap of our fingers. As Shadow spoke, our hair blackened, our skin turned red, and horns sprouted from our heads. Cloven hooves took the place of our feet, pointed tails emerged from our backsides, and our minds morphed into grotesque breeding grounds for diabolical plans. Insert demonic, hallowed laughs here.

Like any great military operation, we had to account for all the items necessary to implement our strategy. If we were going to execute our plan successfully and be properly vindicated, it was absolutely necessary that the entire division know about it, or rather, hear about it. Fuck that, they needed to hear *it*, not just hear *about* it.

We tallied up all the FRHs we had available and scraped together some thick, plastic juice bottles of the alli-*gator* variety. Hint, hint, wink, wink. Bottles: check. Twenty-four heaters: check. Hundred-mile-an-hour tape: check. We had enough wares to produce three FRH bombs. Again, I feel it necessary to ask my fine readers, what good were three makeshift bombs going to do anyone? No good, whatsoever, was going to come of this, but hey, it's the dumb shit that makes for a great adventure.

Then began the daunting task of breaking up the wafers into smaller pieces. We divvied them equally into the containers, and then rolled hundred-mile-an-hour tape around the bottom and sides of each, to strengthen the bomb casing, as it were. We then readied enough tape to secure the cap to each bottle. It had to be enough tape to allow the cap to withstand the pressures of the chemical reaction; otherwise, the cap would've popped too soon, thus deflating the bomb aspect of our plan. This was going to be a high-speed, low-drag mission, that we would call, Operation Scatter…Assholes!

We assigned two men to each bomb. One man to ready the water and steady the bottle, and the second to secure the tape over the cap after the water was added. We had no idea how long the chemical reaction would take, how big or small the blast would be, or what their reaction would be, but we had a plan and we had to trust the plan. Always trust the plan!

As it was still daylight, we ran the risk of getting caught. It was a highly sensitive operation that exposed a lot of troops, but thankfully the sun was setting, so we had that going for us. A GP medium was 16x32 feet, but with two of them together, the structure was 64 feet long, with an access opening on each end. We would have to utilize all of the skills and tactics within the arsenal of our _Specialized High Intensity Training_ (SHIT), if we were to pull this off. Brave souls were we.

We opted for a pincer move with the bulk of our forces, two tank platoons, on one side of the tent and a single mortar platoon on the backside. In essence, walking the enemy into our tank strongholds. Okay, okay, a little dramatic. Two bombs on the front side and another to the rear. We synchronized our watches and moved into position. We staged ourselves at every fourth or fifth stake of 5-77s tent, and at the prescribed time, we poured the water and secured the caps. We staged the bombs and waited…

KABOOOOOM!!! It was fucking brilliant. Those things went off like a civil-war-era cannon. It was a thunderous roar that would strike fear into any unsuspecting victim, and our sister unit was no exception. It was more than we'd ever expected. There were no concussion waves, obviously, but it was loud as fuck. If our intent was to wake up the whole fucking division camp, then I'd say, _"MISSION ACCOMPLISHED!"_

As soon as that first one went off at the backside of their tent and several highly concerned voices could be heard echoing the same thing, *"WHAT THE FUCK WAS THAT?,"* then the second bomb exploded at the front side. That's when the real fun began, because after the second explosion, we started pulling up various tent stakes, allowing their tent to cave in on them as they were bombarded with makeshift munitions. It crumpled in on them like a boot stomping on a wet paper bag. It was beautiful. We beat-feet back to our tent as the third bomb exploded. Those guys were flying out of their tent in their skivvies, barefoot and dumbfounded. They didn't know what to think. They looked back on their collapsed tent with that *what the fuck just happened* look.

We ran back into our tent and scrambled to return to our business as usual persona, the lounging-around-the-tent look we had no doubt mastered this far into the detail. We sat there, angelic faces and postures, as if we didn't hear the three über-fucking-loud explosions that just rocked the entire division camp. Halos floated overhead when SSG Smitten quickly turned into SSG Fury and burst into our tent (unannounced, mind you). It was not pretty. She marched in and, per usual, she spotted me first, laying in my rack writing home to my dear, sweet mother.

"TURNER, I KNOW YOU'RE INVOLVED IN THIS SHIT. GET YOUR ASS OUTSIDE AND WAIT FOR ME," she said angrily. *"Y'ALL HAVE DONE IT THIS TIME…,"* trailing off as she angrily marched through the length of our tent, no doubt towards SGT Travis.

I knew the gig was up. We all did. We formed up outside and waited for her to return. She was livid as she ripped us new assholes. She knew *she* was going to have to answer for this one, as troops from the entire camp rolled in to see what war had broken out in our area. Much higher ranks than SSG were going to get involved.

As pissed as she was, scolding us at sunset, there was an undeniably hysterical aspect to watching our sister unit reassemble their tent in boxer shorts and boots. There were several stifled laughs from our vantage point. As we explained the situation to her, it was difficult for any of us to remain straight-faced. She eventually stopped trying to smile and just grinned, ear-to-ear, giggling while scolding us. Never fear, her golden children of 3-77 Armor were still safe.

Operation Scatter…Assholes was a complete success. We awarded ourselves fictitious ARCOMS (Army Commendation Medals), for TOP GUNNERY PLATOONS—TANK and MORTAR—and BRONZE STARS, for meritorious achievement to all individuals involved.

Silver Knights—3: Steel Tigers—0: SSG Smitten—½.

I had to award her something for being such a great sport about everything. She was pretty awesome to us. After that, we decided that we should calm down as we were nearing the end of the detail. Friendly comradery had won the day…5-77 Armor loathed our existence, and we loved every minute of it. All-in-all, they weren't bad guys, just a friendly rivalry that I am sure they revel in just as much as we do. Hats off to the guys of 5-77; beer and pussy to the guys of 3-77!

41

AMERICANS, GERMANS, & MEXICANS, OH, MY!

On New Year's Eve of 1993, our platoon buddies, Spive and SGT J, aside from being high-speed, low-drag soldiers, were also employed as bartenders. They worked weekends at this now defunct place called Chi-Chi's. It was a Mexican restaurant, located in Germany, but operated by Americans. Yeah, mind boggling. It was a huge restaurant and bar on the outskirts of Heidelberg. I am willing to bet they could easily hold two-hundred and fifty customers in there at one time. There was a huge country & western side of the place, where Germans, and naturally, Americans, could eat American fare, as well as line-dance and whatever else cowboys and cowgirls did in Mexican restaurants in Germany. The place was a hotbed of weird shit like that.

Thankfully, the country & western side was not where SGT J and Spive worked. To the side of the foyer was a separate, but sizable bar. The rock & roll side, we shall call it. I'll bet there were four car loads of guys from 3-77 that night, if there was one. It being New Year's Eve, it was busier than a three-legged cat trying to bury shit on a marble floor. Most were there to eat prime rib, line-dance, and listen to country music. Nothing wrong with country music. I like a lot of it, but not that night.

Enter the main doors, walk through the lobby, maybe a 20x80 foot rectangular space, and then decide which side of the bar to enter. If you went straight, you entered the country & western side; if you took an immediate left, you entered the hallway for the restrooms; and if you passed the hostess stand about thirty-to-forty feet, then turned right, you entered the rock & roll portion. 1970s thru 1990s music blared out of its confines. It was pretty bad-ass, especially with our buddies working the bar.

We entered to find Spive and SGT J dressed to the hilt, in white button-down shirts and black bowties. Very swanky. They were slinging cocktails left and right, and they were damn good at it, too. They made a phenomenal team, though they were definitely on *our* team, as far as customer-bartender relationships went. There must've been eighty-plus people in there, but we could get a drink faster than a hot knife through butter. That should be cause for alarm as we didn't take too many opportunities to actually *breathe* in between cocktails. Disaster was written…no, it was sprawled across this scene; that which would become known as my New Year's Eve debacle.

Some guys, like Spive and Fritz, brought their wives, while most of us were single soldiers looking to get laid. We had a few tables all clumped together, though Support Platoon dominated the room with a nearly twenty-man presence that was undeniable. It was SGT J, Wildman Ward, Spive, Fritz, Duffster, Vegas, O.C., Hamburger, Weatherford, Shadow, Box, Gumby, and several others from 3-77. We were in party mode, as drinks were cheap, thanks in great part to our two in-house *intoxicologists*, our resident *booze chefs*, if you will. These two indulgent dogs of war mixed-up their own brand of a famous drink, the Blue Motorcycle. They had concocted a mean, vile, and wonderful version, which would put an elephant to sleep. I think it had about seven or eight different alcohols in it; 'twas a brutal whistle-wetter, my fine readers.

They were not served in those childishly small cups, either. They were served in large glasses, whose only mission was to maim and murder your brain cells at a break-neck speed. It was the perfect recipe for cirrhosis of the liver. I, rather, we enjoyed every ounce of them. We probably arrived at Chi-Chi's around 1900 hours, in order to get a good arrangement with the rallied tables. Translation: we had five hours to liquor-up before we were to sing Auld Lang Syne. It was a tough job, but someone had to do it.

The boys behind the bar were slinging and singing, with their liquid-liver-killer, delivering a punch worthy of a title fighter. It didn't take long for them to perform their magic. We were running around like headless chickens…on fire. It was a party for the ages, no doubt. I remember someone had a video camera and, at some point, put me in charge of it. I was scaring wives and children alike. Yes, in Germany you can take your children to the bar with you. The law back then, to the best of my understanding, was that if a child could see over the counter to look the bartender in the eye, he or she could order fermented alcohol, like beer or wine, but not hard liquor. I think now it's a child of fourteen, accompanied by an adult, can drink fermented alcohol. Albeit, in limited quantities and at the discretion of the bartender. Otherwise, at eighteen years old, you can legally drink.

Anyway, I remember the motorcycles hitting me pretty hard, and about to knock me out when my buddy Gumby said, *"HERE, TURNER, TAKE A COUPLE OF THESE."*

Again, youth and zeal, or stupidity, however you want to word it, were hard at work on crafting my inner monolog of irresponsibility. Which is to say, any semblance of responsibility was as effective as a gaping hole in a boat hull. I threw a couple of these little white pills into my mouth without thinking much about it. The guy that assisted the ammunitions SGT was giving me white pills with a cross imprinted across their circular form. *Again, I ask you, what's the worst that could happen?*

Like the drinks, it didn't take long for those little white wonders to work their magic and blast me off to another planet. I guess they were, hopefully, a legal form of over-the-counter speed. For about an hour and a half, they opened up a fly-by world for me. It was as if none of the drinks were even registering on my alcohol-o-meter. I was very awake and, seemingly, not near as drunk as I once was. An added bonus was that I had bounds of energy to spare. It felt as if I could ace an Army PT test, drinks and all. Naturally, I went to the bar and ordered up a wonderful concoction of the blue variety. It went down like a cool slice of watermelon on a sweltering summer's day. Then, another, and another, until I was exactly where I was an hour earlier…drunk as fuck!

"GUMBY, CAN I HAVE A COUPLE MORE OF THOSE THINGS," were naturally my next words.

"SURE, TURNER, BUT BE CAREFUL, MAN. THIS IS PROBABLY ALL YOU SHOULD DO," was his semi-responsible response.

Foolhardy, I responded, *"I GOT IT, GUMBY. NO PROBLEM."*

I popped a couple more, all while washing them down with those beautiful blue wonders. I was having a rip-roaring time…until the night sort of took its own little turn into the unknown. I remember having a great time, laughing, singing, and drinking well towards the Eve's festivities. The drinks were flowing, I was impervious to alcohol's effects, thanks to the Beelzebub's aspirin, but, at some point, clearly, I had succumbed to the blue motorcycles. I am thankful for the video footage of this psycho-circus that did survive, and also thankful that the internet didn't exist back then.

It couldn't have been too much after midnight when I was tossed into the back of Duffster's car, a really sweet-sounding M5. That thing sang a beautiful soundtrack in every single, manually-operated gear and at any speed, too. I remember passing out for the evening as I fuzzily eye-balled the back of his passenger seat. I knew I'd had too much to drink, obviously, but I have no recollection whatsoever of the thirty-minute drive from Heidelberg back to Mannheim. At nineteen years old, it was a good night. I was so proud that I had lived up to one of my many earned nicknames, *Iron Gut McKenzie*. I can only imagine it was Vegas Brad that gave me that, as I rarely, if ever regurgitated good alcohol. As my longest running roommate, he would know.

My final memory, at some ungodly hour in the morning, was waking up in the barracks. Problem was, it wasn't in my rack. To enter our building, you'd have to ascend a half-flight of stairs to enter the first floor level. Then a normal flight for the second floor, where I lived. It was dark when I came to, my head was chin-to-chest, and I was still FUBAR and discombobulated beyond belief. There was no inner monolog, only silence, as my brain aroused itself.

A persistent noise gradually hit my partially inhibited consciousness. I could hear two clicks. Two clicks that were almost in unison; ever so close to being perfectly synchronized with one another. It was a distinct and discernible, *cl-click…cl-click…cl-click…cl-click*. My brain began deducing any and all of my known *cl-click* sounds of memories past. It drew a complete blank as my brain was devoid of any computing power, whatsoever. All my hippocampus needed was a room for rent sign, hanging about my neck. Inner monolog began with the normal response to any situation in a soldier's life, *What the fuck is that?* To which of course I replied, *I haven't a fucking clue you über-drunk asshole! What is wrong with you for getting this drunk?* No reply.

Next question: *How the fuck did this even happen, Turner, and what the fuck is that clicking noise?* You see, the cross bars were deployed, the lights flashed, and traffic had stopped, but there wasn't a train barreling down the tracks…for miles and miles.

I opened my eyes to reveal that my feet were floating on air and weren't actually walking at all. I was capable of doing exactly shit. *Had I been canonized?* I thought. No, way. *Had I reincarnated as an angel?* Not a fucking chance, you idiot. *Had I learned to fly in my drunken stupor?* Self, you are a fucking retard.

It was a dream. That's it, a dream, I thought. But a dream, after feeling what could be compared to awakening from a state of comatose? Fuck that, no way. *Self, stop asking and answering questions that are, by sheer participation, idiotic and proof of your drunken lunacy.*

What the, where the fuck, who in the Sam Hell… I looked to my left and saw my hand and arm firmly grasped around another person's shoulder, in order to support yours truly. I clumsily looked to my right to find the same scenario. My head bobbled around like a dashboard doll on a four-wheeler, yet my body seemed lifeless and incapable of functioning. I finally recognized that it was a couple of my buddies carrying me up the stairs. Still, that ever-present noise was in my head. I finally gave up on trying to hold my head up and relaxed it into its original position of chin-to-chest, eyes closed. Like an old specter in a creaky house, the noise returned, *cl-click…cl-click….*

I reopened my eyes to try and see what this incessant noise was. I thought I would let my eyes follow what my ears were hearing. Ingenious, I know. Even with the darkness of both the stairwell and my brain working tirelessly against me, the answer came….It was like a long overdue turd after a week of exclusively eating MREs. As my buddies carried me up each and every step, my lifeless toes were clicking on the riser portion of each step. I laughed out loud, as if I'd just heard the punch line to a great joke. I'm sure it was more akin to a cackling hyena in my self-induced motorcycle psychopathy. I then began an incomprehensible dialog with my brothers until they threw me in my rack and I, assuredly, began dreaming of God only knows. I was down and out for the count. The referee called it as soon as my head hit the pillow.

The next morning, albeit late, I woke up and felt like a fresh pile of dog shit. I felt awful, as I should have for punishing my mind and body as I had. I was never one of those guys that woke up the morning after a hard night's drinking, wailing like a little bitch. *"OH, THAT'S THE LAST TIME I EVER DRINK THAT MUCH. I PROMISE. YADDY, YADDY, YA."* That was never me. I never did appreciate the idea of lying to myself about something I knew damn-well was never going to happen. In the future, I would simply drink more water in between each drink, or drink less (albeit, a rare option, but, an option), and certainly without the assistance of those little white demon-imps.

I stumbled down the hall to the latrine and did some *last eve recycling*. I think my piss was even blue. I returned to our room, chugged some water, and smoked a couple of cigarettes whilst sitting on the couch. I was hell, froze-over. Then, my buddy woke up and started cracking-up laughing at me. *"IT LIVES,"* he said. *"HOW YOU FEELING, TURNER? LIKE SHIT, I BET?"*

I made some small talk with him before he cut in and said, *"YOU ARE A FUCKING ANIMAL, TURNER. HOW ARE YOU EVEN ALIVE TODAY?"* I asked him what he meant. He gave me a confused look and asked if I remembered the fiasco of the night before.

I told him I remembered most of it. *"WHY? WHAT DID I DO?"* This opened an entirely different dialog to what my memory served up, as I now struggled to recall some of my actions.

His eyes widened as he said, *"DUDE. YOU ALMOST HAD ALL OF US THROWN OUT OF THE PLACE."* My mind raced for an answer, but I came up with fuzziness in lieu of hard evidence. He went to the latrine and returned with an eye-opening tale. My mind went in-and-out of memory lane, shockingly reliving my tirade of white crosses washed down with blue motorcycles. My eyes searched the room in failed hopes of it jogging my brain. As he began telling the tale of my evening, I noticed the garish cartoon-like cloud bubbles floating above my head, playing out the events in real time.

Apparently, after round-two of Gumby's wonder drug, they hit my stomach like two-tons of shit bricks. I felt odd, out of sorts in the worst possible way. I had never in my life had these *white-crosses* that more appropriately should have displayed a satanic pentagram on them, given how I started feeling. A couple of my buddies realized what was happening and strode in like the cavalry to assist me. I was weak at the knees, my head was spinning, and my stomach felt as if I'd swallowed something that would make a maggot puke. It was as if God had come down and touched me with his own personal *sick stick*. I was being paid in spades, my friends.

I was so drunk, I couldn't have poured beer out of a boot, with instructions printed on the bottom of the heel. My buddies grabbed my arms and led me out of the rock & roll room and into the lobby. The doors swung open with a swooshed mixture of warm conditioned air and cold wintery air from the restaurant's front doors, hitting me like a lightning bolt. If, by some strange coincidence, we are ever out drinking and I am this drunk, which is highly unlikely at my age, please do not allow me to be overwhelmed with cold, German wintery air. You have been warned! It was nearing an exact fifty-one weeks since my trifle with 1SG Puke-On-Boots in Frankfurt, and again, me with the cold air blues. No pun intended on the blue part.

The mixture of combating airs, white crosses, and blue motorcycles did a number on me like never before, or since. I stood in the crowd of standing-room only guests, in that large, rectangular lobby. I shooed my buddies away, as if to imply that I had the situation *under complete control*. They eased off, but with sound trepidation.

Thankfully, my buddy was there to recall this horrifying event back to me. I listened in bewilderment, as if it were entirely someone else's reality. I sighed, as he continued…

I backed them off, then proceeded to discharge all digestive contents in a full-on geyser mode. It was of epic national park proportions, with wide-eyed crowds gathered around. I violently evacuated a concoction of dinner, white crosses, and blue motorcycles; thereby, smattering the lobby floor with my guttural remnants. Chunks of blue-dyed meat and vegetables were hurled from my mouth like the working end of a hose on a five-alarm fire.

To add insult to injury, I was told that I didn't just spray it out onto the floor in front of me. No, no, that would be way too civilized, and un-like any semblance of my normal self. According to Vegas Brad, I had a rapid-action, rotary-styled, back-and-forth, industrial strength demonic sprinkler-head attached to my neck. It was said that my self-made rain looked as if it'd fallen onto one-half of an umbrella, splayed perfectly into a semi-circle formation around my position—cartoonish, if you will.

People were running outside to avoid the stench, or perhaps spew their own holdings, while other onlookers gasped in horror at my petrifying display of motorcycle mayhem. Then, like a good soldier, I snapped to position of attention. Vegas said to imagine someone standing up an unsupported 4x4 post on its end, and then watching it tumble over. That was exactly what I had done, only I was momentarily in a cata-tonic-like state. One of my finer drunken moments.

I was mortified at what I was hearing. I had been drunk several times in my life, Army drunk, even, but I'd never puked like that, or even *acted* like that. It was, even for me, a bit much to take in. It sounded like a bad dream, but considering how I felt, who was I to argue? He continued…

My buddies grabbed me and raced into the latrine where I continued to wretch my guts out in a Mephistopheles-inspired fashion, as the Angel of Death hovered above, laughing. They said it sounded like a torture chamber in my stall; as if I were being mummified alive, insides removed with a small, cleft hook. In agony, I moaned, grumbled, and groaned for a good five minutes or so, whilst they stood guard at the door like gothic statuesque fiends. I did, however, manage to not spill my guts all over the floor and toilet, or even my clothes. Very much standing in stark contrast to the lobby. I was, at best, proud of that accomplishment.

Then, as if nothing at all had happened, I popped back up and was ready to drink some more. They were in utter shock and complete disbelief. It was as if the cataclysmic possession had simply left my body and I was unaware of any and all happenings afterward.

What was more surprising, was that they allowed me to remain a patron after I'd just made a mess of their lobby. While I was wrenching my guts in the toilet, they'd cleaned-up my blue mess, and my buddies made nice to the manager on my behalf. I certainly have no recollection of having another drink, but I'm certain I'd have been served with Spive and SGT J at the helm. I have a vague memory of feeling rather awesome after regurgitating the white and blue monsters from my system, but vague is, perhaps, too strong of a word. I guess they somehow convinced management that I was okay and *good-to-go* after this, as I continued to drink as if nothing had happened.

I was *never* one to drink until I blacked-out, so I was in a state of disbelief, if you can fathom such a thought from your angelic author. It was very difficult to believe such vile nonsense, especially from my roommate. I thought, *He's fucking with me.* This is a joke on Turner, ha-ha-ha.

Of course, I went into complete denial about everything he said after this stage of the story. Cue inner monolog…*I fell over in my own puke, deflowered an innocent lobby and toilet with white crosses and blue chunks of food and drink? Utter and total bullshit.*

I decided I'd ask someone else about the evening. *I'll nip this shit in the bud, right here, right now.* There is no way these guys could hatch and deliver a cover-story like this, given the condition we all were in, right?

They couldn't get one over on me so easily, as I was always the one getting them with jokes.

My buddy, Spud, confirmed it. Fuck me! It was true. It was all so horribly true, but could *I believe it?* Had they embellished a little bit? I was not a puking kind of guy, but I did ingest something foreign. *What the fuck was that? Did he give me something besides the white-crosses? Was that part of the blur?* Unsettled, I returned to my room with the news of my exploits, yet still not buying into it one-hundred percent. I was notorious for pulling pranks…*Had they finally pulled one on me?*

Reflecting, I plopped back on the couch, drank some water, and lit another cigarette. I grabbed my AFTCAP ashtray (an AFTCAP is the portion of a tank round that remains in the tank after the bulk of the round is expended). Like most tankers that smoke, I still use mine as an ashtray twenty-seven years later. I pulled a couple more drags off my cigarette while slowly shaking my head in contrived disbelief. *Man, my ear itches,* I thought. I swapped my cigarette into my other hand, raised my finger to my ear, and then it happened…

My mind had a flash of events and memories from the previous evening as I pulled this crusty, dried chunk of matter from the confines of my inner earlobe. I pulled out chunks and slices of white crosses, dried booze, and whatever the fuck I ate for supper. All these contents were found in that superlative blue motorcycle hue. The memories of it all flooded back to me like a raging river.

I should have been disgusted at myself, but I wasn't. I laughed it off and took a shower. I don't think I drank for a day or so, but I have never fucked with another pill or white cross again in my life. Fortunately, and with the assistance of my buddies, I managed to piece together the events of that night; moreover, I would say I never really blacked-out, but it was the only time drinking that heavily gave me a good run for my money.

42

AMSTER—OH, FUCK—DAM

One of my favorite four-day weekends that, like so many others, is a bit of a blur was the (first) one Spud and I took to Amsterdam and Paris. There were six of us in total, but the other guys all worked in the sweat shops, or basic building blocks of an Army unit. S1: Personnel; S2: Intelligence & Security; S3: Training & Operations; S4: Supply. Joe and I were the only tankers in the bunch; therefore, we were the only wild ones, which reminds me, how the fuck did we wind-up going to Amsterdam, without permission, with these guys?

The part that made it bad was, they were kind of nerdy, by our Neanderthal standards. Nothing wrong with nerds, but I guess I didn't expect them to completely disregard Army Regulations regarding leave, as we didn't have permission to go to Amsterdam, which makes them less nerdy, really.

The deal was, if we travelled farther than, say, 240 km/150 miles, we had to inform command that we were doing so, in case a war broke out and we needed to be reached, or for a family emergency, etc. We had permission to go to Paris, but not to Amsterdam, which is well beyond said range, which meant we were breaking the law. Any time anyone took leave anywhere near Amsterdam, you could bet your ass a urinalysis exam followed.

You see, in Holland, or Netherlands, depending on how technical you want to get, marijuana had been decriminalized. You could walk into nearly any coffee shop and order a joint, same as you would a beer. I know in today's day and age, walking into a bar and ordering a joint may not seem like a big deal. But, in 1993, it was a huge fucking deal, as the places on earth where this could be performed were extremely limited. We were in the most famous of them all—Amsterdam. *I really mean it this time, what the fuck could possibly go wrong?*

We all pitched in and rented a large, red passenger van. We departed Mannheim shortly after Thursday's 1630 formation, drove straight-through about five hours, and reached Amsterdam that evening. After a decent meal we slept in the van like gypsies. We slept like shit, but we were young and in the original sin city, so who gave a damn?

The next morning we woke up, grabbed some breakfast, and decided to take in the sights. However, the weather was awful, as it was rain-ing, with intermittent bouts of sleet. Like soldiers, though, we trudged through. We walked around, finding shelter in doorways and bars along the historic canals. We visited several world-famous bars, build-ings, and other oddities only found in Amsterdam.

We decided to split up. Joe and I would go our way, the sweat shop guys would go theirs, and we would all meet up again after lunch. One of the guys, whom we shall call SPC Horndog, found himself a little Asian gem in Amsterdam's red light district. He fucked her once that morning. After our lunch meeting, to ensure everyone in the group was still alive, he fucked her again. She must have really been something. In 1993, a Dutch whore would run you about 50 Guilders (currency of the Netherlands before the Euro), or $25.00. But, seeing as Americans were still a hot commodity in the world, with a little haggling, the deal could be sealed for $20.00. It kind of gives a whole new meaning to the phrase Action Jackson, eh?

Our group split up again and would meet for an early dinner. Joe and I took a tour boat excursion on the canal. We saw Anne Frank's house and the narrowest building in Amsterdam. The trip proved a mistake as we exited the canals and entered the rough and tumble bay. The weather, which was already shit, took a turn for the worst, if that were even possible that day. It did offer proof as to why I didn't join the Navy. When we completed the tour and needed a beer to warm-up and calm our stomachs, we found a low-class bar and did exactly that.

What visit to Amsterdam would be complete without a trip to the world-famous Sex Museum? It was a little lame, but seeing the animated pornographic version of a certain princess and her very horny dwarves, seemingly made it worth the admission price. Plus, there was also a certain 1980s–90s pop star that had published a book, explicitly banned in America, but plastered in larger-than-life pictures to the walls of said museum. Hint: she was *definitely not a virgin*, or *touched for the first time*. Whore better describes her exploits.

After that, we visited a couple of the local coffeehouses for more beers: Rick's American Café and the 7th Heaven. They were, I believe, within earshot of one another. We then met up with our brethren and had dinner and drinks at the coolest of cool bars, the Other Place. They had an old Harley hanging from the ceiling, along with years and years of funky stuff hanging on the walls, and still do from what I've read online.

After dinner, we found our van had been broken into. They smashed the rear window and made off with our borrowed video camera. No easy task, as video cameras back then were as large as construction cinderblocks. Thankfully, they didn't take our bags or luggage. With the police notified, we filed a report and had the window replaced. Somehow, I still have a copy of that police report. It's all in Dutch and fuck only knows what it says. We split up again to take in the nightlife of Amsterdam. This is where the story really takes a turn into the deep unknown...

Joe and I found our way back to Rick's for an evening nightcap, or seven, but who was, or could, count after the first six? We decided that while we were in Amsterdam, we should, at least, sample some of the local wares. Joe watched our table, while I, like a swami knowledgeable in all things, sauntered up to the herb bar.

As I ask to see a menu, the bartender, or *herbtender*, however you care to perceive it, starts up a nice conversation with me. I ask him the ins-and-outs of the whole process, and he kindly obliges me. I explain to him that my buddy and I would like just enough for a nice evening, but we didn't want to pass out on the sidewalks, dicks-in-the-dirt wasted. He perfectly understood our plight and suggested the now-world-famous, Northern Lights strain. He said he could loan us a bong or a pipe, which was chained to the bar for our smoking pleasure. I wasn't keen on the idea of placing my lips onto an item that half of the herb-smoking world had salivated onto. I opted to roll a joint, but the bartender insisted I allow him to do it, Dutch-style. *Who could refuse such an offer?*

It took the bartender about six or seven minutes to roll this beast that was part hog leg and part ice cream cone. It was humongous, as it was also rolled with tobacco, to ease the harshness of the herb. It was nice, even had a handy-dandy little filter rolled into the end of it, which I'd never seen before. When in Rome, observe Romans. Joe provided fresh beers for us, while I took care of the *other* order. I'm standing, patiently waiting, when I hear this mature, older voice in perfect American English holler out to me, *"WHAT BRANCH OF THE SERVICE ARE YOU IN?"*

We were well aware of the punishments of smoking herb in the Army, and had even been warned about the different branches of service having lookouts, or spies if you will, in the bars of Amsterdam, purposely sent out to look for assholes like us. We knew the risks and accepted them in this *once-in-a-lifetime* experience. The chances of us ever coming back were, so I thought, minimal. Besides, what were the chances of us running into a military spy? We'd been in Amsterdam all day and had not run into one single American.

My brain froze for a split-second. I acted as though he was not speaking to me, even though I was well aware that he and I were the only ones at that bar. I casually looked up and asked, *"ARE YOU TALKING TO ME?"* complete with a whodunit look on my guilty face and sporting a high-and-tight haircut.

"YES," he responded. *"ARMY, AIR FORCE? WHICH BRANCH OF THE SERVICE ARE YOU IN, YOUNG MAN?"*

I knew this was a crucial moment. There wasn't a chance in hell I was going to tell this guy I was in the Army, and certainly not in Amsterdam waiting on our joint to be rolled a few inches away. He heard me speaking English with the bartender, there was no denying that. *"I'M A DEPENDENT, BUT, I'M NOT IN THE MILITARY, SIR,"* I replied. A dependent is a child or spouse of someone in the military. I looked to be about twelve when I was eighteen, so it was feasible to most, but not that guy.

With a smile across his face and holding up a joint of his own, he said, *"BULLSHIT, I CAN SPOT A SOLDIER WHEN I SEE ONE. I CAN SEE HOW YOU CARRY YOURSELF. I KNOW BETTER THAN THAT DEPENDENT CRAP. I'M NOT HERE LOOKING FOR WRONG-DOERS. YOU'RE AMERICAN AND SO AM I, SO WHAT BRANCH, BUDDY?"*

I grabbed my beer off the table and gave Joe a concerned look before stepping over to meet this stranger, whom we shall name Smokey. He explained that he and his wife were retired USAF (United States Air Force), and living in Amsterdam. Collectively, they'd put in more than forty-five years of service to the Air Force. The more I conversed and listened to him, I knew he wasn't CID (Criminal Investigation Division), the Army's version of an undercover narcotics officer. I relaxed and motioned Joe to the bar. We continued talking to Smokey and found out he was a very cool customer indeed. He did his time and was living the easy life. When we finally parted ways, Joe and I were a little wiser about the ins-and-outs of Amsterdam. He said he would be around and to say hello if we saw him again. Nice guy.

Joe and I returned to our booth and quietly stared at our Dutch ice cream cone. He broke the silence. *"WELL, IT'S NOT GOING TO SMOKE ITSELF, TURNER."* The path to the darker, funnier, snack-food side of life, was about to begin. We maybe smoked a third of it and left its remnants in the ashtray. Given our status as novices, there was still plenty to smoke on that hog leg. This is where the evening also became a blur, as if that would actually shock my readers at this point. We sat there in that booth, beer-after-beer, cracking up at whatever the fuck we were discussing. It was stony as fuck, too.

I know, I know, *What kind of fucking soldiers were we, smoking herb in the Army?* Well, I'll tell you. We were young, adventurous, wild, and it was our first time in Amsterdam, so we partook a little of the local fare. *So, what?* When we were in garrison or the field, we performed our jobs well. Had our nation called us into combat, we'd have served with honor and professionalism. We'd have done our duty as young, freedom-loving Americans.

Remember the words of our forefather, Thomas Jefferson, when he penned in 1787, *"I HOLD IT THAT A LITTLE REBELLION, NOW AND THEN, IS A GOOD THING...."* for *"THE TREE OF LIBERTY."* Perhaps it's a slight misguided use of his words, but it captures the American spirit; a controlled, temperamental rebellion for the greater good. It's not like we were international drug smugglers. *Not Spud, anyway? And that's all I got to say about that.*

As we sat there enjoying our evening through a stupor of laughter, little did we know we were marked for an unannounced inspection by SGT Larry. I watched him walk into the bar looking for the rebellious leader mentioned herein, yours truly, and his partner in crime, Spud. This bar was very long and narrow, so it wasn't hard to spot us, a few mere inches from the herb bar. Larry started shining his own piece of the vinyl seat, as luck would have it, right next to me. Instantly, we thought his presence would be the *coup de grâce* to our fun, a real buzz kill. The remnants of our laughter lay motionless in the ashtray like a 400 pound gorilla stretched out for a nap.

We started bullshitting with Larry as though everything were normal, until he noticed the gorilla staring back at him. He immediately began dissecting our faces. Eventually, he noticed we could have been blind-folded with dental floss. Larry, being the ranking soldier, explained that we would be drug-tested when we returned to Mannheim.

I thought, if I'm caught, I'm going to enjoy it, so I lit up the joint and passed it to Joe. He shrugged his shoulders and physically said what I was thinking, fuck it! We puffed away while we finished our beers. Meanwhile, Larry droned on about the evils of the world, highlighting our wicked ways. You see, Larry was an NCO (E-5), Joe and I were not, so technically, he outranked us. But, me being me, I swiftly took charge of the situation as a young private.

Smoke bellowed from our mouths as we sipped our beers, and I then laid out the dos-and-don'ts of _my_ wicked world, _my_ reality, as I'd seen it at that moment. I asked, *"LARRY, HOW LONG HAVE YOU BEEN SITTING HERE WITH US?"*

"DUH, TWENTY-MINUTES, OR SO, I-I-I...," he responded. Larry really did make these long syllabled moans and mutters before and after each response whether in Amsterdam or in garrison. That was just Larry.

"EXCELLENT ANSWER," I quickly retorted before he could complete his thought. I then continued, *"LARRY, DO YOU HAVE PERMISSION TO BE IN AMSTERDAM?"*

"NO, UHHH…," he said, with a confused look across his face.

"AGAIN, LARRY, EXCELLENT ANSWER," I sounded off, continuing with, *"LARRY, HAVE YOU BEEN BREATHING WHILE HERE AT THE TABLE?"*

First a perplexed smile, then, oddly, a quick, *"YES,"* came his obvious response, with an even more perplexed tone to his voice.

Trying to piece it together for him, I asked, *"LARRY, WOULD YOU SUFFICE IT TO SAY, THAT YOU, TOO, WILL BE DRUG-TESTED UPON OUR RETURN?"* The lightbulb had yet to illuminate.

"YEAH, BUT, I DIDN'T DO WHAT YOU GUYS—" came his matter-of-fact enlightenment.

Cutting him off mid-sentence, I made the connection for him. *"LARRY, YOU HAVE BEEN BREATHING IN THE SAME MARY-JANE-INFUSED AIR THAT WE HAVE. WHAT DID YOU SAY, LARRY? TWENTY MINUTES OR SO? I'M PRETTY SURE YOU WILL PISS HOT, TOO, BUDDY."*

Someone get this man a cigar. With bulb installed, the switch was now in the on position. We, as a collective, knew there was going to be no surprise drug screens. We didn't go up there with the intention of smoking, but it ended up that way. Maybe those nerdy guys, less Larry, were toking it up, too. We'll never know.

Travesty averted, we carried on with our normal evening. Larry was suddenly *very cool* about it all, as I am quite certain a contact high came over him the longer we sat in that bar. He was extremely and unusually quiet. But it was the kind of quiet that made me wonder if he were plotting murder in our midst. He politely drank his beer and followed our lead. We sat there getting more wasted than we should have.

A little later, Smokey passed by and invited us to join him and his friends outside. We happily accepted. We grabbed a fresh beer and sat at this large, round table near the sidewalk. It was us three, Smokey, and four of his local buddies. A very diverse crowd, would be an understatement of epic proportions. We tucked into the group in various positions at the table. Joe sat across from me, out of immediate earshot, but positioned next to Smokey. Larry and I were separated by an English musician in a black leather jacket. He'd just finished a show and was celebrating its success.

Smokey then pulled out a humongous Dutch ice cream cone for us all to enjoy, but not before he explained this was, supposedly, the second strongest strain in the known world. It was from Afghanistan, or South Africa, I simply cannot remember. He instructed the novices, namely Joe and I, to only take a small puff, and then leave it be, as it would, figuratively speaking, paralyze us.

Now, I ask you intelligent readers, after reading this far into the book, do you think I would have listened to the voice of reason in that situation? The same voice that has been nearly devoid in all of my adventures? Yeah, I didn't think so.

Smokey sparked it up and passed it to his left. Joe was to his right, meaning he would be the last of seven to hit the joint, seeing as Larry didn't smoke. I was separated from our buddy, Smokey, by only one person, which meant I was third in line. It was passed to me after many, many fits of coughing. I knew it was strong when I witnessed the professionals coughing their asses off. I took a very small puff on it and coughed uncontrollably, even with tobacco mixed in. Now, I'm experienced enough to know it wasn't laced with anything funny; it was just strong. I passed it to the musician on my left. It skipped Larry and went to two others before Spud grasped it. He looked at me, and I didn't have to say anything, I just nodded and widened my eyelids to imply that it was the serious sticky-icky.

Joe must've missed the memo about this weed. He puffed on that thing like it was junior high school oregano. He coughed uncontrollably, and then coughed some more. We all laughed, just like they did when I was hacking and coughing. We were the novices and it showed, but no one cared. Then it came my way again. I should've listened to that inner voice and just passed it along, but that inner voice was stoned, drunk, and not to be given any rational advice anyhow, so why would I listen to it now. Spud, apparently, had that same inner voice, as he, too, took a second hit. It was a huge mistake on both our parts. We were cata-tonic, glued to the chairs. At one with them, you might say. The real blur kicked in for both of us right about *there*.

The stuff was way out of our league. I remember looking at Joe, and he looked freaked the fuck out as Smokey was telling him about his home-town. Not Smokey's hometown, but Spud's. Spud is from a small town in Idaho. It's next door to that town named, *You've Never Heard Of It*. Joe was freaking the fuck out, and rightly so. The herb was not helping him in this situation; it was only intensifying it. I was so relaxed watch-ing Spud freak out. I was high with beers in my belly, so life was good for me in that moment. I simply sat back and took in all the scenery. Looking, listening, talking, and just being.

However, Larry was doing a bit of freaking out himself, as the musician between us had found a fresh soul in which to regale his own escapades of personal debauchery. The only thing I remember of their conversa-tion was seeing a horrified Larry as the musician said, *"I WAS IN THE WOODS, ALL ALONE, AND THERE I WAS, WRESTLING THIS BIG, BLACK BEAR..."* I quickly chuckled it off as brain fodder and returned to my status of space cadet.

Both Spud and I have *abso-fucking-lutely* no recollection of getting back to the youth hostel. The next morning, we loaded up and headed to Paris, another five-hour drive, due south.

The weather in Paris was shit as well, at least on the first day. We checked into our hostel with a great view of Notre-Dame Cathedral. It's weird looking out of your window and seeing a 700-year-old building staring back at you. Now it is long gone to the flames of history. We had a very nice supper at this wonderful Greek restaurant. I think I remember them breaking some of the dishes as we finished our meal, or some larger group finishing theirs. It was real traditional stuff. Then, as in Amsterdam, we split up to scour the city. The nerd-herd went to test their luck in the discotheques of Paris, while Joe and I searched for a buzz. Somehow, in one of the more sophisticated cities on earth, we found an American teen favorite—strawberry flavored, Angry (sic) Dog 20/20. Somehow, we got wasted and managed to walk most of Paris in the rain, sleet, and snow. It was awful, but fun.

The next day, the weather broke and turned out to be quite beautiful. The sun was out, and the air was considerably warmer, so we took in the sights; Trocadéro Gardens at the Eiffel Tower, Notre-Dame, the Louvre, and Jim Morrison's grave at the Père Lachaise Cemetery, which was fucking closed after walking 8 km (5 miles). Had we a couple of beers in us, we'd have hopped the fence.

I had a caricature drawn of myself at the base of the Eiffel Tower. Long faded and beaten up, it still hangs in my living room. I think it was all of 10 Francs (currency of France before the Euro). Those were certainly the days. The Euro has priced nearly everything out of reach, as I've since returned to France once and Germany thrice since the Euro was introduced. We took in most all the big sights, and even managed to ride one of those red, open-air, AEC Routemaster buses, like the double-decker ones you see in London. We rode down the famed Champs-Élysees and around the Arc de Triomphe. We walked across the river Seine to the Esplanade du Trocadéro, where it offered a splendid view of the Eiffel. After that, we returned to Trocadéro Gardens, where another Larry incident happened.

Larry had to go to the restroom and asked if we'd seen a toilet (or water closet, as the Europeans call a bathroom) nearby. Paris had these outdoor toilets, right on the sidewalks, like porta-potties, that you could pay 2–3 Francs to use. As he'd been holding it a while, he had neither the time nor proper arrangement of coins to utilize the portable John, so I told him to go in the bushes. It was Europe…who cared? At the base of the Eiffel are bushes at each leg, so Larry opted to try and relieve himself at one of the less busy legs. Paris is a filthy city, so trust me when I say, no one would have noticed the smell. We waited in the center, directly beneath the tower.

Larry returned with his hands sort of hiding the front portion of his shorts. Perplexed, but not surprised, we looked at one another as he approached our position. He continued with the lowered jazz-hands. We eyed each other and shrugged our shoulders with a *what the fuck* expression. When asked what the hell was happening, he moved his hands to reveal a sizable piss mark on the front of his khaki shorts. So, like any mature group of adults, we immediately burst into laughter, pointed to his shameful stain, took a picture, and in between fits of laughter and breathing, I yelled, "LARRY PISSED HIS PANTS, LARRY PISSED HIS PANTS AT THE EIFFEL TOWER." We all doubled-over in laughter, and then like someone had turned on the kitchen lights, we scattered faster than cockroaches. It was a great trip, that one.

43

THE BEST MIKE FOXTROT

Once you're in country for a while, you are no longer considered green, or wet behind the ears. You find friends, have experiences, and make some rank along the way. In the lower ranks of enlisted personnel, rank comes naturally after so much time at your permanent duty station, provided you don't make a huge mistake and get caught. You gain more experience as a soldier with several field problems under your belt, especially the big ones: Grafenwöhr—for gunnery engagements; Hohenfels—for force-on-force training; and Wildflecken—for low-mountain training. All are very cold, and located in the free state of Bavaria, or Bayern to the locals. These are definitive proving-grounds for every soldier, his unit, and their equipment. Like training with our weapons in OSUT, these build confidence in oneself and in the brothers you live and work with each day.

As a general rule of thumb, for a soldier to promote past the rank of E-4/ Specialist, it must be earned and attained through schools and training. Back then, and probably today, there were several ways to be promoted. It all depended on the points one had acquired through weapons qualifications, awards and citations, physical fitness tests, evaluations, credits through the Army Correspondence Course Program, time in grade, and Soldier-of-the-Month boards.

I actually enjoyed the correspondence courses, as they covered so many facets of my MOS, as well as several others. We had to learn about tank tactics, in-depth studies into our weapons systems, different vehicles (foreign and domestic) and their weapons systems, like mortars, dragons, and the Mk19 grenade launcher. It also covered in-depth studies into other militaries that we could potentially have been at war with in the, then, future. It was great stuff. As a side note: the Mk19 is a 40mm hybrid machine gun/grenade launcher… it was the real tits to fire.

I decided it was time to stop dicking around and become a SPC4. This PVT shit had to go. I was ready to buckle down and do something with my time in the Army. This was long before the advent of the internet, so I had to apply and wait for snail-mail to deliver these correspondence books. I'd study them, take an exam, mail them back in, and then wait several weeks for them to hit my personnel packet. It took months for this entire scenario to play out.

I was always in great physical shape, youth accomplished much of that, so acing the PT test with a score of *300* was a no-brainer. Easy points. But, when combined with an expert qualification on the rifle, pistol, and grenade, along with my track and wheeled driving awards and mechanics badge, it added up to quite a few points. All these things aided in my achieving the rank of E-4/ Specialist. I worked hard and wanted to be promoted. Years later, in the Nasty Girls, I held the rank of E-4/ Corporal (unit level). During my three years in the National Guard, I moved from California to Florida, and from Florida to Alabama, which never allowed me the time to attend PLDC (Professional Leadership Development Course), a prerequisite for promotion to sergeant.

The unfortunate part for me was our unit was over-inundated with other soldiers all clamoring for the same damn thing. Nobody wanted to be a PVT, as it more often than not, sucked. Everyone outranked you and told you what to do. The running joke is: What is the difference between a 2LT and a PFC? The PFC had already been promoted twice! The problem was there were so many E-2s and E-3s, it was ridiculously impossible to promote them all to E-4. Furthermore, the Army was overpopulated with 19Kilos, making it more difficult to get promoted.

This was the awesome thing about leadership in the Army back in my day—they had a solution! Command decided to marry, if you will, the Promotion and the Soldier-of-the-Month Boards into one, big, beautiful, ball-breaking board designed to test the gall of its soldiers. Son-of-a-bitch, I thought. I'd only planned to attend the promotion board, but now I had to study all sorts of fun stuff.

The Soldier-of-the-Month Board was pretty broad in its subjects covered. I had to learn all sorts of stuff: military customs and traditions, customs for the American flag, history of the Army, regulations and field-manuals regarding our current job duties, leadership skills and chain-of-command questions. It was a lot of knowledge to impart into my barley and hops-filled brain. I bought and borrowed a few books on the subject and went to work. Basically, I had around four weeks to prepare. It wound up being really interesting to learn all that military history. I rather enjoyed it.

I happened to be attending the board with my roommate, Vegas Brad, which helped, as we could quiz one another. Traditionally, a soldier attends a review board in his or her Class-As, or dress uniform. However, given the number of troops attending and the time needed for uniform preparations (time off work), command opted for us to attend in our BDUs. They still had to be in perfect condition, as we were judged on military appearance as well. Our boots had to be highly spit-shined. Younger generations of soldiers may never know this struggle. Haircuts and uniforms had to be well within the standards of Army Regulation 670-1. It was a big deal. Our leadership gave us time off to study and prepare, if we wanted to attempt the board.

The big day arrived, and even though it was cool outside, I was nervous with sweat. The board consisted of a panel of six reviewers: battalion SGM, and HHC's (our Company) 1SG, two PLT Daddies, a section sergeant, and the XO (Executive Officer, or the second in command of HHC Company). It was very intimidating. Given the number of potential candidates, individual reviews were nixed, and instead were conducted three troops at a time. I entered the room first and sat to the far left of the panel's perspective, with Vegas Brad in the middle and some unknown trooper to our left. It was a dog-and-pony show, mind you. We had to report, be inspected, and then be seated, at attention. Yes, for those of you that weren't aware, there is a position of attention while seated. Uncle Sam thinks of everything.

The questions began, covering everything Army: What could be found at the bottom of a flagpole located on post? What, when, and in which engagements, were our unit citations earned? When, and under what circumstances, was the Army formed? No board would be complete without the famed question of: What were our general orders?

It was Déjà vu, OSUT style, less the pushups. We sat answering questions for nearly an hour, soldier-by-soldier.

Finally the questions started to peter-out. We knew the gauntlet had neared its end. At the behest of the SGM, he asked each board member to finish their inquiries with a final question for each of the three candidates. Eighteen questions, or six each, remained. Torture is made in such ways, as we'd just answered every fucking question regarding every fucking thing anyone would ever want to know about the Army, its traditions, and everything under the proverbial Army sun. However, the SGM had the privilege of asking the final question, as he had more time in grade and in service, than anyone else in the room.

The SGM, thankfully, started with the guy on my opposite end. His question was: Why do you, PFC SO-AND-SO, think you deserve to be Soldier-of-the-Month and promoted to Specialist?

He responded with all the accomplishments he'd achieved in his umpteen months in the Army. Citing his PT scores, weapons qualifications, ribbons and awards, etc. It was as if he'd read them from his own personnel file. I thought to myself, *Dude, they know this shit already.*

He then moved to my buddy, Vegas. The SGM asked him the same question, to which he responded with the same recipe as PFC SO-AND-SO. PT scores, time-in-grade, etc., etc. I couldn't believe my ears.

Then the SGM does a little cross-talk with the other members of the panel. I thought, *Fucking great*, he's going to change his final question of the day for yours truly, especially since I'd formulated a ballsy response. Nerves were strained, but, to my great relief, he continued with the same question.

"PVT TURNER, WHY DO YOU THINK YOU DESERVE TO BE SOLDIER-OF-THE-MONTH AND PROMOTED TO THE RANK OF SPECIALIST?"

My mind went blank for a moment, then began the inner-dialog. *Should I do it, or not? Will I get in trouble? No, way. Will it hinder my chances?* This was, after all, the last question of the day, the final question as to whether I got promoted or not.

Fuck it, I finally decided. I looked across the panel, and then back at the SGM, and delivered in the most confident and determined voice I could muster, *"BECAUSE I AM THE BEST MOTHER-FUCKER FOR THE JOB, SERGEANT MAJOR!"*

I could see my buddy next to me. His eyes and brow jumped and rolled at the reply I'd given, then he darted his eyes at me like, *Really, Turner? That's your big plan to get promoted?* The panel wasn't really sure how to take my response. But good ole SGM knew exactly what I said, and why I said it. He repeated it back to me with a smile and a hearty laugh, before the other NCOs chuckled with him. The 2LT dare not laugh at such a thing.

There was no other dialog needed from me, nor did he require any. I told him exactly what he wanted and needed to know. He made some notes, looked to his panel for any last-minute or missing segments, and then promptly thanked us for our time before dismissing us. We hastily made our escape.

Vegas immediately started in. *"FUCKING TURNER. BECAUSE I'M THE BEST MOTHER-FUCKER FOR THE JOB. WHERE DID YOU COME UP WITH THAT SHIT, DUDE? YOU HAD IT UNTIL YOU PULLED THAT STUNT. BEST MOTHER-FUCKER, PHHHFFF. YOU'RE CRAZY, DUDE."* I started second-guessing my decision to include *mother-fucker* in my final answer.

Of course, it didn't take long for the story to make the rounds in the platoon and company. The jury was conflicted on whether it was completely retarded or a stroke of brilliance. The powers that be would certainly decide my fate. Vegas Brad didn't make Soldier-of-the-Month, but he was promoted a couple of weeks later, having an additional six-months' time in grade, and time in service, than either myself, or PFC SO-AND-SO.

I did, however, make Soldier-of-the-Month and was promoted to E-4 Specialist the following month. I was promoted alongside another of our now fallen brothers, Halterman. We were promoted in grand SPT PLT fashion, too.

In the years that have passed since I was in the Army, I realized there were so many little things I simply didn't, or couldn't, retain year-after-year; weapons statistics, Army traditions, hell, I'd even forgotten most of my general orders, that were time and again drilled into me. To ensure the book's accuracy, as well as jolt my memory, I had to perform shit and tons of research, which led me to find a plethora of information, both old and new, regarding the Army.

It has been a wonderful, and often reflective, journey down Memory Lane. However, my research has been profound and disturbing at the same time. I came to realize how much I had changed since then, often struggling to capture and describe the man I once was. A normal process of life, and especially that of time.

Furthermore, what most alarmed me about my research was how much the Army had changed through the years. It didn't immediately hit me, but upon further reflection, I realized there were in today's promotion board gobs-and-gobs of questions related to sexual harassment. It made me realize these stories wouldn't have breathed an ounce of life in today's day-and-age, which perhaps makes me antiquated in a way. What worked in the American Revolution, the Civil War, both World Wars, Viet-Nam, Korea, Desert Storm, etc., is no longer acceptable in today's world…ushering in the era of getting one's feelings hurt at the turn of every corner, but I guess times change, eh?

44

THREE STOOGES TURN SPECIALISTS

Once the short-lived hoopla of Soldier-of-the-Month wore off, I knew my promotion was assured. It was not going to happen as soon as I'd hoped, or was it?

About a month-and-a-half later, on a sunny, beautiful day, some friends and I walked up to the PX for pizza. As we made our way back to the PLT area for 1300 hours formation, someone came up to me and said, *"TURNER, COME HERE. CHECK IT OUT, HALTERMAN AND DEVO ARE GETTING PROMOTED TODAY. WE HAVE A BUCKET OF SHIT OVER HERE THAT EVERYBODY IS SPITTING IN. TIME TO PONY-UP YOUR SHARE."* *Fucking score,* I thought. Who doesn't want the authorized opportunity to fuck with your brothers on this momentous occasion? I certainly wasn't going to let an opportunity like that pass me up.

I stepped over to the side of the building, out of sight from everyone, to observe the bucket of chum they'd prepared. It was, perhaps, the most disgusting collection of shit I'd ever seen. It had old, half-decomposed livers in it, for fuck's sake. It looked like rotten leftovers from the mess hall had been thrown in there and left in the sun for days on end. My buddy paused and held an arm out to keep me from getting in his line-of-fire, as he snorted, hacked, and coughed-up the most disgusting lung rocket he could muster, then deposited it into the chum.

Clearing my path, his arm dropped and I giggled like a small toddler that had just snuck a cookie from the jar. I was giddy. I held my finger up to my nose and blew out a nostril bullet with the kind of force that made it stick like a glob of half-dried glue. I performed the same from the other nostril. I then commenced to clearing my throat and smoker's lungs of any and all lung-butter I could exorcise from the depths of my soul. It was a horrifying sight for even the most putrid of us soldiers. I am pretty sure at some point during lunch, some of the guys may have even pissed into it a little. It wouldn't have surprised me to learn if they had. Nothing at this point could, or would, shock me, especially in the midst of these animals.

Everyone was slap-happy when 1300 hours rolled around. The promotion ceremony was about to begin. Our PLT formed-up by section and squad. The intensity of it all was silly, really. Everyone knew what was going to happen. I thought, *Those poor bastards are going to have that disgusting shit all over them.* The PLT Daddy, SFC Cigarettes & Coffee, posted to our front and brought us to attention, then the snickering began to overpower us. The plan had been finalized, and the trap was set. The PLT Daddy spoke, in his Southern drawl, *"ALL RIGHT, CALM DOWN. I'VE GATHERED Y'ALL HERE TO RECOGNIZE AND PIN SOME RANK ON SOME OF OUR FELLOW TROOPS."* The snickering continued to get louder and louder, nearing uncontrollable. The stifling anticipation was damn-near splitting our sides wide open.

The PLT Daddy continued. *"PFC DEVO. FRONT AND CENTER."* Front and center meant you had to break ranks, or leave the bulk formation and join the PLT Daddy at the front. He continued. *"PFC*

HALTERMAN. FRONT AND CENTER." The laughter worsened for some, but not for them. Like everyone else, I chuckled. Then came, *"TURNER. FRONT AND CENTER."*

What the fuck was going on? Why was I called forward? I wasn't getting promoted until next month. My eyes widened in shock.

I reported front and center, as ordered. As I was up there, I could see the same dread mirrored in Halterman and Devo's eyes that were clearly in mine. It hit me like a ton-of-bricks…we had all been duped. It didn't take long for us all to realize we had all been in on the joke, but failed to comprehend that we were the joke. We were all part of the secret club that had contributed to our own disgusting *specialist-inspired* concoction. The same story that was relayed to me, was separately relayed to Devo and Halterman. They told each of us the other two were getting promoted, thus we spat, hocked, and loogied into the promotion bucket.

There was nothing we could do at this point. We were firmly snared within the jaws of comic-relief, caught like flies in flypaper. As if all connected, our heads shook in disbelief. *"ATTENTION TO ORDERS,"* began the PLT Daddy, reading off the speech to officially mark our promotion. He then pinned one of two of our specialist pins to one collar, while our Squad Leader or Section Sergeant pinned the other. There was a hardy slap to the pin once fitted to our collar. Even with the keepers in place, the backs of our newly pinned rank hurt like a son-of-a-bitch when driven into your collarbone.

They were not like blood wings (Airborne or Paratrooper) or anything, but it was painful enough. Blood wings are earned and then slapped or punched into your chest without the pin keepers in place. It's essentially two little holes punched into your breast plate. I can imagine those are really painful and remembered for life, through that remaining scar. I seriously doubt that shit happens in formation any longer, but assuredly it is performed in the privacy of a soldier's room or PLT area. I hope it continues. Our own form of misery was well on its way.

The PLT Daddy congratulated us, shook our hands, and then turned the formation over to SSG Lomio. He smiled as he ordered the delivery of the bucket. It was then laid at our feet as we remained at the position of attention. He dismissed the formation with the command of *fall out*, meaning freely disperse. The guys all knew they'd gotten us good. The smiles and pats on the back continued until the bucket was finally raised and poured over each of our heads and shoulders. It was awful. It required a couple of washings to rid my uniform of the stench.

I was now a Specialist in the U.S. Army. The hard work and line, *"I'M THE BEST MOTHER-FUCKER FOR THE JOB, SERGEANT-MAJOR,"* had paid off in spades. I was proud. I was no longer a fucking private! After the pictures and laughter, we were dismissed and given the rest of the day off. That shower felt so wonderful. I promptly went to the Class VI and bought myself a bottle of smooth Tennessee whiskey in which to celebrate my promotion. Which brings me to my next disgusting example of life in an armor unit.

45

BIERFEST, BOXING, BUSTED HEADS, AND BRIGADE DUTY ROSTER

No memoir about being stationed in Germany would be complete without one or two bierfest stories. So, hang on, ladies and gentlemen. This one is a doozy.

The local beer, our lovely *Oak Tree* brand, held one of their end-of-summer German-American Volksfest (people's [beer] festival). Not the one where Wildman Ward had me arrested either. I wish I had room in this book for that story. Book Two? I digress. It was within walking, and fortunately for us, within drunken stumbling distance as well. It was one of the larger ones in our area, complete with a huge main tent and several rows of tables within, capable of comfortably holding several hundred guests. They had these wonderful ½L steins, many of which were re-appropriated into our possession. Years later, after Tire Iron lost many of his steins to a soured relationship, I decided to share one of these re-appropriated steins with him. The insignias were not simply etched or debossed into the glass, as were most; it was formed as part of the glass, heavily embossed, real beautiful stuff. It was nearly a ½-inch thick.

We had been given a four-day weekend, Friday through Monday. Officially, it began after the CO's (Commanding Officer) speech. The captain would give us a weekend safety brief. Rather, he gave himself some sense of plausible deniability to any events that would surely unfold. He, and sometimes the 1SG, would have to drone on about us not drinking too much and not getting arrested for something stupid. The CO had standing orders. *"MEN,"* he used to bark out, *"ALWAYS COVER YOUR BUDDY. NO MATTER WHAT HAPPENS THIS WEEKEND, COVER YOUR BUDDY."*

Yes, when you're eighteen or nineteen years old, it seemed leadership was droning on, but in hindsight, I reckon it sank in. Those were not just words said aloud in order to hear themselves speak; they were words to live by, to soldier by. The potential to go to war with those drinking buddies was always a real threat back then. We even had a couple of intense moments where we geared up for war, so, *Roger that, sir. Cover our buddies.* Check.

Much later that evening, PVT B, a soldier in our platoon, was dancing on a picnic table, as was completely normal at a bierfest. What wasn't normal was some asshole approaching his position and snatching him off the table and down to the ground. It was nothing less than a 5-foot fall, straight to his back, knocking the wind out of him. As I stood there with one of those beautiful steins in my hand, still half-full (always the optimist, I am), I thought, *That is definitely one of my buddies.*

Said asshole commenced to wailing on PVT B's head with several unsuspecting blows. As he did so, I slugged that beer into my belly, because I was not wasting a beer, marched over, and delivered my own version of an *unsuspecting* blow to him. The difference was, I used one of those beautiful steins to accomplish it, because unlike PVT B, asshole had four of his buddies there to back him up. My buddy, he was out cold on the floor, so it was myself and one trusty stein to save the day. The glass shattered into the back of his head, and he too, was out cold. With blood oozing down the back of his head and neck, his motionless body went to rest perfectly on top of PVT B.

Enraged, his friends came at me, so I took a step back, held up the remains of my jagged stein handle, and said, *"ALL RIGHT, MOTHER FUCKERS, WHO'S NEXT?"*

It instantly stymied their advance. The crazy must have been strong in my eyes that night. I was definitely covering my buddy, albeit, with the bleeding body of an enemy soldier. Before I could react, an arm came from behind and had me in a full-blown rear naked choke-hold. I wrestled forward to the nearest picnic table and used my leg to spring us both backwards. As soon as his back and legs hit the table behind us, he lost his grip on me. I broke loose and elbowed him in the face, then regained my stance, still wielding my stein handle as I waited for the rest of the cowardly gang. Again, the others opted out of approaching me for a fight, as I'd single-handedly taken out two of their buddies inside of twenty seconds.

Our Mexican stand-off ended when my buddies rushed in and instructed me to pop-smoke and get out of Dodge, as both the *Polizei* and the MPs were in hot pursuit. In the general direction of the barracks, I ducked under the tent and slowly made my way out of the AO. I was out of the woods, or so I thought.

At the time, I was roommates with a guy we called The Boston Brawler. That night, he happened to be working the CQ desk at brigade, which translates to him being privy to any and all occurrences within the brigade. The next morning he informed me I had made the duty roster; which meant, high command would see my name and hear about my exploits at the bierfest. He also informed me both the *Polizei* and the MPs wanted to speak with me. I was, as the old adage goes, *up Shit Creek without a paddle.* Hell, I didn't even have a canoe, and the waters were deep, my dear friends.

Tuesday morning I was in the motor pool, toiling away at my super-high-speed duties, no doubt acting the angel. Did I mention my uniform and boots were pristine? *Well, they were.* I knew I was going to see leadership that day. The situation looked bleak, so I wanted to look good for it.

I first had to explain my story to the Lieutenant, PLT Daddy, both section SGTs, and every squad leader in SPT PLT. As I finished my story, ole SFC Cigarettes & Coffee wasted no time in motivating me to my original summons as he rasped out, *"WELL, WHAT ARE YOU WAITING FOR, TURNER? GO SEE THE COMMANDER."*

That was the question? Look, fuck stick, you summoned me here before going to see the commander. That's what I'm doing here. You wanted the good gossip from the horse's mouth, in case I was never seen or heard from again. That was my answer, albeit, to myself.

My asshole puckered, as it was straight dread coursing through my veins. Shit Creek was about to hold me under and perform a death roll. I marched up to see the company commander, a CPT Donald Vandergriff. We called him CPT Handgrenade or CPT Vanderpatton: an obvious ode to Gen. G.S. Patton. I rapped at the door.

"COME IN," he barked, breaking the intense silence.

Fuck me, I thought. That is when the real internal dialog to the gods truly began. *Lord, please let me get through this ordeal alive.*

I had a very conflicted outlook. I was nervous, but confident, sort of. I felt completely justified in my actions, so I marched in, snapped to attention, rendered a salute, and spoke. *"SPC TURNER, REPORTING AS ORDERED, SIR."*

CPT Handgrenade, beneath his hardened brow, lurked into my soul with angry eyes. I was so nervous and puckered-up, you'd have struggled to insert a honed scalpel up my ass. He finally spoke in a semi-calm, controlled manner. *"TURNER, I WANT TO KNOW WHAT HAPPENED THIS WEEKEND. I KNOW WHAT HAPPENED, BUT I WANT TO HEAR YOUR VERSION OF EVENTS. I WANT THE TRUTH. THE MPs ARE WAITING AT THE FRONT GATE TO TAKE YOU TO COLEMAN CONFINEMENT."*

What the fuck have I done to myself now? It was *BOHICAS* time, folks, or BEND OVER, HERE IT COMES ARMY STYLE! My life *literally* flashed before my eyes.

He continued. *"THAT KID YOU HIT OVER THE HEAD WAS IN SURGERY FOR 3½ HOURS WHILE THEY DUG GLASS OUT OF HIS SKULL. LUCKILY, HE'S GOING TO SURVIVE WITHOUT PERMANENT DAMAGE, ASIDE FROM A NASTY SCAR. NOW, TURNER, THIS IS YOUR ONE CHANCE TO TELL ME THE TRUTH."*

A pause ensued, then he verbally bludgeoned out, *"I'M WAITING."*

At this point, you'd have needed a sledgehammer to drive that blade into my ass. I had one of those out-of-body experiences you hear about…I had never prayed for an alien abduction to happen, but right fucking then, I was praying for any abduction. My balls had retreated deep into my body after he mentioned Coleman Confinement. Time slowed down, his voice kind-of echoed in the halls of my brain, I was woozy on my feet. To us, Coleman Confinement was the Fort Leavenworth of Europe. I cleared my throat, swallowed the dust from my mouth, and spoke. *"SIR, I DID EXACTLY AS YOU TOLD ME TO."*

His eyes blistered, his lips scrunched-up, and his fists slammed onto the desk as he shouted back, *"I DON'T THINK I HEARD YOU, TURNER. WHAT THE FUCK DID YOU JUST SAY?"*

It felt like my body was floating in mid-air right there in front of his desk. I was committed now. Before I answered, and in a John Wayne-esque fashion, I felt my head momentarily twist and return to the neutral position involuntarily, to imply you damn-well did hear me. So, with more gusto and confidence, I responded, *"SIR, I DID EXACTLY AS YOU TOLD ME TO DO! PVT B WAS KNOCKED-OUT ON THE GROUND. THERE WERE FOUR OR FIVE OF THEM, AND I WAS THE ONLY ONE AROUND TO DEFEND HIM. SO, LIKE YOUR BRIEF, SIR…I DID EXACTLY LIKE YOU TOLD US AND I COVERED MY BUDDY,"* emphasizing each syllable while reciting his own standing orders back to him.

There was a momentary pause. My mind raced with questions: *Did I say it convincingly? Was it enough? Fuck, would he accept my answer?* I waited.

Handgrenade jumped out of his chair, extended his right hand, and said, *"AT FUCKING EASE, TURNER. HAVE A SEAT."* He shook my hand and smiled while he said, *"THAT'S WHAT I'M FUCKING TALKING ABOUT, TURNER. THAT'S FUCKING HIGH-SPEED, LOW-DRAG SHIT, SOLDIER."* He was actually excited, I could hardly believe it. I was, to put it bluntly, beyond relieved. *He fucking loved this shit.* I fucking loved that a commander meant what he said.

He jumped on the phone to the awaiting MPs and began a volley of short responses, to what I assumed were a barrage of questions regarding you know who. This continued for a couple of minutes, until he finally barked out like an angry father, *"HE'S MY BOY AND YOU CAN'T FUCKING HAVE 'EM!"* before slamming the phone back to its receiver. I was thrilled. My awesome commander just went to bat for me, big league. He kept me out of military prison after I'd put another soldier in the hospital for 3½ hours of surgery, and an assured life-long scar.

This little interlude led to my being the first in our unit to sign up for the boxing team. I happened to catch CPT Handgrenade coming out of HQs one day, moments after he'd received the directive. He said he wanted to see my name on the top of that list, so I was indeed the first name. Though I was a welter-weight, I wound up boxing in the (heavier) light-middle-weight class, due to the low turnout of volunteers. I won Battalion, Brigade, Division, and eventually won the German finals in Heidelberg.

After the finals, I was approached and invited to join the *ALL-ARMY BOXING TEAM.* It would have meant an instant promotion to the rank of E-5/ SGT. The drawback was it meant an instant change of duty station back to the United States. I heavily considered it, but I opted against. I didn't want to leave my brothers, nor did I want to leave Germany any sooner than I had to. I sometimes wonder what turns and twists my career would have taken had I pursued the boxing route. Most likely, I'd have never seen the inside of a tank or 5-ton truck again, but more importantly, I may not have seen my brothers again.

Even today, I still talk to these fuckers on an almost daily basis. A few years back, I (along with the other founding father, Joe Spud Powell) organized a reunion for whomever wanted to come, and even encouraged the others to host them. A tradition was instantly born. Now, we get together, drink beer, tell old stories, and do a bunch of crazy shit that no one else in this world would even fathom as any resemblance to normal. But, that is exactly why we love getting together; we all speak the same language, have the same humor, and we imbibe in both of the best medicines known to man…beer and laughter with our brothers-in-arms. I am afraid had I accepted that post with the All-Army Boxing Team, I wouldn't have that same connection we all share almost three decades later. Next to my own flesh and blood, these guys are truly my brothers.

I guess this is where I should thank CPT Vandergriff, as we remain in contact to this day. Not only do I consider you a former colleague, but a friend as well. You were the epitome of what a commander should be: fair, but tough, because you wanted us to win. I will always be thankful that you stood up for me. I'd have faithfully followed you into any combat zone, sir. Even today, you earn my devoted respect.

46

KAISER-WILHELM KASERNE

It was the end of summer, 1993, when we were informed our unit would be relocating back to the states late the next year, as well as to temporary barracks in the interim. That meant we would continue to work out of our then current motor pools and platoon bays at Sullivan, but would live elsewhere.

Sullivan Barracks were to be renovated for USAF personnel; we drunken tankers had to go. It was a pain in the ass, but we would be located closer to downtown Mannheim, into what is now a defunct post named, Turley Barracks. They were a twelve-hundred person *kaserne* (German for *barracks*), built in the 1800s and originally named, *Kaiser-Wilhelm Kaserne*. Supposedly, they were the oldest, still-utilized barracks in all of Germany.

Like Sullivan Barracks, the Americans took possession of them after WWII ended. Unlike Sullivan, these were devoid of Swastikas in the handrails, as they were pre-Nazi construction. At the time of their construction, Germany still employed Kaisers and Emperors sporting handlebar moustaches. They were truly beautiful barracks inside and out. By contrast, we were ugly, unruly, and drunk.

It was home to the 181st transportation unit, where real 88Mikes operated a fleet of trucks and trailers. There was going to be hell to pay... for them, not us. We were a combat-arms MOS, and they were not. We were uncaged Tasmanian devils, while they were cute, fuzzy puppies. Yin and yang...Night and day...Good and evil...Black and white...Wild and mild...Tame and fierce. The vivid and distinct contrasts could go on and on. We were definitely carved from very different stock than they were.

We had two floors of one building and three floors of a neighboring one, all to ourselves. The bottom floor of my building housed German (civilian) contractors working for the U.S. Army. Initially they were not alarmed at our presence, but we changed that in a matter of hours, not days or weeks.

We devised some of the best parties at Turley. It was like a consequence-free environment for us. As long as no one died or was seriously injured, leadership seemingly turned a blind eye, which led to our having a worsened attitude of invincibility. We had women practically living in the barracks, which was a big no-no, but no one enforced it. As long as they were out during inspections and didn't fuck with anyone else's shit, why would we rat on our brothers? We had, in some cases, full bars in our rooms. Granted, it was difficult to keep it stocked because we were all drunk most all of the time.

There was nothing out of the ordinary about walking into your buddy's room in the middle of the day, to find his girlfriend splayed out on the bed completely naked, and he with a pair of hair clippers actively trimming her pussy to his liking. There was no shame. Hell, she would say hello and make small talk with you while her bearded clam was being barbered in front of you. With the exception of a few wee hours, Sunday to Thursday, you could always hear someone's stereo system blaring out tunes at maximum volume. There was always a party happening in *some* part of the barracks, and someone, somewhere was drinking some form of alcohol.

After several hours of drinking, we would enlist the help of machinery to aid in our killing of time and brain cells. Buffer rodeo became a common drunken pastime. I know you've all seen the handled-buffers that polish floors. Well, we would unwind the cord, plug them in, sit on the motor, mount our feet on the lower housing, and pull the trigger to see who could ride it the longest. It was truly a wonder that no one got seriously hurt, as buffer and body were often careening into walls and lockers, and sliding across the floor in every direction.

I remember this one time, and I do emphasize *one time,* that I took a sip from a beer and there was an extinguished cigarette in it. It's one of those things you never forget. I thought Hamburger Martony was going to stream beer out of his nose he was laughing so hard. Meanwhile, I was doubled-over and dry heaving. I can *still* taste that awful thing.

TE-QUI-LA SUNRISE. SCRATCH THAT…TO-KILL-YA SUNRISE.

It's been said, time heals all wounds. Bullshit. It's been over twenty-seven years and I've never recovered from my tequila wounds. I bartended in college, and I can tell you, I looked pretty fucking silly making margaritas, extending the tequila as far as my arms could distance the bottle and glass from my nose.

One night, I'd purchased a 1.75L bottle of the *gold* variety of tequilas. For some reason, unbeknownst to me, I decided I was bound and determined to drink the entire bottle by myself. Please, if ever we meet while I'm vacationing, or grocery shopping, please do not ask me what the fuck I was thinking, because, and quite honestly, I haven't a fucking clue if I was thinking at all. I borrowed a salt shaker from the mess hall and bought a few limes to assist my quest.

Oddly enough, as memory serves, Boston Brawler was on CQ duty again, so the room was all mine. That evening, I sat up and poured myself, and anyone who happened by, a full shot of tequila. I damn-near consumed that entire bottle, with a little help from my friends. Oddly enough, my memory was intact, as well as my nickname, Iron Gut McKenzie. I hadn't puked.

Turner—1: Tequila—0.

I woke up about 0830 the next morning. The sun was shining, and it was a beautiful day. I couldn't move, and I felt like death held over so the grim reaper could reschedule. I was in a physical coma from the previous evening's booze barrage. It was nothing I'd ever experienced. Seemingly, I was paralyzed, or *tequila-yzed*, as I've affectionately come to regard that morning. My body simply refused to respond to my brain's commands. Brawler had just come in after working the CQ desk for a full 24 hours, thus he was trying to get some much-needed sleep. From my bunk, I woke him up. *"BRAWLER,"* I grumbled.

"WAT," he asked, in his Bostonian accent.

I begged him, I implored him to please bring me the ½-gallon of water that was in the refrigerator.

"NO. GET IT YAHSELF, TURNAH."

What you have to understand is, we all loved each other in a brotherly way and would have had one another's six, or back, in combat. What that brotherly love didn't include was performing domesticated niceties for one another. You are a grown man and can do that shit yourself. You're getting your ass whipped, I have your six. You need me to lie to our superiors to save your skin, I have your six. You need someone to do something completely stupid with, I have your six. You need me to take a bullet for you, I have your six. You need water from the refrigerator that's ten feet away, fuck off and get your own six on that one. It was that kind of brotherhood.

Long story short, Brawler eventually caved and brought me some water…twice. I had to drink an *entire* gallon of water in a span of ten minutes before I could even get out of bed. After having risen from the dead, I managed a trip to the latrine. I took a leak and headed back down the hall to our room. There was a nice breeze coming through the hallway windows.

Then it hits me. I let loose the foul, vehement spirits of tequila from within my stomach. I leaned out of the window and tried to puke, but instead, only dry-heaves and lime particulates exited my body.

Yes, my body, in that ten-minute span of drinking an entire gallon of water, had absorbed every single drop of it. Obviously, my vital organs were more important than setting free the limes from within. I wanted to die. I have never wanted to die, but that morning I had the thought, *Death may be better than how I feel right now.* And just like that, I was cured from ever drinking tequila again.

Twice after that, I foolishly tried to reacquaint myself with tequila and feel it necessary to be honest with my readers.

Turner—0: Tequila—3.

You win, fucker.

SCHEIßE HIER, NICHT…ARSCHLOCH!

Translation: *Stop shitting here…asshole.* After we were there for a couple of months, we began to notice someone was unloading a case of the dynamite ass in our latrine. He decimated our toilets with the worst case of exploding-ass-syndrome we'd ever seen. As we were our own maids and butlers, it became the topic of many of our conversations. It became our mission to catch the culprit and deal with him accordingly.

As it turned out, one of the German nationals, a fat-fucker that lived downstairs and whom we shall call, Günter, would come to our floor to blow his ass out, leaving the mess for us. It was horrible, as his rectal explosions were catapulted inside the toilet, outside of the toilet, on the walls…everywhere. Apparently, *Exploding-Ass-Syndrome* was a real thing. *Not only was he a member, but he was the fucking president.* I wished the details of this story ended there, but it doesn't.

Günter was also coming into our latrine to wash his junk in our sinks. By junk, I mean he was washing his dick and balls, including his underarms. *In our fucking sinks*!! For the love of God, what was wrong with this guy? We wanted to murder him. I think it was The Brawler that finally caught Günter and kicked him out.

I made these signs in German and English that read something along the lines of keeping one's feces and urine in the toilet, instead of all over it. The signage, coupled with banishment from our latrines, were not having the effect we'd hoped for. We were forced to interpret things into a language Günter could understand. Spud and I had such a plan to ease international tensions.

We had all received a speech or two regarding our behavior when under the watchful eye of the German general public. As federal employees, we were always *American Ambassadors*, acting on behalf of the United States; therefore, we were to conduct ourselves accordingly at all times. It was the stuff that sounded good and looked great on official looking papers.

With this important consideration in mind, we decided to dole out a little well-deserved justice to our German friend, Günter. It was a simple recipe, really. It was seventeen parts alcohol, one part 100-mph tape (Army duct tape), one part expended 40mm grenade shell, and just a smidge of lunacy, for that home flavor like grandma used to make. This is why Spud was my Idahoan partner in crime on so many occasions;

Paris, Amsterdam, Bastogne, why should Germany be exempt?

We got completely hammered, then we used about three rolls of 100-mph tape and toilet paper to stripe Günter's doorway almost completely closed. Between the tape and the actual door was a 12–14" void. Then the real fun began. The unfortunate part of our *downstairs diplomacy tour* was every other German on the floor had to suffer with Günter, as well as every swinging dick on the second floor, where we lived. Maybe it was a stroke of brilliance, as Günter's immediate neighbors (co-workers) would realize what was happening and intervene on our behalf in the future. Our plan, however, was not *that* forward thinking, as the first seventeen parts of our recipe were very much in play.

You might ask what the 40mm shell was for. I will tell you. Günter's door was at the end of a long hallway, maybe twenty-five meters in length. Thus, it made his door the perfect target for a newfound sport, Barracks Bowling. After taping over his doorway and setting up empty beer bottles as bowling pins, we proceeded to the opposite end of the hall and took turns bowling the shell towards Günter's door. Because of the threshold space and the door's opening inward, it forced him to deal with the tape and toilet paper before he could exit the room.

I know I have described some ferocious clamors in this book, but they pale in comparison to the all-unholy, ear-splitting shrill that an expended 40mm round makes when chucked down a hundred-year-old stone-walled hallway at 0200 hours. It is beyond mere mortals' comprehension. It makes such a ruckus and racket that the dead, buried beneath our beloved local graveyard bier brewery, were probably startled by our new sport.

Joe bowled the first shot, falling short of the target. Strike one, for Spud. I retrieved the 40mm. We debated whether to continue, as it fucking screamed, clanged, and banged off both sides of the hallway so loudly, it raised the attention of our buddy, Tricky Dick (SPC Box), who showed up to join in the fun. The debacle of continuing was chalked-up to a momentary lapse in insanity. Our irresponsible and reckless diplomacy carried-on in glorious, American fashion. As they say in the business, the show must go on. I took a stab at it. Again failure. Strike two, for yours truly. Tricky took a turn, also a no-go at this station. Strike three, for Box.

Spud stepped up to bat, football glove in hand. One out, and the imaginary beer-bases were loaded. He carefully aimed before he took his shot towards glory. There was minimal interference from the walls and doorways down 40mm Straße (German for street). It looked sketchy for the visiting team, folks. Is it going to make it? *BOOM!* SCOOOOOOORE!!!! Spud knocked it out of the park. It was a grand-slam homerun for the visiting team.

America—1: Günter—0

Fortunately, we staged someone at his door in order to retrieve the *ball* from any home-team interference. Had Günter procured an expended 40mm shell, it could have spelled disaster for the game. Besides, we still had a few more innings to pitch. Surprisingly, Günter was a heavy sleeper, thus he never came out, and neither did his neighbors. We had a couple of pussies open their doors to yell out some indecipherable mumblings, but they never approached us face-to-face. The *Drunken Jolly Green Fucking Giants* were roaming the *straßes*!

I had to get a homerun, now, as Spud set the bar high. It became my life's mission. The inner monolog of tank gunnery commands began. *Gunner, 40mm, door. Identified. Up. Fire. On the way.* I chucked that shell so hard down the hall, I swore it had gone live, as if fired from the MK19. Possibly even punch a hole through the door. It went most of the way before it started that *swerve,* striking a guardrail or two, mimicking a sour drunk-driving episode, before making its target into Günter's door.

America—2: Günter—0

The only problem was, my homerun awakened Günter. We just did retrieve the shell before he opened his door. Günter ripped, fumbled, and cursed the tape and toilet paper, before managing it into a gigantic sphere that resembled one of those colorful exercise balls you'd find on late-night infomercials, that are guaranteed to change your life. We spied him from behind a slight jog at the other end of the hallway. Uncontrollable laughter ensued. Amidst the shards of glass, he chucked his sphere into the hallway and returned to his room.

Our mission being one of diplomacy, I couldn't help but give a short speech. I then yelled to Günter, *"HEY, ARSCHLOCH, SCHEIßE NICHT, NACH OBEN,"* which is a horrible translation for, *Hey, asshole, stop shitting upstairs.* We did a tactical retreat to grab another beer and discuss our next battle plan. Tricky Dick was the only one in our trio yet to hit a homerun. What kind of buddies would we be, if we didn't see to it that he had, at minimum, a chance to bowl for a homerun? Awful ones, I know. So, we liquored-up a bit more and gave Günter an opportunity to return to his slumber. Diplomacy at its finest.

After a little reconnaissance, I staged myself at Günter's door and waited while Tricky lined up his shot. The bases were loaded, it was bottom of the ninth, and a shut-out was imminent. *Folks, we have a helluva game today at Kaiser-Wilhelm Field....* The batter eyed his target, and like the Babe, king of baseball, he pointed his 40mm high into the bleachers, *calling* his homerun to the adoring crowd. Tricky lined it up, delivered his shot, and we waited while the screaming apparition of Kaiser-Wilhelm himself howled like a bleeding banshee down the hallway.

The tension built, the slumbering Germans leapt from their beds, as the imaginary crowd leapt to their feet. Our lungs held its last drawn breath as that shell twirled and sang towards its target. It was right up the middle; up and over the outfielder's position. It looked beautiful, folks. *SCOOOOOOORE!* Wake up, mother fucker! Like witches over a cauldron, we exploded into a fit of cackles and hisses, as if the 40mm shell had exploded upon impact. Tricky closed-out the game. America had its *V*, for victory.

America—3: Günter—0

I always include this esteemed position to applications when applying for employment: United States Ambassador to Germany, *Kaiser-Wilhelm Kaserne*; House Leader of the Segregated Shithouse Incentive. To this day, I have yet to have anyone question the integrity of such a claim, although I usually pencil it in on the back of some obscure, meaningless form.

Soon after completing our downstairs diplomacy tour towards peace and goodwill to all mankind, and shortly before our permanently leaving country, we had to relocate to the building next door, which meant, to some degree, our diplomatic tour was concluded.

BATTER UP…TOASTER-OVEN BASEBALL!

As our time in Germany neared its end, our happiness soured to rueful mourning. A time when the bars would no longer see our faces drinking glorious Hefe-Weißbier. We could no longer eat warm, moist, fresh Turkish Döners with lettuce, tomato, onions, and tzatziki sauce. Washing down the most awesome of sandwiches with the local wheat beer. Can you see the guy slicing the meat into the bread yet? Can you smell it? Can you sense the powdery texture in the air from the fresh bread? I told you I was an asshole, but you didn't believe me, did you? Don't feel bad. I want one too, right about now.

Our priorities shifted as our departure of Germany neared. It was a sad state of affairs. Don't get me wrong…I was excited to return to America, as I'd not been on actual American soil in nearly two years. I hadn't met a true American woman in nearly two years. Wait, scratch that, I did *sleep* with an American woman I'd met at the Special Olympics. She was an officer's wife and not an actual participant in the Olympics. My Army brothers are reading this sentence and deciding how much they are going to fuck with me about it. Anyway, America raised us, educated us; our primary school if you will. But Germany, oh, Germany, well, she completed our education in all things worldly.

Our time at Turley was a bit fractured, beaten, and bruised. We were the redheaded step-children on post. We were the dogs that had been beaten and left out in the cold. One could say, the leash was severed, the umbilical cut, and the gate left wide-open for those last few days that remained. *"THE BARRACKS WILL BE CLEANED AND INSPECTED BEFORE OUR DEPARTURE, GENTLEMEN,"* the PLT Daddy instructed us. That task ensured, for the post commander of Turley, a grimmer outlook on us, the Silver Knights. The events that followed would have had Kaiser-Wilhelm himself either order us *shot-on-sight*, or he'd have delivered more beer and further funded our antics.

We were instructed to remove all non-military items, such as furniture, decorations, alcohol, women, appliances, and anything else that didn't belong there. We were on it like hair on a gorilla. We were given two days to complete the cleanup, so naturally we spent the first one depleting all the remaining booze, and maybe, just maybe, a few extra that were purchased for the cleaning party.

Couches were defiled in a final blaze of glory with women that would soon weep the tears of our departure. Grease-soaked microwaves poured out the last of its heat waves into frozen chicken dinners, and dirty ashtrays housed the remnants of our $2.00 cartons of cigarettes. I can still see the staircase going up to the main floor, where I'd beaten up the PLT bully. Due to a large amount of blood, I woke up the Brawler to look him over, as he was a medic. Like the wrestler he was, I will give him credit, as earlier that night, he body-slammed me onto the cobblestone streets of Sullivan. But, the MPs showed up so the fight was postponed until we reached Turley. I digress.

Day two, we awoke to find hangovers had overrun our position during the night. It was bitter-sweet. Our last full day in Germany was upon us. Women were doing the walk of shame after their last fucks, hugs, kisses, and goodbyes. We had three floors of shit to flush out and less than a day to do it. With a stairwell on each end, it seemed implausible to think of hauling that shit down, *one-handful* after another. So in honor of soldiers all over the world, we did the only natural thing possible, we took the shortest route. I have had a few experiences in my life where things slow down, like in a movie: running with the bulls, facing time in Coleman Confinement, the tank firing the main gun for the first time, a few close-calls on my motorcycle. Those were scary, but this next one, was awesome.

It was nearing dusk when my roommate and I, along with everyone else, were drunk as all get out. I know, difficult to fathom. We found ourselves outside of our barracks' window at ground level. We set up an AO near the dumpster we'd commandeered in an effort to expedite our house-cleaning party. It was midway between the ends of the building. Instead of hauling all that shit down by hand, we simply dumped everything out of the windows…and there were a lot of windows. There were fans, microwaves, beer boxes, half-eaten meals, bloated garbage bags, stained pillows, coffee tables, chairs, German road signs, televisions, and anything else one could imagine; it was of landfill proportions. It was the accumulation of years and years of soldierly goods and wares of every variety, and all were caked in the assorted bodily fluids of half the breeding-aged populous of women in the Mannheim area.

Another, albeit short-lived, sport of ours that lasted all of exactly one evening was Toaster-Oven Baseball. Vegas Brad and I were there, knee-deep amongst the ruin. I stood shirtless in those earlier mentioned beer-labeled boxer shorts, baseball bat in hand, a cigarette hanging from my mouth, and a beer resting near my feet. Vegas stood there, drink close by, hands clasped to our poor, well-used toaster-oven. A cigarette also hung from his lip as he wound-up the pitch, delivering the goods, and I swung for the bleachers. My only regret is I didn't predict my homerun in Babe Ruth style like Tricky Dick did. The toaster-oven window shattered as I swung through. The screwed and riveted seams loosened, and it lay in a twisted refuge of heating elements and crumb catchers.

TURNER—1: TOASTER-OVEN—0

In-and-of itself, this may not seem like a great credit to our normally sinister methods, of which you've, no doubt, come to expect in this memoir. But, the awful, drunken ways we brought forth to this once peaceful Army post in quiet, Baden Württemberg, Germany, gave rise to our [transportation] brothers-and-sisters detesting our very existence in the moments that followed.

About the time I scored my monumental homerun, someone called us to attention, and *not* in a joking manner either, so we knew it was the real deal. We observed the post commander and his driver approaching our position in his vehicle, thus we were expected to come to attention and render the time-honored military courtesy of saluting an officer. We stood there, beers-in-hand, saluting him as he slowly inched towards us. I observed the commander in the passenger seat, leaning forward and towards the window. What I couldn't tell was whether he was squinting from the setting sun, or from the strained comprehension of what was before him. I presume it to be the latter.

I can only imagine what went through his mind, as he saw this troop of inebriated soldiers saluting him in nothing more than beers, boxers, and baseball bats. He really struggled to make sense of us tankers.

This was where things slowed-down for me. About the time we rendered our salutes, and the colonel keened his sights in on us, a couch from a third floor window fell to the ground about four meters from our position. It smashed to smithereens as it struck the earth. We didn't bat an eye, but the post commander could hardly believe either of his. The look on his gob-smacked, wide-eyed face was priceless. It was as if a nine-headed hydra had appeared in front of him. He could barely move past the scene of this motley crew as he returned more of a *half-salute,* and a half *oh-my-god* what am I seeing?! I will never forget the look on his face as he took it all in. The mess, the debaucherously absurd example of soldiers that stood before him, left him looking as dumbfounded as we were drunk. It was the epitome of a proper Silver Knights departure.

Later on that evening, we decided to hit the town for some final beers in Der Vaterland (German for The Fatherland). We didn't frequent our normal bars on the economy, as we didn't want to get stuck with DMs on the last night, so we visited one of our own haunts, the *Pirates Cove Bar*, at Taylor Barracks in the suburb of Vogelstang. It would prove to be a fatal mistake for our brother, SGT Paine.

There must have been thirty of us there that night. It didn't start that way, but by strange coincidence, it ended up that way. I met this cute brunette woman that, naturally, wanted to bear my children. It was one wild night in that bar, in the hours before we departed for America. As Taylor Barracks were very close to our old barracks, Sullivan, we simply walked to Sullivan and had a bus ride to Turley when happy-hour ended. That meant no taxis, no Straßenbahn. We simply drank and allowed the bus to do the driving for us, which was very wise for leadership to have provided.

We drank our normal excessive amounts until about 0230 or so, before we decided to head back to the barracks. We were flying to Ireland in a matter of minutes, so it was probably a good call. Before leaving, I remember that SGT J and I, among others, were trying to convince our buddy, SGT Paine, to come with us. Like the rest of us, he'd had quite a few drinks, so we wanted to make sure he was not left behind. He assured us that he was having one more beer, then departing with some other guys from our unit. Efforts aside, he was a big boy and could handle himself, so we left.

We said our goodbyes to buddies and bartenders, along with my little brunette, then made our way out. We left in packs of four or five, heading to Sullivan. You could either take the safe route, or you could finagle your way through a hole in the fence and literally run across the Autobahn on foot. Yes, actually running across an active German Autobahn on foot. We were that stupid.

We arrived at Sullivan and caught the bus back to Turley. We woke up the next morning and prepared ourselves for the flight to Ireland. There were a few guys (I'm so jealous, Spud) that stayed in country for a couple of extra weeks to clear out the barracks, complete some administrative stuff, and take care of last-minute dealings. We stopped in Ireland for a spell, then continued on to Fort Lewis, Washington, in the United States of America.

Two days after we arrived, they formed us up to divulge the news that we'd lost one of our brothers in Germany. They had pamphlets made, and a service was held to honor his memory as one of our comrades. He was a good man, a great soldier, and a dear friend.

Until Valhalla, Brother Paine.

47

AMERICAN CONQUISTADORS OF THE SPANISH INQUISITION & OTHER VILE ODDITIES

It was 1994, and we had in-hand our marching orders to Fort Lewis. Our fate back to the states was sealed. We asked the Army if we could take a thirteen-day trip to Spain, to follow in the footsteps of famed author Ernest Hemingway in his book *The Sun Also Rises*. We trekked from Paris, France, to run with the bulls in Pamplona, Spain, also known as the *Fiesta de San Fermin*. This would be the feather in our caps before exiting Germany. The Army, thankfully, approved our request. There were six of us: Tricky Dick, Vinny, SSG Special K, Tom Dever, SGT Larry, and myself. I'm still not sure how I managed to never really hang out with Larry in garrison, but always managed to find myself paired with him on so many adventures. Spud should have been there, but couldn't make it.

We rented a station wagon for the 1800-mile round trip through Germany, France, and Spain. Had yours truly not packed four CDs, we'd have been forced to listen to fifty-year-old French classics for days on end. This was truly going to be an adventure of a lifetime.

It was early in the morning when we picked-up and tightly loaded-out our station wagon. We'd purchased shit and tons of cigarettes, booze, beer, shitty canned foods, crackers, snacks, and anything we didn't want to purchase on the economy. As we didn't know what the exchange rate was going to be on any given day, we were on a tight budget. We had our Army sleeping bags, pillows, clothes, booze, and groceries packed like sardines into the hatchback area.

It was about 0700 hours when we were ready to depart. As we said our goodbyes, Dever's wife said, *"WAIT. I HAVE SOMETHING FOR YOU, BUT IT'S FOR ALL OF YOU...TO USE ON YOUR TRIP."* It resembled a large book wrapped in brown grocery bags. Dever opened the package, and low and behold, it was a large book, but not just any book. It was a road atlas of Europe and all of her highways. A road atlas is how we old folks used to get ourselves around in the world. It was the perfect gift for our journey. It being my third trip to Paris, we didn't need the atlas for the first leg of the trip. So Dever opened the hatchback and placed the book between some bags of food and booze.

I was one-of-two authorized drivers of the rental car, so I took the first shift. The trip we'd planned for months was finally upon us. It was surreal. It would be the last time I would ever drive into Paris for a two-night stay before going to Spain; the last big trip before return-ing to America. We were on our way, cruising Autobahn 6 towards Saarbrücken, Germany, then on to Paris. The weather was perfect—sunny and warm. Our car had a sunroof, so it was wide-open, as were the windows. We had some 1990s Seattle-based grunge blasting out of the speakers; life was awesome. I felt on top of the world.

That morning, I noticed a funny thing about the French...they still held a grudge from WWII. I had travelled from Amsterdam to Paris and noted that there were maybe two toll stops along the way. However, when travelling from Germany to Paris, there were six. Six fucking toll stops. It wasn't much, maybe 5-10 Francs each, but it was the principle of it. We still averaged 120–130 km, or 75–80 mph.

The music seemed to fit each curve of road like a glove. It was shaping up to be an awesome day. We paid the second of many tolls, and continued cruising across the beautiful French countryside. In my rearview mirror, I soon noticed a nice *seven-series* car flashing its headlights at me. I waved them around, as traffic wasn't heavy, especially on a four-lane highway. In our personally owned vehicles, adorned with US/German license plates, we were easily identified as Americans, but we were in a rented vehicle, so we looked like every other swinging dick from Germany.

We reached the next toll. I threw the money into the basket and continued down the highway, business-as-usual. I assumed we'd lost our fanatics in the congestion of the toll stop. No such luck. They continued their tirade, flashing their headlights at me. I motioned for them to overtake us, as I'd grown weary of them in my mirrors.

They pulled up beside us, and we noticed that they were an older German couple. The woman was persistently motioning for us to pull the car to the shoulder. I gave her a bit of local sign language; palm-in, I waved my hand in front of my face, which in Germany means, fuck you or you're crazy, depending on the situation. I'd hoped to imply both meanings to the old bat. They sped around and placed their vehicle in front of ours. I thought, *Fuck my life. How did I manage to draw-in the crazies this time?*

Oma and Opa (German for grandma and grandpa) were now in front of us, laying on the brakes with their turn indicator signaling to the shoulder. I thought, *What the fuck do these assholes want with us?* They maintained a reasonable speed, but continued with the brake-lights and the turn indicator, before Oma motioned her arm out of the window for us to pull-over to the shoulder. After a short discussion with the boys, we decided that unless they were armed, we could overpower them should they try something funny. I pointed out that it was daylight, there were plenty of people around, and there were five of us, as SSG Special K was in a separate vehicle with his wife and son. I instructed them to exit the car like mobsters, like we meant business. All agreed.

I put on my indicator and eased to the curb. I stopped our vehicle well-short of their position. We exited the car like a movie in slow-motion, like five gangsters getting out of an old 1930s car with suicide doors, but in reality, it was five soldiers from an Opel station wagon. Yeah, we were bad-ass and we knew it.

Then a funny thing happened. This little ole Oma climbed out of the passenger seat and started yelling to us in German. None of us could hear her over the traffic whizzing by. With trepidation, we inched forward in an attempt to hear her. No luck. She started pointing at us, which confused us further. Dumbfounded, we looked at one another in search of an answer. Mouths agape, eyes squinted, we then tried to decipher her sign-language.

She motioned to imply there was something over us, beyond our position. A heavenly beam illuminated our thick, Cro-Magnon skulls. Then, as if our bodies were tethered to a set of hands in the sky, and also in slow-motion, we turned around to face the horror of our open-air station wagon…literally! The hatchback lid was *wide-ass-open*. It wasn't ajar, or just shy of closing, oh, no, the hydraulic supports were fully-fucking extended to the *n*th degree. That meant, all of our clothes and groceries, but more importantly, our cigarettes and booze were exposed to the elements.

I turned to Oma and bowed while I screamed, *"VIELEN DANK, VIELEN DANK,"* which means, *Thank you very much*. I waved, and we broke into a full-on race, not sprint, to the rear of the car.

There was strange magic at work that day, folks. The number of bumps and curves that we'd navigated since the ass end of the car was wide-open was, quite frankly, unfathomable. We sifted through our belongings and groceries, and to our gleeful delight, every-single-thing was present and accounted for. It was a miracle. Every drop of alcohol, every cigarette remained inside of that car. I started believing in Saint Anthony, the patron saint of lost things. Nothing was lost on that open stretch of French highway. We were so relieved. Then, Dever asked, *"HAS ANYONE SEEN MY BOOK?"*

Every single item, less the road atlas, survived the hatchback debacle. It was easily a DM100/$70.00 book. This may not seem like such a catastrophe to my younger readers, but in 1994 it was somewhat of a catastrophe. We didn't have the technological luxuries of today. Hell, no. We had to actually navigate our way through places like Paris, Pamplona, Munich, Berlin, Prague, Amsterdam, and so many more, all without the aid of instant information. We noted landmarks, read signage, and did what manly men do; *when needed, we asked complete strangers for directions.* There is nothing to read back there. Keep moving along, folks. We were modern-day Magellans of land navigation. We were barely two hours into our trip, and our atlas was splayed out and made into tire fodder on some strange French roadway. Our trip was, seemingly, doomed…NOT.

I delivered us to the youth hostel in Paris with no more hiccups. It was the same one I'd stayed in before, that offered a spectacular view of Notre-Dame. We unloaded our vehicle, and hit some of the usual tourist sites; the Eiffel, Notre-Dame, etc. Tricky and I went to *Pont de Grenelle*, along the river Seine. It is home to the smaller Statue of Liberty, the one America gave to France in 1889. We sat quietly, taking in the summer sun, as I enjoyed a smoke with Lady Liberty.

The next day we took in a few more sights and decided to hit the town for drinks. The French thought us crazy, as we carried our own 1.75L bottle of American bourbon, occasionally mixed with our semi-warm sodas. The French are weird. I am pretty sure we were thrown out of, or politely asked to leave, a couple of different cafés. Later that night, we returned to the hostel to continue our belligerence. As we couldn't finagle a room together, we had to rent two. Tricky and I shared a room, while Larry, Vinny, and Dever split a room with a couple of unknowns. We were partying in their room, when in walked their roommates. They were Scotsmen and about as inebriated as we were. They shared their scotch, and we shared our bourbon. It was a match made in heaven. We had a noise complaint issued…twice.

We drank heavily and exchanged stories with them about soldiering and life. They were curious about being American, and we were curious about being Scottish. It didn't take long for Tricky to start feeling the effects of the international parade of booze. Hell, it had pretty well hit us all. We still had another day in Paris, so we opted to turn in for the night.

We were about to leave when another drunken conversation started and another drink was poured. This was my chance to jot down some of the Scottish slang I'd learned that evening, as it was funny stuff. With drinks finished and exit in sight, Tricky in true drunken fashion looked over and asked one of the Scotsmen, *"HEY…WHERE ARE YOU GUYS FROM, ANYWAY?"*

Almost in unison, they replied, *"AYE, WE'RE FROM SCOTLAND."*

Tricky looked down for a moment, then back and asked, *"WHERE DID YOU GUYS LEARN TO SPEAK ENGLISH SO WELL, THEN?"*

It was classic Tricky.

OFF TO ESPAÑA

The next morning, we grabbed some orange juice and a hostel favorite, French bread, marmalade, and salami. After breakfast, I opted to make the much dreaded phone call back to our unit. A condition of our leave was that we were to check-in to the unit, via telephone, at least once during our thirteen-day hiatus. The boys loaded the car, while I made the call. I did, however, have the inside scoop.

My old partner-in-crime, SGT Travis, told me he would be working the first weekend of our leave and to call him for our mandatory check-in. It was maybe 0800 hours when I telephoned the unit and asked to speak to him. He asked his aide to run an errand, as he quickly clued me in to what could have been a total disaster. He informed me I was not to, under any circumstances, call back to the unit, unless it was serious, dire even.

Naturally, I asked why. He explained we had some new general in charge of USAREUR (U.S. Army Europe). No big deal, I thought. Then, he informed me that the new commander issued a sweeping directive that put us directly in his crosshairs, as any and all leave to within 300-miles of Pamplona, Spain, was to be either denied or re-voked, _immediately_. Fuck my life.

He said the letter came in shortly before 0700 hours, but he would annotate us _calling-in_ before the directive arrived, at say, 0645. It saved our asses. I seriously doubt any branch of the military, especially these days, allows any of its members to run with the bulls in Pamplona. I reckon it safe to say, we were among the last service members to le-gally run, though legally is a stretch, because we knew our leave was cancelled. And I quote no one in history, "_You make awesome stories by following the rules to a tee._"

Next stop, _Orléans_, via the AutoRoute 10. About 40 km out of the city, we took the split south. The highway opened up into this beautiful, four-lane highway. The scenery was absolutely gorgeous, and the roadway was as straight as an arrow. We were cruising along at a good speed, with minimal traffic. Near ghost-town-like proportions. We cruised upwards of 140mph, sometimes closer to 150.

I was in the right-hand lane, where drivers are supposed to be, unless they're overtaking someone (Lord, please allow Americans to grasp this concept, Amen), when I motioned for SSG K to drive alongside of us. With no other traffic around, he obliged and eased his vehicle next to ours. With his passenger window down, he looked at me like, *What is it?* Above the 140 mph winds, and to joke he was one (not that he was), I yelled, *"I WAS JUST LOOKING FOR ASSHOLES!"* He smiled and eased off the throttle to his original position. Good times!

Later that night, exhausted, we managed some sleep in the parking lot of a little truck stop, until daylight, when the French police ran us off.

We crossed into Spain that afternoon and quickly exchanged some dollars for *potatoes*, our nickname for *Pesetas* (Spain's currency before the Euro). Soon, we found ourselves at the Bay of Biscay, located in the beautiful resort town, *San Sebastián*, famed for its beaches and cragged hills stemming from the Pyrenees Mountains. After the long drive, we decided a swim was just what the doctor ordered. Have I mentioned how awesome it was to have been a young, dashing American soldier in Europe during the early 1990s? Well, I will say it again. It was awesome. As we walked along, we soon realized we were at a nude beach. Of course, it didn't take me long to undress…when in Rome and all that jazz.

As we meandered down the beach, taking in the scenery, we naturally could be overheard speaking American English. Wow, did that ever elicit a response from the local women. In Spain, upon an introduction, it's customary for a woman to hold your hand, bring your bodies close together, and kiss one another on both cheeks. I don't have to explain anatomy to say how close we had to be for our bodies to touch. Wow! It was incredibly awesome, but weird too. It wasn't anything I was expecting. *Did I mention that Spanish women are absolutely lovely?* They are not like our lovely friends to the south [America], with dark hair, eyes, and skin; Spanish women are more akin to the European bloodlines. Translation: blue eyes, green eyes, blondes, brunettes, and redheads. They are a beautiful mixture, for sure. I'm afraid with how the world is going, the cheek kiss will soon be a thing of the past.

With a swim under our belt, no pun intended, we needed to find accommodations. We asked a local for directions and were directed to a campground atop the mountain. It was a wonderful collection of people from all over the world: New Zealanders, Asians, South Americans, Russians, and everything in between. We easily made some acquaintances with nearby campers.

Later that evening, I had Larry drive me into town, to meet up with the lovely women on the beach, as they'd invited me to party with them. We found the discotheque, although Houston had a problem…I didn't bring discotheque-worthy clothes for our trip. I was no longer a well-prepared soldier.

I was not allowed into the club, as it was kind of swanky. Oh, well. Larry and I started our return to the campground. On the way down, I'd spotted an über-seedy bar along the roadside. Naturally, on our return, I suggested we stop in for a beer, to which Larry vehemently protested. Being me, I quickly feigned an upset stomach to force Larry to slow down. I lied and cried, *"LARRY, STOP. I THINK I NEED TO PUKE."* Foolishly, he stopped. I jumped out and said, *"LARRY, PARK THE CAR AND MEET ME INSIDE."*

I proceeded to walk into the bar and order a beer. It was, *in-double-deed*, a seedy bar. It was for rough customers only. In hindsight, it probably was a bad idea, but when you're a nineteen-year-old soldier, you think you're invincible. I received some strange looks from the other patrons. I was definitely not a working-class hero like them, and I was much, much younger and, how shall I say, better held together. I had enough sense to order my beer the right way, though. The problem was, it depleted my entire command of the Spanish language in one fell swoop, *"BUENOS DIAZ, SEÑOR, UNA CERVEZA POR FAVOR,"* or, *one beer, please, sir.* It was day one in a country I'd never been, and where I spoke practically none of its language. *What could possibly go wrong for a young, cocky, good-looking American soldier in a seedy mountainside bar in the heart of Basque Country?*

My beer was delivered, but not without a discerned ogle from the bartender. He gave a hard, mean look to the lone white-boy that walked in and ordered a beer with a strange Spanish accent. What I did have going for me was that I had a dark tan, brown eyes, and black hair. It gave the impression I may have been of Spanish descent, but who was I to dispute that fallacy on a sunny Spanish evening?

He spoke to his buddies, assuredly about me, then they eyeballed me, too. My inner monolog started up like a Chatty Kathy doll. *Turner, what have you done, now? Was this a bad idea? Am I in big trouble?* I was standing there like James Dean in my American blue jeans, white t-shirt, and black shades. I looked and acted the part. I gave a confident nod and tipped my beer to the bartender and his buddies when they looked over at me. I then returned to minding my own fucking business like a good little boy in a bad-ass place.

I was holding my own, considering the circumstances. Then, like flying pigs, Larry walked in. The gig was up. His big, loud, goofy voice made us out to be the ink blot on the table linen. I was standing about seven meters from the door, and Larry starts in, *"I DO NOT THINK THE CAR IS SAFE HERE. THIS IS BAD, TURNER."* My eyes must have turned into cue balls, as I darted them over to him like, *You fucking idiot, keep your voice down.* My lips pursed as my eyes bored a hole in him through the smoke and bad lighting. It worked though, as he quickly piped down.

I motioned him over, and again, even though he outranked me, I took immediate control of the situation. Larry was book smart, whereas I was street smart. I muttered, *"KEEP YOUR FUCKING VOICE DOWN, LARRY. DON'T ADVERTISE THAT WE ARE AMERICANS, YOU IDIOT."*

I noticed that the guys were really eyeballing us now. Two of the guys looked as if they would murder their best friend for five bucks. They feverishly began to talk amongst themselves about the elephants in the room. I should have turned around as soon as I walked in, but pride… no, it was stupidity that kept me walking right up to the bar, Larry in tow.

The group of men then walked towards us. I said, *"LARRY, GIVE ME THE CAR KEYS AND BE PREPARED TO RUN."* He gave me a weird look and started to speak, when I curtly repeated my orders to him.

Larry chimed in, *"DUH, WHAT, TURNER? UHHH, WHAT DO YOU MEAN?"*

I said, *"IT IS TOO FUCKING LATE NOW. BE PREPARED TO RUN, DUDE. THESE GUYS ARE COMING OVER, AND THEY DO NOT LOOK HAPPY."*

Larry was still computing my words. *"DON'T FUCKING MOVE, LARRY,"* I said, emphasizing each syllable, as I worked out a plan. One beer bottle for one of the big guys. One barstool for the other big guy. My fists for the other three guys. The bartender would just have to wait his turn. *We were fucked.*

The ring leader asked, *"AMERICANOS?"*

I really exhausted my command of Spanglish, when I responded, *"SÍ, AMIGO."*

They were not smiling at this point, so it was extremely intense for me, and Larry certainly hadn't grasped the situation yet. The conversation then continued haphazardly. The ringleader, with much trepidation, asked me if I understood Spanish, to which I replied, very little. I was still nervous as fuck, but they didn't know that. He smiled and in his best English, *"HELLO, MY FRIEND. WELCOME TO OUR BAR!"* I think I needed a change of drawers.

I was flabbergasted as I watched them all inch closer to shake our hands. My guard was still up, but it started to relax as the non-English speakers wanted the two English speakers to translate their questions to us. *Where were we from? What were we doing in Spain? Why did we come into their lowly bar?* I eased up and ordered them all a beer, as they were less than a dollar a piece. With that token of generosity, we were their new best friends.

As it turned out, they were extremely grateful we'd visited their bar to purchase beers. They were true, working-class heroes and very patriotic members of their culture and background. They were *Basque*, the oldest, still-living culture in Europe, with a history spanning more than seven-thousand years. Some theorists claim the Basque were in Europe before agriculture was introduced. I was as curious about them, as they were about us. They were only too proud to regale their history with us.

They were friendly and excited an outsider wanted to learn their story. They shared with us so many of their customs, their struggles, and some of their rich family history; how they didn't want all the riches in the world, only a place to call their own. They said most Basque were a simple, but happy people, herding sheep and raising crops to support themselves and their families. Given the untold generations of Basque that occupied the lands in the north of Spain and south of France, most wanted a sovereign country of their own. Some factions even resorted to terrorist-like measures to coerce the French and Spanish governments to relinquish these lands to the Basque.

The gentlemen we met that day admitted over a few more beers, that they were on the cusp of being regular citizens and also members of the resistance, but certainly not terrorists. They accepted my first beer, and attempted to buy my beers after that. I told them that it was hard for me to come in and spend my money if they were going to insist on buying my beers. They smiled, and I made the bartender take my money to buy another round. It was a wonderful evening hanging out with the *real* locals, and a moving experience getting to know these guys.

During our many conversations, the leader imparted to me a very valuable piece of advice for our journey through the Pyrenees. He said, that if we encountered a very simple looking people, they were, in all probability, Basque. He taught me to say hello in their language (Kaixo) and encouraged me to make every attempt to speak it when confronted with Basque, that our efforts would be met with great generosity.

It was growing late, so at the behest of Larry, we decided that we should rejoin our brothers on the mountaintop. I wished I'd have had my picture taken with them, as they'd done with me, thanks to the bartender. I am hopeful, that if that bar still stands, my picture proudly hangs in it. They shook our hands, and the biggest one threw his arm around my shoulder and asked our translator to relay a message to me. He said, *"WE WANT TO MAKE YOU HONORARY BASQUE MEMBER, MY FRIEND, MY BROTHER. WELCOME TO OUR BROTHERHOOD."* It was so nice for them to take a stranger under their wing and accept me as an honored guest that evening. I bought them another round of beers before we departed.

The decision to go into that bar turned into one of the coolest experiences I ever had with the locals in any of the many, many places I visited in Europe. Blind stupidity certainly paid off that evening; greater were the number of roads found to Pamplona than were annotated on our map. Saying hello in the Basque tongue proved invaluable beyond measure. In honor of my Basque brothers, I shall, for the remainder of the book, use the traditional name of *Iruñea,* in place of Pamplona, for without those brothers, we'd have surely been Lima Lima Mike Foxtrot. We returned to the campground and partied the night away with our new world-wide acquaintances.

The following morning and very hungover, we began our journey to Iruñea. The drive through the mountains was absolutely gorgeous. It was rugged country, but spectacularly scenic through the twisty, switch-backed roads. We were surrounded by scorched golden earth, rocks, and small, but lush trees of what I believed to be a form of sage brush. We were comfortably cradled in the valley of, in land navigation terms, one saddle after another. We found very little traffic, but managed to find a few villages in which to *stop and ask for directions*. Keep reading, nothing to see back there. We were men, in man's country. We were a proud brotherhood of mighty seekers of strange places and people. If life offered another opportunity to drive through these beautiful mountains, I would take it in a heartbeat.

FIREWORKS...ENCORE IN IRUÑEA!

We arrived in Iruñea for what was to be four fun-filled days of imbibed indulgence and depravity. We found a parking lot in which to set up camp. It was in the heart of town, near all the craziness. We planted ourselves right across the street from a large carnival with rides, games, and other fascinating Spanish festivities. There were approximately 500 to 600 cars in that parking lot.

Us being thirsty, we ventured into the carnival to procure some local beer. On the outskirts, we found a gypsy-style tent bar; dark, smoky, and full of low-life folk, like us. Naturally, we walked right in and ordered a beer—a wonderful concoction that boasted an alcohol content of 13%. It fell right-in-line with our German standards. We were bullshitting and remarking about how happy we were the road trip was finished. That's about the time we noticed we were the *only* males in the place. Now, one might think we'd hit the jackpot and walked into the largest nest of hot women in Europe, but one would be wrong. It was the anti-sausage party from hell. These women looked like they could and would take us on in a fist-fight. We had been in Iruñea for all of an hour, so it was way too early to get arrested. Beers in-hand, we promptly popped-smoke and beat feet out of there.

We walked around the carnival a little while, getting tipsy along the way. I met a group of guys and gals, a mixture of Americans and Australians. I wound up *cuddling* in a sleeping bag with one of the Aussie girls. Yes, it was a fast affair and not as noteworthy as I'd hoped, but still a *g'day* for this mate! We didn't even mind the few night owls walking around. Not that we drew an audience, but it's more difficult in a sleeping bag than imagined. I'll leave it at that. *Night one* was in the [sleeping] bag.

The following morning, the 6th of July, we woke up shortly after sunrise, as our parking lot hotel was unencumbered by curtains and walls. We walked into town, perhaps a mile, toward the bull-related festivities. We grabbed some grub to sober up a bit. It was more of a plan, than a goal, as sobriety didn't last long. Soon, we found ourselves in a great plaza, in the heart of the old city, surrounded by buildings of wonderful architecture.

Shortly before noon and in a matter of a few moments, we were surrounded by hordes of other partiers. We quickly hashed out a plan in case we were separated. I was, again, found in James Dean attire; blue jeans and a white t-shirt. I seamlessly blended-in, as most everyone there wore a white shirt and trousers, adorned with a red, waist-worn sash. With over one-million people in attendance, it was a sea of white, striped with red. I quickly purchased and donned a red bandanna for my neck and a sash for my waist, as is the customary attire for the running.

The horde quickly expanded into a massive score of people, as if flood gates were violently flung open. The next thing you know we had bottle after bottle of champagne being passed around. It was partly to drink, and partly to shower folks around you with. Then, a hypnotic spell seemed to have been cast over the crowd, as they began an ancient chant while a trance-like dance was performed in unison. It was incredible to be part of a 600-year-old tradition. At times, I was literally swept off my feet in the throngs of the swaying mass. No shit, there were so many people crowded shoulder-to-shoulder into this plaza, my body was actually elevated off the cobblestoned streets. Hands-down, it was the largest, craziest, wildest party I had ever experienced.

I was mid-day-drunk on champagne and beer, my eyes were closed, and I was, sort-of, vertically crowd surfing, as my body was defying gravity for seconds on end. It was like a loud, but silent din of rapturous noise, until I was belted in the side of the face with chocolate powder. Yes, like the kind you mix with milk. I was pissed for a split-second, before realizing that everyone was covered, head-to-toe in champagne and chocolate powder. The entire crowd gloated in smiles, as did I. It was the wildest party of my life, and I only had five friends in attendance, and it was literally impossible to find them in the crush. Before we were separated, I remember Tricky and I were indulging in one of the local customs by throwing champagne corks at the photographers.

Wild is an understatement. The party continued until around 1400 hours or so, then, poof, it was gone. The crowd dispersed so quickly, it was as if we'd witnessed a mass-abduction, followed by the sidewalks being rolled-up. This was normal, as it was *siesta* time, where businesses close and people rest before the night-life ensued. Seeing as we were struggling to purchase any alcohol or food, we decided rest would be a good idea. When in Rome…

We must have looked pitiful as we slept inside, on top of, and beside the car in the makeshift Spanish shade, but it was a wise course of action. It seemed like it was for only a few minutes, as we hid from the boiling hot rays, but it was a couple of hours of much needed time for us to clean-up and *semi-sober-up*. Hot, sweaty, and thirsty for more beer, we ventured back into town. We found what was known as the British bar section, where most of the English-speaking countrymen and women would hang out. It was an entirely different animal to what we expected to find in Iruñea.

It was located at the *Plaza de la Navarrería* (place). It was a medium-sized plaza surrounded by tall, red-roofed buildings. Lined with bars, their storefronts met at three intersected roads, with the *Fuente de la Navarrería* (fountain) in the center. The fountain is a cylindrical shaped statue that stood about six-to-seven meters. Mostly, we met Brits and Aussies, but also quite a few non-English (first language) speakers from around the globe. Most were between the ages of 18 to 30. The sun had yet to set on the square, so we had a good layout of the place upon arrival. Soldiers always take in the scenery and find an escape route in just about every situation. This was a very packed and busy intersection, so naturally, we were on guard.

We went into several bars before we met up with a few fellow soldiers from Australia, thus the drinking commenced on an epic level. We quickly mitigated sobriety before dark. That's when we noticed something strange happening outside. These idiots, and yes, the same ones we were drinking and partying with, were climbing this fountain in order to attempt a leap from its crown. I could hardly believe my eyes. I would highly suggest a video search of jumping from the fountain in Pamplona, in order to appreciate the demented acts I am about to describe.

They started their ascent from these large diameter bollards designed to keep cars from [accidentally] hitting the fountain, though there were no cars present during San Fermin, as they were forbidden, given the amount of people present in the streets, bars, balconies, and every space in-between. Tricky and I looked at each other like, *These assholes are crazy…crazier than us, even.*

I told him, *"IF OUR ENTIRE BATTALION WERE HERE, SOBER, I STILL WOULDN'T LEAP FROM THAT THING."*

He responded, *"NO SHIT. ME EITHER, DUDE."*

The premise of it was you'd climb to the top ledge, over twenty feet high, position yourself with arms overhead, and allow yourself to fall naturally with an erect body posture. During the fall, the elapsed time and distance allowed gravity to *level-out* your body into a horizontal position, so the alcoholically destroyed crowds below could catch you…hopefully!

I know it sounds insane, because it is. This is where strong terms like *alcoholically destroyed* are justified. Some of these assholes were so inebriated, they tried to leap, or dive, off of the statue. Big mistake. Again, they did not have the luxury of the internet to teach themselves how to gracefully fall off. Trial and error were the victors. They kept the genepool in check during this affair.

We watched from the base of the fountain. It was like a bloody train wreck from which one could not avert their eyes. It's difficult to explain the stupidity of mixing human beings and alcohol, in an even worse light than I have already painted myself and others, some of whom I consider my closest brothers. We were truly humbled by their sheer idiocy that evening. This kind of stupidity was light-years beyond licking the glass of the short bus, through your protective helmet, because you ate too many fucking crayons. Sorry, Marines, I had to go there. No

Army memoir of mine would be complete without at least one Marine joke. Seriously, I couldn't even begin to make fun of the other branches of our military, albeit in jest, that would describe this sort of brainless lunacy.

One idiot after another mounted and failed Spanish flight school. Yet, others knew exactly how to do it…crack-pilots they were. We were positioned fairly close to the fountain, for a front-row seat to the action, when disaster struck. This guy, drunk-as-fuck, dove, head-first into the crowd. A brief hush washed through the crowd, but it was a momentary lapse in humanity. Que the ambulance, as he was done for. Others tried to jump, feet first, and you could hear their bones snap through the noise of the crowd, as they hit the aged, cobblestoned streets. It was beautiful watching alcohol thin the herd. We inched closer yet.

Just after dark, we were right next to this guy that began his stellar ascent atop the bollards, making his way atop the fountain. He scraped, scrounged, and clawed his way to just beyond the halfway point, when his grip failed him. A gasp came over the crowd as he fell about eleven feet through the air before the back of his head landed squarely on a bollard, like a hammer to a nail. It was as if a melon had been dropped before splaying its innards across the floor. With his head cracked open, he spat, stuttered and frothed at the mouth whilst his body convulsed, before eventually going limp. His body lay corpse-like until an ambulance, readied at the top of the hill, could make its way through the crowd to retrieve him. One of the Spaniards near us started cracking-up laughing, as they loaded him into the meat wagon. He had no mercy whatsoever regarding this dimwit and his air-headed (pun intended) blunder. Tricky took pictures of the whole affair. It was a bloody, gruesome mess.

The ambulance left, and the party continued. The locals thought it ridiculous, because it truly was; therefore, they made fun of them right to their faces, too. It was rather comical when you think about it, as no one was forcing these fucktards up-and-onto the fountain. It wasn't a tiptoe-to-cliff, pike pointed into their backs, sort of affair. They gambled, and they lost. I like to think of it as Mother Nature performing natural selection and thinning out the population a wee bit. In the spirit of the brave yet stupid, we, as good soldiers, drank their share of the beer that they couldn't enjoy that evening. Besides, the night was young, as were we. If you dare, look up videos and watch the pain unfold.

Soon thereafter, I met this gorgeous white woman from South Africa. Oh, my, her accent was different, but sexy as fuck on her. She had green eyes, long brown hair, and tanned skin. I'm sure she had a name, almost positive she did, but I have long since forgotten it. I have, however, not forgotten our evening together. We drank many, many beers that night, despite the language barrier. She spoke Afrikaans, a West Germanic language with some Dutch and other flavors thrown in. I spoke German very well at this point, so I could make out enough of her Afrikaans, and between what little English she spoke, we made it work.

Later, she asked if I had a hotel we could adjourn to? She wanted to further speak the language of love, because her bus was leaving at 0030 hours. Naturally, with our car in mind, I told her a resounding, *Yes*. We departed the plaza around 2300 hours and walked the short trip back to the parking lot. It wasn't what she'd had in mind, but given the fact we'd both invested the time and energies into wanting one another, she accepted. I do appreciate a woman that knows what she wants and is willing to go to such lengths to get it. We climbed into the backseat of the car, despite the near insufferable summer heat. I couldn't remember the last real shower I'd taken, perhaps it was Paris, more than four days ago. I'm sure I was quite ripe.

The car was almost dead-center in the parking lot, and it was like a ghost town, complete with rolling tumbleweed. As luck would have it, her tour bus was parked at the edge of our parking lot, directly in front of the carnival. I still exercised some measure of modesty during our flight of passion, by installing makeshift curtains into our *shaggin' station wagon*. I installed t-shirts into the manually-operated backdoor windows and shoved a few sleeping bags into the head rests that separated the front and rear seats. There being no real visibility from the hatch area, I opted out of placing any barriers at the rear headrests. I cracked the front windows and the sunroof for some air, and we started in on the business at hand.

Less my sixteen weeks during OSUT, at nineteen years old, I had over four years' experience at donning a condom, and I was quite adept at it, too. The Army even showed us graphic videos on diseases and how to protect ourselves. Real eye-opening shit. To reference the chapter titled, *"Gas, Gas, Gas…Chamber,"* and information regarding MOPP gear, I quote one of my old 1SGs. *"GENTLEMEN, KEEP YOUR ONE-EYED WONDER-WORM IN MOPP LEVEL-4."* Army slang for wear a condom.

Good advice didn't always immediately sink in, like CPT Handgrenade's standing orders of covering our buddies. There was definitely no pun intended on that one…though, it works. Maybe, that's a bad example, as that was exactly what I had in mind. I was going to be covering my best buddy and pal in the whole-wide-world, *George,* also known as my pecker. The only problem was, I was about to cover my buddy with two condoms, instead of one. Okay, I admit, I was drunk off my ass and not thinking clearly. *I was being safe, right?* I did have enough, albeit, *just enough,* sense to cover my pecker in such a situation.

TURNER—1…rather…TURNER/GEORGE—2:
LIFE LESSONS—0

Anyway, we are in the backseat conducting our business as the world around us buzzed along none the wiser. I knew the car was rocking and the windows were steamed-up, because it was hotter than twelve hells in that moderately sized backseat. The air stifled us, but when you're young and in the throes of passion, you could care less. Speaking of youth, we were finding positions in that car that I didn't think possible. No doubt, another telling testament to youth, as well as alcohol. Necessity is, *after all*, the mother of invention.

Our time together was, as they say, nothing to write home about, but there was something special about it, nonetheless. Two people, each in a foreign and strange country, fluent in differing languages, born and raised on entirely different continents, with completely opposite backgrounds, finding passion in the backseat of a station wagon in Spain. I know it's not exactly how a Hollywood tear-jerker begins, because it was nothing like that, but think about this: This is something you only do in your youth, not as you age into maturity. Okay, never mind, there will be no soul searching here. I am only trying to justify my semi-responsible, yet reckless, I-got-out-alive behavior.

Now, where was I? Oh, yeah, positions! We were regular circus sideshow contortionists in the backseat of that station wagon. I was behind, she was on top, hands and lips were all over the place, but even the best liquor dick syndrome has its limitations. I knew my time had come, pun intended. After some carnival-like sex, I returned her to the missionary position, but given the time it took to rearrange ourselves, I bought myself a few extra minutes. Her hands were pushed out over her shoulders, which prevented her head from being crumpled into the door console. I was riding her like a bronco cowboy on a bucking bull, only longer than eight seconds, I might add! I could feel the car violently rocking to and fro. *Damn, I'm good*, I thought to myself.

I was nearing the end, as I was about to finish up with Miss South Africa. In the heat and under the influence, I was getting light-headed (no pun there, folks). It must've been the stroke of midnight when the fireworks started, not that I stopped to check my watch, but that *stroke* of midnight (this is too easy) started the seventh day of the seventh month, the day of the bulls. Yes, the carnival across the street started an actual fireworks show to celebrate the festival's actual beginning, just as I was concluding my business.

I swear I am not so talented to make this up, which explains my writing a non-fictional memoir, versus a fictional spy-thriller. It was as if fate had peeked in and said, *Turner, you get fireworks tonight, buddy.* Seeing as the moment was not lost on either of us, we both smiled with shit-eating grins, then broke into uncontrollable laughter as we continued our Spanish soiree. Moments later we were done, rather, I was done, which in turn meant, *we* were done.

I wound-up behind the driver's seat when the *deed* was complete. I removed my doubled-up condom collection, tied them into a knot, rolled down the window, and tossed it up and behind the car, out of the parking spaces and into the main aisle of the parking lot. I then began round-two of contortionists school as we proceeded to get dressed. Once class was dismissed, I wound up behind the passenger seat. It was *hot as fuck* in that car, pun not intended. Upon completion, our skin had nearly melted into the crevices of the car's interior.

The shirts and sleeping bags were still in place as she dressed herself. I only had to don my boxers before exiting the epicenter of the shaggin'-wagon-turned-nuclear-reactor. I climbed out, still eyeing her, when I was startled by roars of cheers, whistles, and a grand round of applause.

I looked up to find that a crowd had gathered, but not for the *Turner and stranger love show.* No, they were there to observe the *actual* fireworks celebrating San Fermin. As a matter of fact, the parking lot had filled-up quite dramatically during the *double-header* attraction…pun, obviously intended. As were most of the cars in the parking lot, ours was also nose-to-nose along an aisle of 80 to 100 vehicles, and, by strange coincidence, facing away from the carnival. So, the crowds that were gathered to watch the fireworks, leaning on the row of cars ours was nosed to, were also privy to our show of testing the vehicle's suspension.

Embarrassed? Me? Wrong. I formed a large smile, and in an accepting manner, I tilted my head back with pride and opened up my arms to rake in the accolades of my many, many adoring fans, as there were shit and tons of them. Applause reigned over me, so naturally, I casually raised my left arm into a position across my mid-section and gracefully extended it outward, taking a graceful bow for my cheering fans.

Through the darkness, I saw her eyes widen distinctly, revealing their whites. She instantly understood the situation, but faced with such adversity, she knew she still had to exit the car to return to her bus. She had to face the crowd at some point. I smiled, kissed her lips, and made a cringe on my face like, *No problem, own it*. She did just that. I took her hand to help her out, we stood for a moment to even more applause. We held hands as I took another bow, and she, a make-shift curtsy. It was brilliant. I walked her to the edge of the parking lot, gave her a long, warm kiss, we hugged, and said goodbye.

TURNER/GEORGE—1: STRANGER—1

I then proceeded back to the British bar section, to imbibe the remainder of the night away. It must have been around 0400 hours when we returned to our automotive hotel turned love nest. With only three hours until we were to test our dodging prowess against six large bulls and six large steers, it seemed a wise and logical choice. I am not sure we really slept, as much as laid there. We were sprawled out in each of the seats, one on top of the car, one in the hatch portion, and another on the ground beside the car. We looked like dead cockroaches splayed out on the kitchen floor, the morning after an exterminator's visit.

I believe it was SSG K that stirred us awake around 0600, as he was the soberest of the bunch. The sun was just breaking through the buildings and trees—it was going to be another beautiful day in Spain. We knew we had to get to the main square of town. I believe it was City Hall, or its equivalent, where we'd previously been covered in champagne and chocolate powder, popping corks at photographers.

We were stirring about getting our shoes and such donned, as I fired up my first cigarette of the day, rather, of the daylight hours of that day. I think I'd slept in the backseat, as I wasn't the kind of guy to let my buddies sleep in the aftermath of my bacchanal. I was an asshole, but not that kind of asshole. I believe it was Vinny who said, in his Big Easy New Orleans accent, *"WHAT THE FUCK? SOMEONE DUMPED TWO USED CONDOMS OUTSIDE THE DOOR. THEY'RE TIED-UP AND FULL OF CUM. FOLKS IS FUCKING DISGUSTING."*

For the life of me, I couldn't stifle my laughter. As I began an uncontrollable cackle, my body doubled over. It was the kind of laughter that feels both painful and therapeutic at the same time. He chimes in again, *"ARE THESE FUCKING THINGS YOURS, TURNER?"*

In our more than inebriated state in the hours leading up to that morning, I had yet to divulge the details of my backseat bungalow. My laughter incited the others to join in, even though the guys were not positive the condoms were mine…yet. A feeble attempt to hold my guts together with my arms crossed over my belly, all I could do was *nod* my upper torso in an up-and-down fashion, confirming they were, indeed, my condoms. I had to explain the situation, in-full, as to why the condoms were beside the front door of the car. That was what was so funny to me, and later, to the guys.

In my drunken condition, I thought I had full range of all my physical abilities, especially as a young soldier, but I was, apparently, wrong on some accounts. My throwing abilities *after* the aforementioned parking lot porno show, were not as precise as I'd hoped. In fact, they were strained, and calculations suffered severely. I thought I'd thrown the condoms into the aisle of the parking lot, far, far away from the shaggin' wagon, but I was wrong. They ballooned up and over the car—a perfect arch from the driver's side to the passenger's—and forward about eighteen inches. The standing ovation I'd received, all became so clear to me now. In essence, the crowd knew, what I would learn in the light of day. Even so, that is fucking impressive, despite the disgust of it all. I rest my case.

SEVENTH DAY OF THE SEVENTH MONTH

With no coffee, no breakfast, no water, no sleep, and still drunk from the night before, we readied ourselves to flee from twelve charging bulls on an 825M/ 2,706-foot dash over ancient, cobblestoned streets. A dozen angry bulls chased us through maze-like streets for just over a half-mile, so again, I ask my readers, *Do you realize what mayhem could have befallen us drunken idiots on this adventure?* Sure you do. As we didn't have the luxury of doing an internet search for the madness we were about to fling ourselves into, I highly suggest to my readers a search now for what the running of the bulls is all about.

The streets were filled with men from all walks of life, mostly young ones, though. Women and children were forbidden to run with the bulls, and the police surveilled the crowd with extreme scrutiny. Women's liberation and equal opportunity had yet to spearhead this ancient ritual. I did see one young woman, hair tucked neatly beneath her baseball cap, discreetly blending into the crowd, before hawkeyed police officers escorted her from the corralled streets and into the spectator area. However, during the run, I did see one woman running, and thought, *Fucking, bravo! Good for her! She got through security, and she's doing it!* Most of the people that attended the festival did not actually run with the bulls. It is definitely reserved for the brave and *stoopid.*

Tricky and I managed to remain together for the entire run into the arena. He and I were on the boxing team together, so we were in excellent physical condition, so the run wasn't a problem for us. Throughout the run, we managed to keep just ahead of the gory fray, screams, and the overpowering din of the frightened crowd. Terror stayed well on our heels, though. It was after straightaways and into the corners where people were tripped-up and captured by the bulls. Alas, we rounded the final corner. We'd made the home-stretch. I momentarily looked over my shoulder and saw the bulls inching towards us, as they were much faster than us on the straightaways. I turned to Tricky and asked, *"WHAT THE FUCK ARE WE DOING HERE, BOX?"*

He responded, *"I DON'T FUCKING KNOW, PUNK ASS* (one of my nicknames), *BUT WE'D BETTER KEEP RUNNING, OR WE'RE DONE FOR, DUDE."* I couldn't have agreed with him more as the infuriated hooves clopped closer and closer to our backsides. Despite our *drunk-overs,* we managed to put a little more oomph into our step. We witnessed several people ditch the course altogether and hop the barriers into the crowd of spectators. Tricky and I, remained.

Once we'd reached the statue of Earnest Hemingway, of which I barely achieved a glance, the entrance to the arena became a hazardous chokepoint. *Hazardous,* what a provocative word used to describe something *other than* the actual peril of running from twelve fucking bulls. The gap that once separated us from the ever present melee, had now closed-in on us. The screams and shouts now had us in a stranglehold, a cacophony of horror. We knew these 1500–1800 pound bulls were going into that arena, despite any puny humans that may have impeded their path. We were trapped like fish in a barrel, as we shoved, pushed, and prodded our way through the multitudes of terror-stricken runners.

At that time in my life, there were instances, few and far, that truly scared the hell out of me. I mean, for fuck's sake, I thought I wanted to go into combat with enemies trying to actively kill me, but at that moment, I was absolutely scared *for my life*. I didn't want to be skewered by a bull, as death by impalement didn't sound very noble, or honorable. The fear coursing through my veins that morning was, quite honestly, unlike any I'd felt before. Absolute shrieks of terror could be heard directly behind us. In fact, they were blood-curdling shrills of horror. I wondered if, indeed, we were going to die inside of that cobbled entrance, near the statue of my literary hero, Hemingway. In the years that have passed since then, I can count on one finger, the number of times I've heard screams that rivaled that morning in Iruñea.

As soon as we entered *Plaza de Toros de Pamplona* (place of the bulls), the world's fourth largest bullfighting arena, Tricky and I instinctively shoved each other in opposite directions. We never discussed it, as it was simply to avoid our being gored. We both fell to the ground, mere milliseconds before the first, second, and third bulls charged in. The first two found their way into the openness of the arena, but the third fell onto its front-quarters, paused, and then twisted its head as if taking in the spectacle before rising and continuing into his pen with the remaining bulls and steers.

After that, it was something more akin to rounds of boxing. A fight, with breaks in between. The difference being, we never knew how many opponents we'd have, or for how long. Sometimes, there were two bulls, three, and even up to six bulls in the arena at the same time. I was, on two occasions, nearly gored by a charging bull, but adrenaline subsided most of the fear at that point. Miraculously, and by complete accident, I managed to snap off two pictures, the bull's eyes perfectly reflected in my lens as he converged on me.

During the breaks, the bulls were corralled beneath the bleachers, hidden behind an up-swung door. The Spaniards would then, purposely, sit cross-legged, just outside of that door. When the doors forcefully swung open and let loose an untold number of bulls, all charging like bats out of hell, it became a game of rodeo poker, or he who flinched last. Pure insanity.

Once the bulls were still, or deciding their next target, runners would slap their asses with newspapers. Seeing as I didn't have a newspaper, I, like many others, used my hands to slap the bulls. *What was I thinking?* My hands smelled awful afterward. I know, more insanity.

That year, one person died, three were seriously gored, and several injured. The wonderful thing about running was, nothing else in the world mattered, except to stay alive and avoid being impaled. It was like leaving the body and looking down on yourself, as if in a lucid dream. It was hurried, but in slow-motion at the same time. Time, space, and everything else in life seemed to have melted away during those dreadful and intense minutes.

The next morning, financially exhausted, along with our bodies, minds, and livers, we decided to not run with the bulls again. Instead, we accepted that our luck had held out, and we headed back to Mannheim. We were ready for a much needed break, as we had escaped death, impalement, foreign jails, disease, and any other sort of serious mishap. It was good not to tempt the gods with another day of imbibed debauchery, especially with 900 miles of highway ahead of us. Once again, we trekked through the National Park of the Pyrenees, and with Paris off the to-do list, we travelled through Toulouse and Lyon, a more direct route home. After managing a slight *Lima Lima Mike Foxtrot* mishap in Rodez, France, we arrived home intact.

This would be our last great adventure before leaving Europe. For me, it was one of the last *awe-inspiring* moments for a long while. The draw-down of U.S. forces in Europe was right around the corner, and we had a one-way ticket to the land of the free, the home of the brave… The United States of America.

Farewell and adieu to you, Spanish Ladies.

Farewell and adieu to you, ladies of Spain…

For we have received orders to drive back to old Deutschland,

But we hope in a short time to see you again….

48

LADIES AND GENTLEMEN, THE BAR IS CLOSED!

Things would never be the same for me, or any of us, after living in Germany for so long. We knew very little of what was coming; what a post-9/11 world looked like. Without sounding naïve, before that tragic event, the world still had an innocence to it. We didn't have terabytes of information at the swiping behest of our fingertips. I think that is part of what I wanted to capture in this book, the last of a simpler time in history…knowing things would never be the same.

Even at their inception, I always wanted to chronicle my experiences in the Army, for reasons of laughter and posterity, but until now, never made the time to do so. It was more than a quarter of a century in the making, and I truly hope you've enjoyed reading the pages of my former life. I know it's not a world-class literary masterpiece, but it's a part of the history of how I became who I am today and why my buddies from 3-77 Armor are the best brothers I will ever have in this life. It's how I saw the world in the last days before instant information and gratification and quick, easy porn…come on, we have kept it real this far in, no need to stop the carnage now.

During the weeks and months of researching, remembering, and articulating the details of these stories, I realized I'd cracked open Pandora's Box in the process. I was forced to think about the very brothers I was idolizing. Those alive, and those no longer with us. I thought about their nicknames, and their faces at the time of a particular event. Some of these brothers I will never see again, while others, I see regularly at our reunions. Time is beginning to show on all of our faces and bodies, as youth has escaped us in many respects. Yet, I still see their youthful faces from so long ago—the smiles, the eyes of my brothers, and I'm still proud to call these gentlemen my very best friends and brothers. They know how much I appreciate their role in my life, as I've tried to make it known at each and every opportunity.

The paradigm in all of this, is that I, too, remembered the stories and faces of the brothers that are no longer with us, the ones that are now seated in Valhalla: SPC M. Box, SPC J. Halterman, SGT Paine, and SSG J. Melo. These are but a few examples in the great scheme of life. At the second reunion I'd organized, meeting at an even larger veteran's reunion in Melbourne, Florida, we found SSG Melo's name on the 3rd plaque from the left, on the 77th line from the top. He'd passed away many years after we served with him in 3-77, but to us, it was a sign, a fitting tribute to our old buddy.

Having helped me edit this book, my Uncle Chris was inspired to reach out to some of his old brothers to reconnect as I did with mine. I would encourage the same for every veteran, suffering or not, but especially for those that are suffering. Please reach out and reconnect with your brothers and sisters in arms, as you will never make connections like these again in your life. Take it from an old man…they are some of the closest people to your soul, and I don't even have the experience of combat like so many of you do upon which to preach, but I know the truth when I see it. They will heal your soul and lift your spirits better than any doctor or therapist.

They will not judge you or turn you away, and neither will I. I believed the Army when they said, "This We'll Defend." I believe they were talking about the veterans, Americans, kind souls, the ones you never knew you'd meet, because I haven't met a bad one yet.

Although, the [combat] title of the book is meant in jest, its intent was never to depreciate the true heroes of America: the men and women, my brothers-and-sisters-in-arms that have stared the enemy squarely in the face, only to *never* come home again, whole or otherwise. These are the true heroes. Honor these men and women by being a good American, a good neighbor, and a good human being.

When people thank me for my service, I think to myself, *You're thanking the wrong person*. Granted, I took the oath and signed the dotted line, but I never sacrificed near as much as the ones that sacrificed their lives for the greater good; for our American way of life. Honor their memory, because without these selfless souls, we wouldn't have the opportunity to be Americans.

I miss you, Deutschland. I will always love what you did for me, for us, the Silver Knights of the 3rd Battalion of the 77th Armored Regiment, First Armored Division, "OLD IRONSIDES," Käfertal-Wald, Deutschland…*Life in an Armor Unit circa 1993–94*. Hint-hint. Wink-wink. Fast-forward some towards the end of the video.

I think of the joke we had throughout my time in service…US ARMY spelled backwards was, YMRASU, or to frame it into yet another acronym, *Yes My Retarded Ass Signed Up*. But, after serving something larger and far more important than myself and growing up (years later), I realized that was one of the few jokes that actually wasn't a joke. Like my DS promised, *They would be the best times of my life*!

Like the old days when television stations would end the day's programming with the "Star-Spangled Banner," I, too, would not want to disappoint the patriots reading these pages.

O say can you see by the dawn's early light

What so proudly we hailed at the twilight's last gleaming

Whose broad stripes and bright stars through the perilous fight

O'er the ramparts we watched, were so gallantly streaming

And the rocket's red glare, the bombs bursting in air

Gave proof to the night that our flag was still there

O say does that star-spangled banner yet wave

O'er the land of the free and the home of the brave

Goodbye, Auf Wiedersehen, adieu, Vaarwel, and adios to America, Germany, and the world we once knew. And that, folks, is (NOT) last call, for alcohol. Thank you, be kind to one another, goodnight, and God bless these beloved United States of America!

Ac· ro· nym. /ˈakrə,nim/ noun—An abbreviation formed from the initial letters of other words and pronounced as a word.

Also an acronym for *acronyms*…the **A**rmy **C**ould've **R**econnoitered **O**bscure **N**icknames **Y**ielding **M**ore **S**ignificance!

A:

AAM:	Army Achievement Medal.
AIT:	Advanced Individual Training.
AO:	Area of Operations.
ASVAB:	Armed Services Vocational Aptitude Battery.
AWOL:	Absence With Out Leave.

B:

BDU:	Battle Dress Uniform.
BOHICA:	Bend Over, Here It Comes Again.
BOHICAS:	Bend Over, Here It Comes Army Style.
BT:	Basic Training.

C:

CIB:	Combat Infantryman's Badge.
CID:	Criminal Investigation Division.
CIF:	Central Issue Facility.
CPL:	Corporal. Okay, an abbreviation.
CQ:	Charge of Quarters.
CVC:	Combat Vehicle Crewmen.

D:

DOD: Department of Defense.

DM: Deutsch Mark.

DS: Drill Sergeant.

E:

EFMB: Expert Field Medical Badge.

ETS: Expiration of Term of Service.

F:

FNG: Fucking New Guy.

FRH: Field Ration Heater.

FTX: Field Training Exercise.

FUBAR: Fucked Up Beyond All Recognition.

G:

GP: General Purpose.

H:

HEMMT: Heavy Expandable Mobility Tactical Truck.

HMMWV: High Mobility Multipurpose Wheeled Vehicle.

HQ: Headquarters.

J:

JAG: Judge Advocate General.

L:

LLMF: Lima Lima Mike Foxtrot or Lost Like a Mother Fucker.

M:

MEPS:	Military Entrance Point Station.
MER:	Maximum Effective Range.
MG:	Machine Gun.
MOAI:	Mother Of All Inspections.
MOPP:	Mission Oriented Protective Posture.
MOS:	Military Occupational Specialty.
MRE:	Meals-Ready-to-Eat or Micky D's Ready-to-Eat.
MP:	Military Police. The last two letters to spell wimp.

N:

NATO:	North Atlantic Treaty Organization.
NBC:	Nuclear, Biological, and Chemical.
NCO:	Non-Commissioned Officer.
NVA:	National Volks Armee.
NVD:	Night Vision Device.

O:

OSUT:	One Station Unit Training. How boys become bad mother-fuckers.

P:

PLDC:	Professional Leadership Development Course.
PLT:	Platoon. Okay, another abbreviation.
PT:	Physical Training. Gimme some. Hun-ga.
PU:	Push Up. Shit and tons of them.
PVT:	Private.
PX:	Post Exchange.

R:

RPM:	Rounds-Per-Minute.
RTB:	Ranger Training Brigade.

S:

SAW:	Squad Assault Weapon.
SHIT:	Specialized High Intensity Training.
SNAFU:	Situation Normal, All Fucked Up.
SOS:	Army = Shit-On-a-Shingle.
	Navy = Save Our Souls.
	Marines = Can't spell SOS.

T:

TC:	Tank Commander.

U:

UCMJ:	Uniformed Code of Military Justice.
USAF:	Uncle Sam's Airplane Fuckers. I mean, United States Air Force.

V:

VCR:	Video Cassette Recorder. Rewind fees –look it up! The struggle was real, folks.

PHONETIC ALPHABET

Alpha	Bravo	Charlie
Delta	Echo	Foxtrot
Golf	Hotel	India
Juliet	Kilo	Lima
Mike	November	Oscar
Papa	Quebec	Romeo
Sierra	Tango	Uniform
Victor	Whiskey	X-ray
Yankee	Zulu	

CPSIA information can be obtained
at www.ICGtesting.com
Printed in the USA
LVHW020346140121
676451LV00014B/297